Learn to Write Badly

Modern academia is increasingly competitive yet the writing style of social scientists is routinely poor and continues to deteriorate. Are social science postgraduates being taught to write poorly? What conditions adversely affect the way they write? And which linguistic features contribute towards this bad writing? Michael Billig's witty and entertaining book analyses these questions in a quest to pinpoint exactly what is going wrong with the way social scientists write. Using examples from diverse fields such as linguistics, sociology and experimental social psychology, Billig shows how technical terminology is regularly less precise than simpler language. He demonstrates that there are linguistic problems with the noun-based terminology that social scientists habitually use – 'reification' or 'nominalization' rather than the corresponding verbs 'reify' or 'nominalize'. According to Billig, social scientists not only use their terminology to exaggerate and to conceal, but also to promote themselves and their work.

MICHAEL BILLIG has been Professor of Social Sciences at Loughborough University for more than twenty-five years and has written books on a variety of different subjects. Among his books are *Freudian Repression* (Cambridge, 2009) and *Arguing and Thinking* (Cambridge, 1987 and 1996).

Learn to Write Badly

How to Succeed in the Social Sciences

Michael Billig

Department of Social Sciences
Loughborough University

CAMBRIDGE
UNIVERSITY PRESS

CAMBRIDGE UNIVERSITY PRESS
Cambridge, New York, Melbourne, Madrid, Cape Town,
Singapore, São Paulo, Delhi, Mexico City

Cambridge University Press
The Edinburgh Building, Cambridge CB2 8RU, UK

Published in the United States of America by Cambridge University Press,
New York

www.cambridge.org
Information on this title: www.cambridge.org/9781107676985

© Michael Billig 2013

First published 2013

Printed and bound by CPI Group (UK) Ltd, Croydon CR0 4YY

A catalogue record for this publication is available from the British Library

Library of Congress Cataloguing in Publication data
Billig, Michael.
Learn to write badly : how to succeed in the social sciences / Michael Billig,
Department of Social Sciences, Loughborough University.
    pages   cm
Includes bibliographical references.
ISBN 978-1-107-67698-5
1. Communication in the social sciences.   2. Social
sciences – Research.   3. English language – Writing.   I. Title.
H61.8.B55   2013
808.06′63–dc23

                                                                2012049260

ISBN 978-1-107-02705-3 Hardback
ISBN 978-1-107-67698-5 Paperback

To Ari, Monica, Hannah, Elsie and Artie

Contents

Acknowledgements

I would like to thank colleagues and friends who have kindly read and commented on chapters of this book: in particular, Charles Antaki, David Deacon, Derek Edwards, Jonathan Potter, John Shotter and Tom Scheff. I very much appreciate their helpful advice. Particular thanks to Cristina Marinho who read all the chapters and even seemed to enjoy doing so.

As always, I am grateful to Sheila and our family. The last decade has seen a shift in our family. The older generation has now passed and a new generation has begun to emerge. I dedicate this book to our new generation. In this book, I criticize the present, but without looking into the future with optimism. That is my failing because, when I look at our grandchildren and see the joy that they bring, it is easy to be optimistic.

1 Introduction

This is a book which complains about poor writing in the social sciences. The author is not someone who is offering criticisms as an outsider looking in upon a strange world. I am an insider, a social scientist, and I am publicly criticizing my fellows for their ways of writing. Anyone who does this can expect to have their motives questioned. Readers may wonder whether the author is embittered, having seen younger colleagues overtake him in the race for academic honours. Perhaps he has been slighted in the past by senior figures and now he is determined upon gaining his revenge. Or possibly the author is deeply flawed as a person, a serial troublemaker, who is constantly picking quarrels and seeking to be the centre of attention.

So, I should begin with a few personal remarks. I am not a young scholar, rebelling against the establishment, but I am approaching the end of my working life, having spent almost forty years in continuous employment as a university teacher. It has, for the most part, been a wonderful job. Not only has the work been relatively well remunerated, but it has been a privilege to be paid for reading and writing; and it has not been a hardship to teach bright, young people, some of whom have even been interested in the topics that I have taught. I cannot imagine a better way to earn a salary; but that may say more about my lack of imagination than it does about working as a modern academic in the social sciences.

Doing the job has not always been easy or free from insecurities. There are some academics that one cannot envisage in any other line of work – they seem to belong so perfectly to the world of scholarship that they would be misfits in the so-called 'real' world. Some of my colleagues and students might think that of me. It would be nice if they did, but I should say that for me it has not felt that way at all – and this is relevant to my reasons for writing this book.

When I was a student of philosophy and psychology at Bristol University in the late 1960s, it did not occur to me that I would ever stay at university after I had finished my undergraduate degree. I was doubly fortunate that Henri Tajfel, one of the greatest social psychologists in the discipline, was my teacher, and that he persuaded me to consider doing a doctorate under his supervision. Without that encouragement, my life would have been considerably different. As a doctoral student, however, I never felt that I properly belonged to the world I was entering. My big problem was that I could not master the academic language which I was expected to use. I would struggle to read articles and books with complex, technical terminology. I would try to translate the unfamiliar words into simpler ones, into the ordinary language that I used in daily life. Sometimes, I succeeded in doing so, and sometimes I didn't. And occasionally, when I'd finished the translation, the ideas and the sense seemed to dribble away, leaving truisms and little else. Then, I would be perplexed. Was it my failure to understand or was it that a writer, who had actually been published, really had so little to say? I could hardly believe the latter possibility.

I would look with envy at my fellow postgraduates who could use the terminology easily and who did not seem to suffer from my problems. Not only could they speak fluently in this strange, unfamiliar language, but they could even think in it. And that I most certainly could not do and I still don't know why. All I know is that I never got past the stage of translating the big words into smaller words: I never became a fluent speaker, let alone a thinker, of the academic dialect. Even after I obtained a post in the psychology department at Birmingham University, things did not become easier: I still could not use or understand the words that a young social psychologist should use. After a while, I stopped reading the journals that I ought to have been reading. The superb library at Birmingham had so much else to offer. I still remember the first time I read Hannah Arendt's *Eichmann in Jerusalem* (1963), and feeling so utterly changed. Few books have affected me as deeply and shown me how little I knew. Or, on a more pleasurable level, I remember reading C. L. R. James's *Beyond a Boundary*. Later I would have similar feelings of delight when reading Freud, although I was always aware that he could simultaneously be wise and silly.

Despite their intellectual differences, Arendt, James and Freud share one thing in common: none was a professional academic, writing primarily for other academics. The academic terminology, which I could not master or take into myself as my own, seemed paltry by comparison to their words. George Orwell's wonderful essay 'Politics and the English Language' helped put things into perspective. I felt heartened: perhaps the fault wasn't mine but that of some academic social scientists who, by using long words, were dressing up banalities as profundities. Maybe – and this was too liberating to say out loud – my strategy of translating academic words might not be a sign of shameful inadequacy, which I dare not admit to others, but possibly I had stumbled unwittingly upon a strategy which would protect me. After all, I did not need to translate Arendt or James or Freud: study, re-read, struggle to understand, yes, often; but translate into simple words, never.

So it has continued over the years. I have avoided reading the technical journals which I should read and which I occasionally publish in. I have never taken on the technical terminology as if it were my first language. I still have to translate if I wish to understand the academic articles that I do read. But I no longer feel ashamed. Today, I can see young post-graduates struggling to understand what they know they must read. Sometimes, I see their confidence draining away in the face of big words, as if they were failing the test that defines whether they are fit to think intellectually. I want to tell them to trust their own supposed inadequacies, for their failings might protect them from the onslaught of big words. I hope that some young academics, who are today as uncertain as I was years ago, may take some confidence from this book.

The nature of this book

This is by no means the first book to criticize the use of academic jargon either generally or more specifically in the social sciences. Just over forty years ago, Stanislav Andreski (1971) caused a stir with his *Social Sciences as Sorcery*, a book which took social scientists to task for their inability to write clearly. In his ferocious onslaught, Andreski claimed that intellectual standards were declining: compared with half a century ago, there was, he suggested, an 'abundance of pompous bluff and paucity of new ideas' (p. 11), and that this was another reflection of modern society's 'advanced stage of cretinization' (p. 17). It was gloriously ill-tempered stuff but very much the voice of an embittered person.

Much gentler was Brand Blanshard's *On Philosophical Style* (1954), a delightful little book in which the distinguished American philosopher argued that philosophers should try to write as clearly as possible and that it was bad manners not to try to do so. More recently, we have had the physicist Alan Sokal castigating postmodernist theorists, both literary and social scientific, for writing in a wilfully obscure manner (Sokal and Bricmont, 1999; Sokal, 2010). When Sokal revealed that he had success-fully submitted a spoof article to a postmodernist journal, which had published it in all seriousness, a public brouhaha ensued with much anger and accusation on both sides.

I hope that my book will differ from these earlier works in a number of respects. Unlike Sokal, I am not attacking a particular viewpoint in the social sciences. I am not implying that if we could only get rid of continental philosophy and its adherents, all literary wrongs would be put to rights. In fact, I will hardly be mentioning postmodernist theorizing at all, not because I find the literary styles of Derrida, Lacan, Deleuze and their followers commendable for the social sciences, but because they are not the issue. Even if we lanced the Lacanian boil, as Sokal would wish, the patient would still be suffering from a serious rhetorical sickness.

Besides, I have criticized Lacan and his style of writing elsewhere and there is no reason to repeat those criticisms here (Billig, 2006). Lacan famously considered his work to be a return to Freud, but rhetorically this could not have been further from the case. Lacan was an obscure writer, who seemed to delight in making things difficult to grasp, offering few examples to illustrate his allusive points. Freud could be a wonderfully clear writer, who tried to draw his readers in with beautiful metaphors, jokes and, above all, clear examples. As I will suggest later in Chapter 5, Freud could also write in a pseudoscientific style, much to the detriment of his theory. Brand Blanshard has a lovely remark that is apposite, in my view, to Lacan and others like him: 'Persistently obscure writers will usually be found to be defective human beings' (1954, pp. 52–3). Blanshard was saying that authors, by their style of writing, are showing how they treat their readers and, thereby, how they treat other people. The persistently obscure writer can be like a bully, who tries to humiliate others into submission. Personally, as a reader, I would rather be charmed, even seduced, by a Freud than bullied by a Lacan.

My criticisms, however, are much wider than criticizing the style of an individual author or of a particular school of social scientists. In this respect, my book is closer to Andreski's onslaught than to Sokal's. Andreski was criticizing the mainstream social scientists of his day, rather than a comparatively small group of exotic radicals. Principally, he was gunning for respected figures like Talcott Parsons, Robert Merton and Robert Linton. He was not suggesting that they were defective human beings, although he was not so kind about their followers. Regarding Talcott Parsons, Andreski wrote that 'the Grand Master' was an honourable man, who, like all 'effective sorcerers', sincerely believed in what he was saying and who 'takes no part in the intrigues and machinations rampant among the academic jet-set, and for this reason he has been cold-shouldered by the common run of manipulators since his retirement, despite his great fame' (1971, p. 162).

Andreski could certainly turn out a good sentence, but I hope that my tone differs from his. The real difference between my critique and his – and also between my critique and those of Blanshard and Sokal – is neither tone nor target, but in analysis. Andreski's book, it must be said, is stronger on rant than analysis. Blanshard's arguments about the need for authors to use concrete examples to illustrate theoretical points are still valid and sociological theorists today could do far worse than read his largely forgotten book. However, Blanshard does not discuss the pressures of modern academic life that may lead to hasty writing; nor does he analyse precisely what may be amiss in current styles of academic writing. Although Blanshard cites William James approvingly – quoting Whitehead's praise of 'that adorable philosopher' (Blanshard, 1954, p. 17) – he does not mention that James criticized the academic system of his day, suggesting that it was encouraging young academics to write poorly. Later, I will be referring to William James and his critique of the division of the academic world into different disciplinary territories. His observations are still pertinent for understanding the relations between academic life and academic writing and, of course, they are wonderfully written.

My analysis will have two threads: the first is to examine the conditions under which academic social scientists are working; and the second thread is to examine the linguistic nature of what we produce as writers of the social sciences. I will be suggesting that the two threads are connected. The first part of the argument will be familiar to anyone working in higher education today: academics work in an increasingly commercial culture, as universities, disciplines and individuals compete economically. In this competitive culture, it has become second nature to promote oneself and one's work.

The second part of the argument may not make for comfortable reading: this culture of competition and self-promotion is seeping into the content of our academic writings. This is a culture in which success and boasting seem to go hand in hand. When we write, we are constantly boasting about our approaches, our concepts, our theories, our ways of doing social sciences and what these products can achieve. It is boast after boast, but we scarcely notice that we are writing like academic advertisers and that we are training our students to do likewise. And we boast of our big words which have become part of the product portfolios that we promote.

In the following chapter, I will begin analysing the conditions under which modern social scientists work. There has been a massive expansion of higher education and in the production of research, such that academics are expected to publish continuously and voluminously. There is so much publishing going on that the academic world is inevitably divided into smaller and smaller circles. In order to keep up with the pressures of work in an increasingly competitive world, academics are producing hastily written works. As the old saying goes, easy writing makes hard reading. William James once said that if there was anything good in his own style of writing, then it was 'the result of ceaseless toil in rewriting' (quoted in Richardson, 2007, p. 298). Such toil in rewriting is not possible when academics have to publish ceaselessly. It is not merely the style that suffers, but so does the content. When writing for audiences of specialists, it is easier and certainly speedier to reach for the common technical terminology than to try to clarify one's thoughts. Hence big words are circulating in decreasingly narrow circles.

In Chapter 3, I will be looking at the way that young social scientists enter the academic world – how they progress from being undergraduate students to being fully-fledged members of the trade. Because social scientific disciplines are so diverse today, the young apprentice academic has to do more than become a 'sociologist' or an 'anthropologist' or a 'psychologist'. Typically, they have to associate themselves with a specific approach, a theoretical perspective or an already existing body of work. To do this, they have to accept the technical terminology of their chosen world, as well as the assumption that this technical terminology is superior to ordinary language. And then they are expected to promote their own work, their approach and the language of their approach.

As I look at what is happening in the social sciences in these chapters, I will be citing studies which social scientists have produced about current university life, its commercial culture and the ways that postgraduates become professional academics. These studies are important for what they contribute to our knowledge about universities, but I will also be using them as examples of the ways that social scientists use language. I want to avoid going out of my way to look for imprecise, over-technical writing, for then I could be accused of selecting extreme examples just to fit my case. Instead, I will be using examples where I find them.

I will continue this strategy in the subsequent three chapters (Chapters 4 to 6) as I look at the linguistic features of contemporary academic writing. Those who examine current trends of writing will at times become my examples of those trends. In the first of these three chapters, I will be discussing the reasons that social scientists some- times give for using technical terminology. They claim, for instance, that ordinary language is too imprecise or that it is too infected by the philos- ophy of common sense. However, the defenders of technical jargon seem to overlook that academic terminology is heavily weighted towards nouns and noun phrases, with verbs, by comparison, hardly getting a look in. For me, that characteristic of contemporary academic writing is highly significant.

In the following two chapters, I develop the linguistic themes that I have introduced in Chapter 4. Basically, I consider why a noun-based style of writing, which is entirely appropriate for the natural sciences, is inappropriate for the social sciences. Although current styles of writing can be awkward and unlovely, my argument is not primarily aesthetic. The trouble is that when we use noun-based styles in the social sciences, we run the risk of rhetorically turning people into things – of reifying people. Significantly, sociological theorists, such as Peter Berger, who have looked at this topic, tend to use the noun 'reification' rather than the verb 'to reify'. When theorists write in this way, they treat the problem as a thing, and thereby, even as they warn against the dangers of 'reification', so they contribute to the problem.

Here, then, is the centre of my argument: the big concepts which many social scientists are using – the ifications and the izations – are poorly equipped for describing what people do. By rolling out the big nouns, social scientists can avoid describing people and their actions. They can then write in highly unpopulated ways, creating fictional worlds in which their theoretical things, rather than actual people, appear as the major actors. The problem is that, as linguists have shown, using nouns and passive sentences is a way to convey less, not more, information about human actions.

The paradox is that both bureaucrats and natural scientists use heavily nouny styles, often because they can avoid specifying who is doing what. In my view, it has been disastrous for social scientists to follow them. I will be giving examples from critical linguists, who show how bureaucrats and ideologists use particular linguistic constructions, such as 'nominalization' and 'passivization', to avoid specifying who does what in the world. But, just as sociologists prefer to write of 'reification', rather than people 'reifying', so linguists talk of 'nominalization' not people 'nominalizing' and, in doing so, they produce examples of the problem that they are critically examining. At root, there is a problem in preferring the big technical noun to the shorter, humbler verb.

In Chapters 7 and 8, I finally depart from the strategy of taking my examples where I find them. Instead I present some case studies of current rhetorical trends in sociology and experimental social psychology. In Chapter 7, I look at sociological writings, with my case studies initially coming from three articles, which the editors of a major sociological journal have singled out as representing work of particular importance. Then I look at a way of doing sociology – conversation analysis – which seems to be the antithesis of those other three pieces of work.

In Chapter 8, I analyse the rhetorical practices of experimental social psychologists. Perhaps, more than any social scientists, experimental social psychologists try to write as natural scientists do. The end result is not that experimental social psychologists write precisely, but that they routinely exaggerate their results and conceal aspects of what occurred in their experiments. In common with other social scientists, they use their big, nouny concepts incredibly loosely.

In my final chapter, I make some recommendations about how to reverse these patterns of loose, imprecise writing. Having identified the linguistic basis of the problem, it is not difficult to make recommendations: basically the recommendations point to the importance of using ordinary terms where possible and using verbs in the active voice rather than nouns which theorists have formed from verbs. Making recommendations is the easy part, but I have few expectations that they will have any effect. The conditions of academic life, which I analysed in the earlier chapters, will persist and so long as they do, we cannot expect great changes in the ways that social scientists write.

I cannot imagine how my book could possibly change these conditions. A few readers may take heart from what I say; a handful might even try to change how they write; many more readers will find reasons to disagree with me, especially in relation to their favourite big words. The vast majority of social scientists, however, will not read this work, or even know of its existence, and they will carry on as they are.

Some caveats

Having remarked on the book's contents, I should now offer some caveats about what is not in the book. I write loosely about 'social scientists', and, in consequence, readers might expect me to analyse all the social sciences. However, I will only be examining a very circumscribed set of social scientists. It is part of my argument that the social sciences have expanded so rapidly and individual disciplines have become so diversified, that no individual academic can keep up to date with developments within their own discipline, let alone neighbouring disciplines. When Andreski was making his criticisms, sociology was a much more unified discipline, and everyone could recognize who were the senior figures. Now there are diverse sociological approaches, each with their own set of major figures. In the current chaos of social scientific disciplines, we can all be somewhat egocentric, imagining our particular interests to be central, while other approaches are marginal. So, inevitably some readers will take exception to my choice of examples, complaining that I have not discussed the really important approaches. I will return to this in my concluding chapter. However, if I use the terms 'social sciences' and 'social scientists' more generally than I should, then I apologize in advance.

A second caveat is that I am not arguing that social scientists should be public intellectuals. It is true that I am arguing that social scientists should write more simply, and it is true that those social scientists who wish to address the public also need to write simply. And, as Michael Burawoy has argued, there are good reasons why social scientists should seek to address the wider public (e.g., Burawoy, 2005). Because I suggest that academics should write more simply, this does not mean that I am arguing that they should be addressing the general public. Most public intellectuals are bilingual: they use one language for addressing the public and another for addressing fellow specialists. I am suggesting that we address our fellow specialists more simply, whether or not we seek to address the general public. It would be strange were I arguing that we all need to be public intellectuals in a book, which is itself aimed at academics rather than at a wider audience. I will not be rushing to the television studios to tell viewers: 'Did you know that some linguists write about nominalization without telling us who is nominalizing? Isn't that shocking? Aren't you appalled?'

Another advance apology is in order for all the occasions when I might give the impression that all social scientists are poor writers. In consequence, here is another caveat: there are exceptions, but for the most part I will be overlooking the exceptional writers in the social sciences. I will not be trumpeting the stylistic merits of an Erving Goffman or a Richard Sennett or a Deborah Tannen and then saying 'We should all try to be Goffmans, Sennetts and Tannens'. Largely, it would be useless to say this. Notably good writers in the social sciences, as elsewhere, are notable because they have their individual voices which others cannot properly copy. Sadly it is easier to copy really poor writers, than really good ones. Therefore, I am hoping to identify faults in the writings of workaday social scientists in order to say 'We should be trying to avoid these faults'. For the rest of us, who are not Goffmans, Sennetts or Tannens, this is a more manageable, more realistic message. It is certainly more manageable for the large number of academics, whose native language is not English but who find themselves being pressured to publish in English. They have a hard enough job to write clearly in a second or third language without having to aspire to write with aesthetic elegance in that language.

A further caveat is that I am not trying to formulate a theory about the relations between the specialist language, which academic social scientists might use, and language that is more ordinarily used. When I use the terms 'specialist language' and 'ordinary language', I hope that my meaning will be apparent, even if I do not offer exact definitions. Generally, I will be referring to 'specialist language' as the terminology and phrases which tend only to be used by groups of academic specialists; by contrast, 'ordinary language' refers to the vast stock of concepts and phrases whose use is not restricted to speakers or writers belonging to particular specialist groups. The distinction between the two is not absolute, not least because ordinary language contains many words and phrases that started their semantic life as scholarly terms. The verbs 'minimize' and 'maximize' were created by Jeremy Bentham, an inveterate inventor of new words. Today, we can use these words without reference to their intellectual origins – indeed, without even knowing about those origins. Because I am concerned with the ways that academic social scientists are writing today, I am not interested in predicting which academic terms might eventually transcend their narrow circles of origin. I feel confident that the overwhelming majority of specialist terms, which academic social scientists are producing in such profusion, are unlikely ever to trouble the eyes or ears of the general public. However, I will also be discussing some in-between words, such as 'reification', which are neither purely specialist nor purely ordinary terms. When I do so, I will be interested in how academic social scientists, not laypersons, are using these words.

My last caveat is that I am not wishing to obstruct innovation, whether academic or linguistic, nor am I defending the use of old-fashioned English. I have mentioned Orwell's 'Politics and the English Language' as an inspiration, but Orwell's essay has a weak spot. At one point, Orwell recommends authors to choose English words of Anglo-Saxon origin over those with Latin roots. I can understand why Orwell made this recommendation, but it is no part of my argument. When I criticize the use of 'reification', I do not suggest that it would have been better had social scientists used 'thingification'. From my point of view, the problem lies in the suffix – 'ification' – rather than in the etymology of the first part of the word. All my arguments about the use of 'reification' would apply equally to the word 'thingification'.

What I do contest, however, is the assumption that, in order to have original thoughts, you must inevitably create new nouns – or, correspondingly, if you create new words, you are being original. Those assumptions are historically unjustified, for in the past there have been outstandingly original thinkers who have used existing words. Plato's dialogues – and most particularly the character of Socrates – are obvious examples. In the seventeenth century, John Locke rejected the scholastic jargon of philosophers like Ralph Cudworth and wrote clearly and originally using the ordinary language of the day. Also, there are two writers, whom I have already mentioned – William James and his namesake C. L. R. There is another thinker whom I have not mentioned: Ludwig Wittgenstein, who not only transformed views about language, but never used a technical term to do so. His work shows that it is possible to use ordinary language originally, even using it to show how we ordinarily use ordinary language. Although I do not mention Wittgenstein again in this book, his influence runs throughout.

The example of Wittgenstein suggests that big, technical words can restrict, rather than aid, our understanding. This is especially so in current times when self-declared experts can commercially market big new words as big new ideas. Academics, too, often act as if we cannot have a new approach, theory or insight, unless we have a new noun to promote. We should not automatically think that this way of writing is radical. As social scientists, we might feel that we must stand outside current, commercial trends if we are to understand the world, in which we live; if so, that is all the more reason why we should try to use fewer, not more, specially manufactured, competitively promoted big nouns.

Lastly I should add a brief word about the book's title. *Learn to Write Badly: How to Succeed in the Social Sciences* is not the type of title that one would expect for a serious, academic book. Quite apart from anything else, its ratio of nouns to other parts of speech is low – the one solitary noun is even outnumbered by verbs. This is not accidental, for grammatically the title matches my underlying argument. It also parodies the titles of those 'how to succeed' books that are so popular nowadays. But this expresses an underlying dilemma. By exploring the nature of academic writing and by taking apart some of its constituent features, I am inevitably running the risk of providing a manual, which instructs readers how to write in the very style which I am criticizing. I can see no way around this dilemma, except by parody. Nevertheless, even the parody has a serious point. The bad writing, which I am writing about, has not been produced by too little education. Quite the contrary, you have to study long and hard to write this badly. That is the problem.

2   Mass publication and academic life

If we want to understand why academics today write as they do, then we should bear in mind one simple fact: in current times academics are writing and publishing as part of their paid employment. We will not get near to understanding what might be going wrong in the social sciences unless we accept this. By and large, academics today are not writing in answer to a higher calling or because they have dedicated themselves to the pursuit of truth. We are, to put it bluntly, hacks who write for a living. This is the unflattering reality from which we need to start.

Later, I will be examining what social scientists are writing and the styles that they consider normal to use. However, I am not going to start with the writing itself, but with the conditions of academic life today. By doing it that way round, it might be easier to resist some myths that will get in the way of understanding what is going on. Stanislav Andreski in *Social Sciences as Sorcery* (1971) argued that too many young persons were being educated to become academic social scientists, whereas, in his opinion, only a tiny minority possessed the talent to write well or to think originally. Because talent was being spread so thinly, the level of intellectual literacy was sinking disastrously. In my view, the problem does not lie in supposed talent, or lack of it, but it lies in the conditions in which we all are working. To listen to some critics, we might get the impression that all the faults of the social sciences are to be heaped at the door of continental philosophers. If only young social scientists could resist the pretentious nonsense that has been coming from French and German philosophers, then we would be able to get back to robust, empirically minded, good social scientific writing. Again, that is an over-simplification, for there are problems with the so-called robust, empirical way of writing.

In my view, the sorts of rhetorical faults, which I will examine later, are connected with the conditions under which we are working as academic hacks. To adapt a famous phrase, social scientists today are writing in conditions which are not of their choosing. We need, therefore, to ask: 'What are the conditions under which social scientists feel the need to produce the sort of writings that they do?' In this chapter, I will be examining how universities and other institutions of tertiary education have been expanding; how we feel pressure to keep writing and publishing; and how we do so in highly competitive environments, in which we feel it to be quite natural to promote our products. Given that our products are academic words, then we learn how to promote our academic words as part of our employment. These are conditions where the rewards do not go to those who only write when they have something to say and who then take trouble to write as clearly as possible. This is an age of academic mass publication, and certainly not a time for academic idealists.

Disciplines and the modern university

It has been a long time since universities were small, cohesive communities, comprised of male scholars, most of whom were unmarried and practically all of whom were cut off from the world of active affairs. Before the nineteenth century, European universities were not structured as they are today, and one of the biggest differences was that the universities of old were not divided into separate disciplines of study. A student did not enrol to study a particular subject and then receive tuition only from professors who studied that particular subject. As late as the eighteenth century, students would often be taught by a single tutor, who would be responsible for teaching subjects as disparate as classical languages, chemistry, astronomy, philosophy, geometry and theology. In addition to being repositories for all that counted as learning, university teachers were also expected to instil appropriate moral standards in their young charges. In their turn, students would hope to leave the protected world of the university, equipped as young gentlemen, ready to take their place in society. A few might remain in university life. They would tend to lack private incomes as well as the means to find useful employment in the service of their social superiors; they would also be likely to be social misfits who preferred the company of books to that of young women.

The job of an academic has certainly changed since those distant times. The transition has not been sudden, but the foundations for the recognizably modern university date back to the mid-nineteenth century. The German universities were among the first to change and the rest of the world then followed the German model. The old type of university was not meeting the growing need for professionally skilled young graduates, able to enter professions such as engineering, law, medicine etc. Also, with the expansion of knowledge, it was becoming harder to hire teachers who could teach all that needed to be taught. More and more universities had been hiring professors to teach limited ranges of subjects. However, if the universities were to produce new, professionally skilled graduates, then they would need to employ new types of teachers, who would possess sufficiently specialized knowledge to teach a single subject in depth. Throughout Europe and America old universities began to be reorganized, and new universities were founded along the German model. The result was the emergence of the modern research university, structured around separate disciplines (Altbach, 2005; Russell, 2002).

Academic disciplines have continued to provide the basic structure of most universities to this day (Kreber, 2009). One sociologist, who has studied American universities, has commented that 'academic departments are the foundational unit of U.S. colleges and universities' (Hearn, 2007, p. 222). Many university teachers today consider that they owe their primary loyalty to their discipline, or to their department, rather than to the institution that gives them employment or to a wider, undifferentiated community of scholars (Locke, 2008; Poole, 2009). So segmented have modern universities become that they have been described as being composed of competing disciplinary tribes, each battling to possess and enlarge its own territory at the expense of its neighbours (Becher and Trowler, 2001).

In another important respect, the universities of the late nineteenth century differed from their forebears. The members of the new university departments were not only expected to transmit disciplinary knowledge to their students, but part of their remit was to contribute to the production of that disciplinary knowledge. University departments became places where the disciplines were to be developed through research and publication. In the early part of the nineteenth century hardly any of the employed teachers at American universities, such as Brown, Harvard or Yale, were publishing, at least in the areas of their academic appointment. By the 1870s and 1880s about half the academics at major American universities were publishing in their discipline or were active in the learned societies of their discipline (Schuster and Finkelstein, 2008, pp. 25ff.).

Dividing universities into separate disciplinary departments has left its mark on the way that academics write. In the old days before this division, when academics wrote books or articles, they could imagine that they were addressing all their colleagues. For example, Adam Smith did not write his *Wealth of Nations* for specialists in economics. Nor was this a 'popularizing' book in the modern sense: Smith had not first published his theories in specialist journals, using difficult language that only his professional colleagues would understand; and, having done this, then was writing popular, money-making books, using non-specialist terminology to communicate his ideas to a wider audience. Smith expected any educated reader to understand the ideas of *Wealth of Nations*. It had been the same when he had published his first book *The Theory of Moral Sentiments*. Using today's disciplinary categories it would be difficult to categorize the latter book. Is it psychology? Or is it philosophy? One thing is sure: it is not economics. However, Smith was not using one set of jargon for *The Theory of Moral Sentiments* and another for *Wealth of Nations*, as if addressing two distinct sets of reader. In moving his intellectual interests from the nature of moral feelings to the ways that nations create wealth, Adam Smith had not swapped tribal loyalties, but he was doing what any intellectually minded person in the eighteenth century might have done. He was pursuing his intellectual interests where they took him and communicating his ideas as widely as possible. Previously, Descartes, Locke and Berkeley had done just the same, crossing without a second glance those barriers, which today seem insuperable, between sciences, social sciences and humanities.

We might say that someone like Adam Smith was writing in small words for big circles. He was not addressing a small group of specialists, but he was using non-technical words that he thought all educated readers would understand. Today, it is not so easy to move at will from area to area, topic to topic, because disciplines are not just separated by loyalties and administrative structures, but also by divisions of language. Those who work in one discipline will possess a different set of technical terms than those in another discipline, just as carpenters and metalworkers carry different implements in their respective toolboxes. One academic has commented that 'we could probably all recall incidents of attempting to communicate with someone from another discipline and finding that we were using different terms to talk about similar phenomena' (Donald, 2009, p. 37). Or we might find ourselves using the same words to talk of very different things (Hyland, 2009; Hyland and Tse, 2007; Martinez, Beck and Panza, 2009). Mark Waldo has likened the modern university to a Babel, filled with numerous disciplinary voices and he comments that 'as academics we are mostly unable to talk to one another, at least in the languages of our work' (Waldo, 2004, p. 3). The words have become longer and the circles, in which they circulate, have become smaller.

Many academics welcomed the new independent, disciplinary states of the research university, especially those academics who were establishing new subjects such as psychology or sociology. They often sought to create unified disciplinary voices, so that their new disciplinary states would resemble the new nation states of Europe, which were establishing official languages at the expense of provincial dialects and unofficial languages. Some academics, especially those who liked to roam wherever their curiosity took them, felt uncomfortably constrained within the new structures. One such restless roamer was William James. At Harvard, James belonged successively to the departments of medicine, psychology and philosophy before finally leaving the university to work independently. He mocked the new disciplinary perspectives and he particularly mocked Wilhelm Wundt, the psychologist, who, in James's view, embodied the very essence of the German professor – unstoppably pompous and devoted to his discipline (or *Fach*). Wundt wrote voluminously about every branch of psychology, from physiological psychology to what he called 'folk psychology'. James, in a letter to a friend, claimed that Wundt aimed to be a 'Napoleon of the intellectual world', but he would never meet his Waterloo, for Wundt lacked 'a central idea which, if defeated, brings down the whole fabric in ruin' (1920, Vol. 1, p. 263). James continued: 'He isn't a genius, he is a *professor* – a being whose duty is to know everything, and have his own opinions about everything, connected with his *Fach*' (p. 263, emphasis in the original).

As we will see later, William James had another gripe against Wundt. James believed that Wundt used unnecessarily long words to describe simple psychological states of mind and that the great German psychologist did this to impress the impressionable. In criticizing Wundt for this, James was right in thinking that the new disciplinary thinking was creating new opportunities for pomposity. But, in another respect James was wrong to think that Wundt represented the future. When Wundt was working, it was still possible for professors to know virtually everything that was happening within their discipline, but this would soon change. When Wundt became a professor, there were very few journals devoted to publishing articles about psychology. In 1881, Wundt founded *Philosophische Studien*, principally to publish reports of the experiments that were being conducted in his laboratory at Leipzig University. Soon other centres of psychological research began to produce their own journals. *American Journal of Psychology* (1887), *Zeitschrift für Psychologie* (1890) and *Psychological Review* (1894) were established to cope with the growth of psychological research and the development of different schools of psychological research.

Wundt was establishing a pattern, which, when repeated again and again in the coming years, would ensure the impossibility of future Wundts. The great German psychologist did not write for scholars in general but his primary audience was other psychologists and their students. As such, he was using some very large words for moderately small circles of readers, and the circles would become smaller as rival schools developed their own terminology. With time, there would be far too much published within psychology, as well as other disciplines, and this would make it impossible for any individual academic, even one possessing the persistence of a Wundt, to read everything, let alone have opinions on all they read. Future professors, by necessity, would become specialists within particular areas of their discipline. In this regard, neither William James, wandering restlessly from discipline to discipline, nor Wilhelm Wundt, doggedly trying to command everything within his disciplinary state, were early versions of the modern professor. Today, the disciplines are simply too big to control and too powerful to avoid. Size, as we shall see, really does matter; and the intellectual circles, which specialist professors address in their writings, are becoming ever smaller.

The massive expansion of higher education

Although the research university, which developed in the late nineteenth century, might resemble today's universities, there were also important differences. When William James was complaining about Wilhelm Wundt, only about one per cent of young people in the United States received higher education. By 1925 that figure had tripled, but was still well below five per cent of the population (Russell, 2002). Now over eighty per cent of Americans receive some sort of tertiary education. Nor is the United States unusual amongst the developed countries: Finland, Greece and Slovenia, for example, have even higher levels (Altbach, Reisberg and Rumbley, 2009; Kivinen, Hedman and Kaipainen, 2007; Thomas, 2005).

Over the past 100 years, tertiary education has not expanded at a constant pace but there have been sudden spurts and stops. What has been remarkable – and out of proportion to previous increases – has been the rise in students in the past generation. According to the figures of UNESCO, the number of students attending institutions of higher education has been rising in every continent for twenty-five years. It has been estimated that across the world in the early 1990s, there were about 70 million students in higher education; by the end of the decade the figure was around 140 million (Altbach, Reisberg and Rumbley, 2009). Even in sub-Saharan Africa, where the overall level of tertiary education has historically been low, the proportion of young people attending university has been sharply rising (Mohamedbhai, 2008). So great has been the spread of tertiary education, that it has become commonplace for academic observers to talk about 'the massification' of higher education (e.g., Gumport et al., 1997; Trow, 2005).

In passing, I would like to point out that 'massification' is just the sort of concept that I will be complaining about later. It is a big, multisyllabic technical word, built upon an ordinary small word ('mass'). It seems to indicate a 'thing' that social scientists have discovered and, in consequence, need to name. Actually, nothing has been discovered as such – everyone knows that more people are going to university and college than ever before. Social scientists have provided the numbers to back this up. It might be thought that perhaps the concept of 'massification' provides a precise way of talking about these numbers: up to an agreed figure, we still have elite education and beyond a particular point, we can say precisely that 'massification' has taken place. But again there is no agreed tipping point and social scientists disagree about what percentages might constitute 'massification'. In fact, they use the word in very different, and not very precise, ways. I will be returning to this in Chapter 5.

With the sharp increase of students has come a parallel increase in the number of universities, with the numbers of institutions of tertiary education doubling, even trebling and quadrupling throughout the developed and developing worlds over the past fifty years (Altbach, Reisberg and Rumbley, 2009). To give an example from a single country: in 1962 there were twenty-five universities in the United Kingdom, serving around 125,000 students (Lomas, 2001). Thirty-seven years later, there were ninety officially designated universities, together with another forty institutions that award degrees (University Standards Report, 2009). These institutions enrol in excess of 2 million students. In the developed world, Britain is pretty middle-ranking in terms of the numbers of students and universities per head of population. Around the world, new and old institutions of tertiary education are welcoming droves of students whose parents and grandparents would never have imagined receiving higher education.

These increases bear testimony to a worldwide demand for skilled labour. This expansion may owe its origins to the world's changing economic circumstances, but it also has consequences within the world of higher education. More students and more universities inevitably mean more university teachers. According to UNESCO's Institute for Statistics, the numbers of tertiary education teachers across the world rose from just under 6.5 million in 1999 to over 9.5 million in 2007. The United States alone has over 1 million tertiary education teachers. China's increase has been particularly dramatic, with numbers more than doubling between 1999 and 2007. China has now surpassed the United States as the country with the greatest number of higher education teachers. One expert predicts that the number of university teachers, as well as the number of students, will continue to rise in the next twenty years (Trow, 2005). In the light of the present economic downturn, such predictions may need to be tempered. Even if the numbers of students and professors do not continue to rise as they have done, and even if they possibly decline, they are highly unlikely to return to the levels of half a century ago.

Although many of UNESCO's figures are based on estimates, rather than firm data, one thing can be said with confidence. These days, the professor is no *rara avis* to be put on the world's list of endangered species. Throughout the world professors can be easily spotted, flocking in most towns, both middle-sized and large. Every time someone attempts to conduct another census of the species, there seem to be even more of them. Professorially, it is the best of times. But if you were to ask the professors, many would tell you that it is the worst of times.

Mass producing research

Superficially all seems to be well in the academic world, for, along with increasing student numbers, research is booming as never before and, as we shall see, never have academics been publishing so much. This is an age where research, across all disciplines, is being mass produced. Of course, with more academics working in higher education, one might predict an increase in research and academic publication. However, the boom in research is far too big to be accounted for simply by the increase in the number of academics. The job of many academics has changed so that they are now expected to publish as well as teach.

Around the world, universities no longer match the old image of unworldly tutors, sitting in common rooms and engaging in intellectual chit-chat over glasses of sherry. Instead, modern universities are businesses with constant competition between institutions, between disciplines and between individuals. In common with managers working in other industries, university managers today see it as their job to extract ever greater productivity from the employees of the institutions which they manage (and to remove insufficiently productive elements from their workforce). Given that universities are being run on 'business lines', it is little wonder that some observers have described higher education today as 'academic capitalism', with university managers acting like venture capitalists (Slaughter and Rhoades, 2004 and 2009).

There is evidence from the United States that academics, unlike other public professionals, are working longer hours than they did thirty years ago (Schuster and Finkelstein, 2008, pp. 78f.). Certainly, academics have to teach more, so that their institutions can receive more income from student fees per academic member of staff. University managers also see research as a means by which their institutions can obtain extra sources of revenue. There has been a trade-off in the working lives of academics. In return for doing more teaching and research, academics have been relieved of some of the administrative tasks, which they regularly under-took a generation ago. The result does not necessarily mean that today's academics feel liberated to concentrate on the academic matters that interest them the most. Instead, they often feel as if they are losing control over their own working lives and they complain that universities are being run by non-academics, who value the entrepreneurial spirit more than scholarship (Lee et al., 2005). On the other hand, the financial rewards have seldom been greater – at least for a minority of university teachers. The pay differentials between run-of-the-mill university teachers and the academic superstars in elite research universities are growing wider (Lee et al., 2005; Rumbley, Pacheco and Altbach, 2008). Senior managers of universities are, of course, extremely well remunerated.

The great expansion of higher education may have principally been funded by the increase in undergraduate students, but the big financial rewards are going to successful researchers. Those who gain promotions or who obtain the more prestigious appointments are likely to be the most active researchers. This is even true at institutions which have weak traditions for doing research. In less prestigious universities, appointing a senior academic with an established research record of grants and publications is often seen as a means to stimulate research; typically such institutions have to offer large financial inducements and small teaching duties to attract a notable researcher (Lee et al., 2005). Generally the super-paid are the super-researchers, especially in the super-rich disciplines, like business studies or medicine. The result is not just competition but also endemic frustration. Because individual academics are aware that successful research, rather than successful teaching, brings the big rewards, many feel frustrated that they do not have sufficient time to devote to their research (Schuster and Finkelstein, 2008).

On an institutional level, it might seem contradictory that universities and colleges reward individual academics for their performance in research when the income of the institutions comes largely from teaching. However, the position is not altogether contradictory, for the world of higher education is riddled with status and hierarchy (Altbach, 1997). University managers know that their institution would benefit financially from having a good reputation for research. Widely publicized league tables rank order the so-called 'best' universities. Managers want to see their institutions ranked highly and they certainly do not wish to be seen to be slipping down the rankings. The better ranked an institution is, the greater its chance of attracting student fees from wealthy parents, securing lucrative research contracts from outside organizations, and receiving bequests from alumni.

By and large, most league tables, whether providing national or international rankings, give a heavy weighting to an institution's reputation for research. For example, QS World University Rankings publishes a yearly ranking of the world's 'top' 500 universities. Its findings are widely reported in newspapers. In its current publicity material QS quotes a senior figure from the City University of Hong Kong, who says: 'Many senior managers of leading universities around the world now include the QS rankings in their strategic plans because they provide useful, practical targets.' For its rankings, QS uses a series of measures, of which sixty per cent relate to research. A university with a poor or average reputation for its research would not find its way into the QS high rankings.

Governments are well aware of the importance of research for the modern university. In May 1998, President Jiang Zemin of China proclaimed his country's 'Leaping Forward Development'. The aim was to create several world class universities within ten to twenty years. Acknowledging that a world class university needed to be strong in research, the President announced that the top Chinese universities would be funded as research universities. At these selected few institutions, academics would publish at the level expected of international academics, publishing their results in major international journals and writing in English rather than Chinese. The latter proposal drew protests from some traditionally minded Chinese academics in the humanities (Ngok, 2008).

New universities, as well as successful old ones, will be anxious to boast about their achievements in research. In the United Kingdom, the University of Winchester was established in 2005. Its current publicity stresses not only its expertise in teaching and the friendliness of its campus, but also the university's strengths in research. The university's website (in December 2011) claims that 'Winchester has scholars at the very forefront of their disciplines'. The site refers to a national league table, which ranks British universities in terms of their performance in research: 'We moved from 99th to 78th place on the THES (Times Higher Educational Supplement) institutional league tables.' Onwards and upwards, it boasts – as do all Britain's universities, whether long established or just starting out.

The ethos of research has spread throughout the tertiary educational system and even institutions, where teachers have historically done little or no research, now encourage their faculty members to undertake research (Lee et al., 2005). In the late 1960s, only a minority of those working in American four-year higher educational colleges tended to publish regularly; today over sixty per cent do so (Schuster and Finkelstein, 2008, p. 474). In 1992 the majority of lecturers in British colleges of higher education clearly saw their priority as being in teaching; fifteen years later, more than half the respondents claimed to have interests in both teaching and research (Locke, 2008). In Norway the trend is similar: state colleges were originally established to provide vocational education, but now their faculty are regularly engaging in research (Kyvik and Skodkin, 2003).

Individuals employed in less prestigious institutions have a personal interest in doing research, because, not only can they enhance their chances for promotion, but a good record of research can be the entry ticket to a post in a more prestigious institution. Institutions with little previous tradition for research also gain from encouraging their academic employees to take up research. It is not only prestige that they gain, although one should never underestimate the power of snobbery in the academic world. Attracting research grants, whether from public or private financing, is a means of boosting an institution's income (Slaughter and Rhoades, 2004 and 2009). Even academics in the humanities are encouraged to think 'entrepreneurially' (Gascoigne and Metcalfe, 2005).

Institutions may differ in the type of research that they encourage their academic staff to conduct. In the United States, research universities will tend to attract funds from prestigious research councils and their faculty will be more likely to engage in international projects and theoretical developments. The research in community colleges is much more likely to be funded locally and the research projects are more likely to relate to local, rather than national or international, issues (Lee et al., 2005; Hearn, 2007). Such research may be less prestigious – at least in the eyes of the elite superstars – but nonetheless it is a source of income and it will validate the claim that the institution is a serious research institution. Both money and self-promotional claims are crucial in the entrepreneurial culture that is sweeping through institutions of higher education.

Expanding publications

If more research is being conducted then more academics are publishing. In 1969 only half of American academics in universities had published during the previous two years; by the late 1990s, the figure had risen to two-thirds, with even higher proportions in the research universities. The number of prolific publishers is increasing. In American universities the proportion of faculty, who had produced five or more publications in the previous two years, exploded from a quarter in 1987 to nearly two-thirds by 1998, with the rise in the natural and social sciences particularly noticeable (Schuster and Finkelstein, 2008).

In non-university institutions, such as community colleges, the relative numbers of those publishing may be lower than in universities but the numbers are still rising. Over ten per cent of American academics working in non-university institutions are now estimated to be prolific publishers (Schuster and Finkelstein, 2008). Similar patterns can be found in other countries (e.g., Kyvik, 2003; Locke, 2008; Smeby, 2003). Schuster and Finkelstein comment that the system now 'expects research and publication almost across the board'; overall this means that 'not only are more faculty publishing, but more faculty are publishing *more*' (2008, p. 103, emphasis in original). These figures might be somewhat inflated because they do not take account of the growing numbers of part-time teaching assistants that work in the research-based universities and whose employment is designed to ease the teaching burdens of the full-time, permanent academics (Lee et al., 2005).

Individual academics, of course, have much to gain from being seen to be prolific publishers and it is a sign of the times that academics have attempted to quantify the financial rewards from publishing. Tonette Rocco, writing in a book that aims to help and to encourage academics to publish, quotes an economist, who claims that a quality article in a good journal might be worth $200 for every year that the author works as an academic. Questioning whether the financial gain can be calculated quite so precisely, Rocco nevertheless claims that 'a well-placed and well-received article can generate other opportunities with a financial benefit, such as being invited to speak at a conference or other professional event, expenses paid' (Rocco, 2011, p. 4).

Research and publishing have not only spread from universities to colleges but also from richly funded universities in the western world to less-endowed establishments in developing countries. In order to encourage their academics to publish, some of the poorer universities in the world offer financial assistance for research and publication. For example, the University of Ouagadougou, in Burkina Faso, has created financial incentives for its academic staff to conduct research and it has financed two journals in which they can publish their papers (Mohamedbhai, 2008). This is not vanity publishing, pandering to the self-esteem of academics who might find it difficult to publish in the leading American journals of their discipline. There is a potential economic pay-off for the institution. The university's managers will know that the reputation of its research groups – and hence the university's ability to attract research contracts from local and national sources – is enhanced if its members are seen to possess their own portfolio of research publications.

The rise in publishing has been affected by the 'audit culture' that affects universities as it does other public institutions (Shore and

Wright, 2000). The audit culture ensures that institutions and the individuals who work within them are regularly assessed in terms of their performance – and, for academics, performance includes publishing. To receive good ratings, academics must show that they are publishing at, or preferably above, a suitable rate for their institution. Similarly, universities must demonstrate their collective success in publishing if they are to nudge their way up the relevant league tables. Inevitably, the culture of auditing is not just a culture of inspection and managerial control; it is also a culture of boasting. There are good economic reasons not to be modest or to trust that virtue will gain its own reward. In the audit culture, individuals and institutions must proclaim their achievements vigorously.

As far as individual academics are concerned, continual auditing maintains both a constant competitiveness, as well as constant uncertainty, even fear (Brennan, Locke and Naidoo, 2007). Academics will worry about being judged to be publishing at an inadequate rate, or to be slipping behind others. Moreover, the managers are finding, and academics are producing, sophisticated ways to audit and rank publications. 'Citation analysis' has become increasingly important for the auditors, who want to grade academics on more than just their number of publications. The measures of citation analysis appear to identify which publications are most often cited in other articles and, thus, the auditors can claim to distinguish between academics, whose publications are being used by others, from academics whose publications are having little effect. Citation analysts can also produce figures to distinguish journals with high 'impact scores', indicating that on average these journals publish articles that are more likely to be cited in other articles within five years of their publication. The auditors can then reward those who publish in journals with high impact scores (for an excellent, critical discussion on the use, misuse and statistical assumptions of citation analyses, see the report published by Adler, Ewing and Taylor, 2008, for the International Mathematical Union).

Not everyone can place an article in the most prestigious journals with the highest impact scores and, consequently, some publishers are specifically catering to those who wish to publish but find it difficult to place articles in the established academic journals of their field. For example, Frontiers specializes in publishing web-based, open access journals in a number of scientific fields. It claims to take 'a 21st century approach to academic publishing'. Because it is open access, it does not charge subscribers or readers. Instead money is made by charging authors through what the publishers euphemistically call an 'article processing fee'. For some individual academics, this might be their only way to publish and they will see the fee as an investment for future rewards. Institutions, keen on developing their research profile, might subsidize academic employees by paying the fee for them. Either way, those behind publishers like Frontiers believe that they have detected a profitable gap in the market. As long as university libraries continue to pay high subscription fees for journals, paying to publish in electronic journals will be considered by many to be a low status form of publishing; if it is not exactly vanity publishing then certainly it is desperation publishing.

The phrase 'publish or perish' has become a cliché in academic circles, where not publishing is seen as a form of academic death. *Publish or Perish* is the name of a website which enables academics to calculate their own 'citation scores'. The site enables academics to compare their own scores with those of other academics. A few years ago, *Publish, Don't Perish* was used as the title for a book, offering guidance to academics about how to publish their work successfully (Moxley, 1992). There has been a rash of such self-help books recently and this in itself tells us how anxious academics can be to publish. In one of these guides to academic publishing, the author claims to be helping young academics 'so they can flourish not perish' (Belcher, 2009, p. xii). On the opening page of a guidebook for writing in the social sciences, the writers begin by declaring that research is a sort of game with rules and players, 'even winners and losers' (Northey, Tepperman and Russell, 2002, p. 1). In another such book, the authors advise young academics to adopt a strategy for publishing: 'In today's competitive academic environment postgraduate students who want to continue their research career often need to adopt a strategy that separates them from the rest of their peers' (Kitchin and Fuller, 2005, p. 6). In this way, publishing is not seen just a matter of communicating ideas or findings: it offers a means for competing successfully against rivals, and for winning, not losing.

Even the guidebooks do not openly recommend some of the practices that academics use to increase their lists of publications. To do so would be to sacrifice all illusions, to be utterly cynical. Experienced academics know that teaming up with other academics can be a means to increasing their collective output and thereby the total number of papers of which they can be credited as an author (Kyvik, 2003). In a field such as economics, jointly written articles were rare before the 1970s but now they are commonplace (Shaw and Vassileva, 2009). Journal editors, as well as those who have studied academic publishing, recognize the phenomenon of 'salami slicing'. Academic authors will cut their research findings thinly, so that they can maximize the number of publications they can obtain for a single piece of research. In an editorial for the journal *Learned Publishing*, Scott-Lichter (2011) writes that academics are seeking to publish 'the least publishable unit'. Another expert on academic publishing argues that, because citation counts and impact factors are now so important for assessing contributions in the academic world, scientists are routinely opting to salami-slice rather than trying to be original (Souder, 2011). Many researchers, knowing full well that promotions and other rewards can hang on overall citation figures, are careful to boost their citation scores by citing their own work, while denying that this is their motive for doing so (Hyland, 2001).

Not only do academics believe that they must publish voluminously but that they also must publish speedily. In a short article, which concentrates on the state of British universities, the historian Anthony Grafton (2010) has compared modern universities with fast food outlets. Grafton argues that slow scholarship, like slow food, is deeper and richer than the fast stuff. However, the push nowadays is for fast scholarship. This is where the conditions of work directly affect the style of academic writing: fast scholarship means fast writing. It is easier to dash off another piece, resorting to the same old theoretical clichés, rather than struggle to work out new ideas and, above all, to express thoughts clearly.

In a study of British academics, members of all types of institution agreed strongly that the pressures to increase the productivity of research were threatening the quality of research that is being produced (Locke, 2008). The pressures are hard to resist, even when we know them to be harmful. There is auditing from above, asking us to list our publications. At each audit, we will try to ensure that we have sufficient publications to satisfy our managerial superiors. But we cannot put all the blame on the managers. We are also the agents of our own betrayal. Our worries can bring us pleasures. We fret that we are not producing enough publications and we fear that rivals are publishing more than us; our worries drive us onwards; and we experience moments of pleasure when editors of journals accept our papers or when we are invited to international conferences.

And there is pleasure when we enter yet another title to our own immaculately maintained list of publications. We watch with pride as our list grows longer. There is continual anxiety, along with moments of pleasure and pride, but no stopping point. So, we produce our papers, as if on a relentless production line. We cannot wait for inspiration; we must maintain our output. To do our jobs successfully, we need to acquire a fundamental academic skill that the scholars of old generally did not possess: modern academics must be able to keep writing and publishing even when they have nothing to say.

Increase of publications

With more academics publishing more, it is inevitable that the volume of academic publishing should be hitting record levels. As John Thompson has detailed in his excellent *Books in the Digital Age* (2005), academic publishing is now big business. The largest profits come from undergraduate textbooks, but the major academic publishers compete with one another to expand their lists of academic journals. Thompson estimated that more than 12,000 international, scientific journals were published per year. The numbers keep rising, with between 200 and 300 new titles each year, and this estimate only takes into account journals from mainstream publishers. It excludes e-journals, which academics are establishing without the assistance of publishers. The number of academic articles published per year has been rising exponentially in the past fifteen years. Precise figures are hard to obtain, but the broad estimates are staggering. It seems that in 1996 there were over 1 million academic articles published; in 2009 there were probably a million and a half (Campbell and Meadows, 2011; Jinha, 2010).

Faced with the volume of published work, academics must become specialist readers, for, at best, they can read only a small fraction of the material appearing in their discipline. It is difficult to be precise about how many journals are published within each academic discipline, but the abstracting services offer an indication for the social sciences. *The Social Science Citation Index* claims to index regularly 1,950 journals across the various disciplines of the social sciences. This means that it deals with 2,900 new articles per week. *Current Sociological Abstracts* claims to monitor regularly over 1,800 journals, which publish material of relevance to sociologists. It divides these journals into three categories: core journals, priority journals and selective journals. The core journals are 'published by sociological associations, groups, faculties, and institutions, and/or have the term "sociology" in their titles'. At present, there are, according to *Current Sociological Abstracts*, 329 core sociology journals.

No sociologist could read all these core journals, and rough calculations would show the impossibility of attempting to do so. Let us assume that each core journal is published four times a year and that each issue contains six articles. That means there would be 7,896 articles per year. If each article takes an hour to read, then, a reader, working a forty hour week for fifty weeks of the year, would need three-and-a-half years to read all the core sociology articles for any single year. This would allow no time for anything but reading – no writing, no lecturing, no research and without time allowed for sickness or public holidays. Because the rate of publication exceeds the rate of reading, the reader would be continually falling further and further behind. And that is only the 'core' journals: it does not include the 'priority' journals.

The figures for sociology may seem daunting, but they do not compare with those for Wundt's old discipline of psychology. In recent years a number of companies have offered services, surveying psychological and psychiatric journals. *Psychwatch* claimed to have produced a 'comprehensive list' of more than 1,000 psychology journals, separated into twenty different 'disciplines'. *Psycline* advertises that it keeps track of more than 2,000 psychology and social science journals. Information sources, such as these, seek to provide a service to hard-pressed academics who do not wish to waste their time wading through thousands of irrelevant titles just to find a handful of papers of interest. Most academics, however, do not pay to use such services, but they develop their own strategies to find relevant articles. They look for articles with their specialist topic in the title; they tend to select articles written by researchers whom they have heard of; and, above all, they are likely to read articles that are available online (Tenopir et al., 2011). Nowadays, academics do not seem to have the time or inclination to wander around libraries, pulling books or journals from the shelves. They want to access reading matter from their desks. And they want it now.

The pressures for quick, focussed reading are reflected in a curious anomaly in the state of current academic publishing. Despite the overall expansion of academic publishing, the market for academic monographs has collapsed (Thompson, 2005; Steele, 2006). Given the increase in university teachers, one would have thought that the potential market for monographs would have increased, especially in the social sciences. Compared with the natural scientists, social scientists cite a higher proportion of books in their published articles (Huang and Chang, 2008). So, the more articles that academics write in the social sciences, the more academic books have to be read and cited. But, it seems that publishers are finding they are selling proportionally fewer monographs. That means that fewer social scientists are buying and/or reading books. It seems that they prefer to access information electronically in much smaller units and, in this, academics are acting like other people, who use their personal computers to obtain information quickly and efficiently.

In general academics are no longer thought to be special people. The title 'professor' does not carry the cachet that it did in Wundt's day: there are simply too many of us about for that. Nor are our working environments particularly special. We have managers, who use the same management jargon as the managers of non-academic corporations. In requiring us to increase our productive outputs, our managers do not handle us as if we were special beings, engaged in an almost sacral mission to discover truths and to uphold ancient values of scholarship. The days for such claims are long past. Even as we work, we resemble non-academics: our habits of academic reading resemble the way that non-academics – including ourselves when we are not working – consume the products of mass culture.

'Mass culture' is somewhat of a misnomer, for what was once broadcast to a mass audience is now targeted at specific segments. There are specialist channels for particular sorts of music, comedy and other forms of entertainment. It is easy to select just what one wants and to ignore the rest. If we want to listen to country-and-western music or jazz or hip-hop, there are stations to cater for our wishes. We can download particular songs without having to listen to whole CDs. The media are targeting their audiences, aiming newspapers, magazines, television channels, music and so on at particular types of audience. The net result is paradoxical. There may be more variety available than ever, but we are becoming narrower in our reading and viewing habits.

Samuel Becker, the distinguished analyst of contemporary media, has made this point forcefully. We can have what we want and we can avoid what we don't want. We must make a special effort to encounter variety, for, according to Becker, 'it rarely comes about serendipitously'. In consequence, we are developing ways of living 'within our own, restricted cocoon of information and experiences, with insufficient knowledge of the experiences of others' (Becker, 1999, p. 25). The sociologist Eric Klinenberg (2005) makes a similar point when he claims that we live on 'informational islands', receiving the news and information that media producers are targeting at people like us. The more we gain our news from the electronic media, the more that we can avoid the variety of material contained traditionally in newspapers. In theory, we could use the electronic media to widen our tastes but, in practice, we use them to narrow our experiences.

Becker and Klinenberg could have been writing about academics. There may be a greater volume and variety of academic work being published today than ever before, but this does not mean that we have a new generation of enlightened academics, who have broader knowledge than their forerunners. The reverse is the case. We have to ignore all but the publications relevant to our own specialist island. We have little time to wander at will around the library, browsing haphazardly. Search engines direct our attention to 'relevant' articles, which we can then download. We do not have to subscribe to whole journals, whose contents we might browse as we physically hold a complete issue in our hands.

As professional academics, we must extract the small nuggets of material relevant to our interests from the mass of stuff that is being produced. Finding what we need to read necessarily means overlooking so much else. The more that is published in our discipline, the more there is to ignore. In consequence, the sheer volume of published material will be narrowing, not widening, horizons, containing us within ever smaller, less varied sub-worlds. It is important to remember that no one has designed this system. There was not a moment in history when a group of powerful figures sat down in secret around a table and said: 'Let us create a situation where academics have to read narrowly and to write at speed; that will stop them making trouble.' No secret meeting deliberately planned all this. But this is where we are now.

Fragmenting disciplines

So far, I have been writing about what has been occurring generally within higher education. The push for more students, research and publications affects social and natural scientists alike. But the consequences for the state of academic disciplines have not been uniform. All the traditional disciplines have become so large that they are inevitably federations of subdisciplines and sub-subdisciplines. There are tribes within tribes. But not all the disciplinary, or tribal, federations have the same sort of structure. In the social sciences, the fragmentations have been particularly sharp, with the fragmented elements often seeing themselves as intellectually incompatible with one another.

My focus, here, is on the social sciences, not the natural sciences. One can imagine the disciplines of the natural sciences to be divided principally by topic, rather than by philosophy or ideology. For example, in botany, specialists on tropical plants, pollens, agronomy, fungi and so on will be interested in different aspects of the discipline. The experts on pollens will read different journals than the experts on fungi. They may even compete for funding opportunities, research students and professorial positions. On the other hand, they may collaborate on the occasional research project. Mainly, they can imagine that their intellectual interests, while not overlapping, sit alongside each other. There is no mortal incompatibility between the mycologists with their fungi and the palynologists with their pollens. Both can see themselves as developing parallel knowledge, contributing to the overall development of botany.

In a number of ways, the social sciences tend to differ from the natural sciences, for in the social sciences, knowledge is not as cumulative as in the natural sciences. Social scientists, when examining contemporary problems, will often return to old classics for inspiration, especially if they are embarking in new directions. Natural scientists tend only to cite recent journal articles in their papers, ignoring old books and articles. In doing this, they are assuming science to be cumulative: new findings are built upon slightly older findings and there is no profit to be gained by going back to really old stuff (Crane and Small, 1992; but see Kyvik, 2003). To a much greater extent, social scientists will be liable to believe that their contemporaries have taken wrong turnings and that there can be great value in returning to the old classics, in order to renew the discipline and to construct fresh approaches. In consequence, the disciplines of the social sciences are frequently divided into opposing camps, rather than parallel ones. These opposing camps are likely to hold divergent philosophies, to have different intellectual origins and to propose mutually incompatible visions for the overall discipline.

There are parts of the social sciences – most notably, economics and experimental social psychology – where the practitioners try to follow the model of the natural sciences. Their articles tend to follow the patterns of citation that the natural sciences use – namely, citing recent journal articles, rather than older articles and books (Crane and Small, 1992; Kousha and Thelwell, 2009). Even in these comparatively harmonious sections of the social sciences, there is a growing sense of fragmentation. The distinguished experimental social psychologist, Albert Pepitone (1999) has reflected on the development of social psychology since the 1950s, when he began his career. Pepitone comments that today's social psychology is much more differentiated than it was in the past. Nowadays one becomes an expert in a particular topic area, rather than in social psychology itself. Moreover, the various sub-groupings tend to be isolated from each other. Their members do not read the work of the other sub-groups and they do not attend the same conferences. The result is that the sub-groups sometimes develop different technical terms to describe the same things; for Pepitone, and other experimentalists of his generation, this is a cause for regret.

The sub-groups, about which Pepitone was talking, share similar basic principles, using similar experimental methods and adopting similar practices for writing their reports (in Chapter 8, I will be discussing these practices critically). Pepitone does not mention that there are other social psychologists, who reject the methods and practices of the experimentalists and who are seeking to build very different forms of social psychology. By and large, the mainstream experimentalists ignore these non-experimentalists, treating their way of doing social psychology as not being 'proper' social psychology. Most of the large American textbooks of experimental social psychology do not mention their work at all. The image of social psychology, as an internally coherent experimental discipline, is maintained by banishing the dissidents to the cold Siberian outlands, where they can be conveniently forgotten.

In sociology, by contrast, the divisions are much more openly marked, for sociology is, to use the terminology of Andrew Abbott (2001), a 'fractal' discipline. It does not posses a single, dominant approach but instead it comprises various sub-groupings that are often theoretically and methodologically at odds with one other. Some sociologists might regret this lack of unity, believing that the discipline should aim to unify itself (Scott, 2005). Others may celebrate sociology's increasing 'hybridity' as a sign of its vitality (e.g., McLennan, 2003; Stanley, 2005). There tend to be more conflicts about appointments, tenure and promotions in fragmented disciplines, such as sociology, than in more unified ones (Hearn, 2007). Despite all this division, sociology is not about to collapse as a discipline, for the proponents of its various disputatious sub-units are not seeking to break away in order to form their own independent disciplines. In the main, their professional positions depend upon them working as 'sociologists' in sociology departments, teaching students who have enrolled for courses in 'sociology'. Rather than seeking independence, the sub-units are battling for status within, and control of, their fractious, fractal discipline.

In this regard, the differences between the sub-groups of sociology are not analogous to those in botany. For example, the relations between epidemiological sociologists and the post-colonial theorists are likely to differ from those between mycologists and palynologists. Differences in sociology can take on the complexion of mortal conflicts and one notable sociologist has written of 'the sociological wars' (Burawoy, 2009). One type of sociologist will often believe that their opponents have a misguided, even worthless conception of what sociology should be. They will argue as if they want to tear down each other's edifices. It is as if the mycologists wanted to rid botany of all pollens, so that the fungi could rule unchallenged.

On the other hand, the warring sociologists are likely to hold temporary ceasefires, especially in the face of common enemies. When university managers propose to close down a sociology department, or when government departments announce that they are cutting funds for sociological research, the competing factions will come together to present a publicly united front against the threat. They will declare that they are protecting sociology in all its valuable variety. When the various factions have no struggle against powerful outsiders to unite them, then they return to their normal state of civil, and sometimes uncivil, warfare.

Competing approaches and journals

Observing the state of German philosophy in the first half of the nine-teenth century, Marx and Engels wrote wryly that 'mighty empires have arisen only to meet with immediate doom, heroes have emerged momentarily only to be hurled back into obscurity by bolder and stron-ger rivals'. They continued: 'Principles ousted one another, heroes of the mind overthrew each other with unheard-of rapidity' (1846/1970, p. 39). Marx and Engels might well have been describing the state of modern sociology, but for one point. The great socialists were imagining that the academic revolutions had to follow one another in quick succession, as if the next revolution could not live alongside the previous one. At a time when academic work is being mass produced, the rival approaches do not have to appear successively, one at a time. Instead, the various sociological alternatives will be made available together; any good sociology department will stock a wide selection of approaches.

Once disciplines become fragmented – or fractal – then an academic's disciplinary loyalties are neither simple nor fixed. It is not sufficient just to be a sociologist or a psychologist. The type of sociologist or psychologist will matter, both in terms of the topic to be pursued and the approach, or approaches, to be taken. In the social sciences, you will be expected to take an approach, rather than just view the world directly, naively or hopelessly eclectically. In taking your approach, you will be expected to join the subdisciplinary, even sub-subdisciplinary, tribe that comprises others like you and that officially shares, defends and promotes the approach that you take. As a tribal member, you will meet fellows at special sym-posia, read each other's papers and comfort one another when the bullies from rival approaches sneer at the ideas that you hold dear. You will hope to join a friendly, supportive community, where you will make lots of new friends; but, even if you do, you should still aim to scoop the big prizes for yourself.

Generally the mutually incompatible sub-groupings of sociology and of analogous disciplines will be competing with each other – whether for influence within the disciplinary associations, funds from grant-awarding bodies or just to be heard above the din of all those other academic voices. The multiplicity of journals reflects this. Having one's own journal becomes a way for those academics, who are developing a different approach or opening up a new topic, to establish their sort of work. They will no longer have to struggle to publish their pieces in unfriendly journals, battling against the presumptions of editors who might prefer a different sort of approach. A new, specialist journal will be a visible sign that your approach has arrived and that it has recruited enough followers to mount its own independent challenge to existing approaches.

Amongst the journals in the social sciences, there are some whose titles indicate that they are forums for a particular sort of approach. This includes some journals which the *Current Sociological Abstracts* list as being 'core' journals: for example, *Qualitative Sociology*, *Studies in Symbolic Interaction*, and *Critical Sociology*. The last named declares itself to 'be committed to publishing scholarship from a Marxist, post-Marxist, Feminist, and other critical perspectives'. Authors submitting papers, which are written from other perspectives or promoting other ways of doing sociology, are likely to have their work rejected regardless of its quality. Anyone wishing to publish in *Longitudinal Surveys of Australian Youth*, another 'core' sociology journal, will know that both their topic and their methodology will need to fit the highly specialized focus of the journal.

Two examples from social psychology show how journals can take explicitly partisan stances within disciplinary debates. *Papers on Social Representations* is a forum for social psychologists, following the theory of social representations, which Serge Moscovici originally formulated (1961 and 1963). Supporters see this approach as constituting a new form of social psychology that opposes mainstream, American-based social psychology (Moscovici, 2000, pp. 54f; Marková, 2003 and 2008). *Papers on Social Representations* is involved in promoting international conferences and other activities that bring together sympathetic researchers into what the editors call 'the social representation community' (Editors, 2003, p. 3.1; see Billig, 2008a). The editors of *The International Journal for Dialogical Science* outline their editorial hopes on the journal's website. They state that their journal 'aims at the development of a "dialogical science" as a future goal'. They comment that a central concept in any such a dialogical science is 'the "dialogical self" that brings together, in innovative ways, theoretical traditions regarding "self" and "dialogue"'.

It is not only new journals that are involved in such promotional work. Many, if not most, journals have their own character and that means that their editors and their editorial boards exercise preferences for certain sorts of work over others. Some of these preferences can be quite explicit, even if they are not expressed in the words of the journal's title. *Research on Language and Social Interaction* bears a title that indicates its general topic, but the editors favour qualitative approaches, particularly studies using the techniques and ideas of conversation analysis. Authors, who examine language and social interaction through other methods, such as experimental social psychology or psychoanalytically influenced social theories, are unlikely to have their papers accepted for publication in the journal. *Theory, Culture and Society* does not deal in the sort of predictive theories that quantitative researchers might formulate to explain large-scale data about societies and cultures. The journal specializes in philosophical theories, particularly those associated with continental social philosophy. In this regard, *Theory, Culture and Society* is situated at the furthest end of sociology from *Longitudinal Surveys of Australian Youth*. One might predict that these two journals share few, if any, editors, authors or readers in common.

The various communities or subdisciplinary tribes are, to an important extent, groupings with their own academic codes and vocabularies. As David Russell has commented, academic communities develop their own 'conventions of argument, evidence, diction, style, organization, and documentation which allow those familiar with the conventions to recognize and understand the writing of a particular community' (2002, p. 13). Communities can also have their own special terminology, and some concepts may be accorded protected status for their existence is vital to the existence of the approach. As will be discussed in Chapter 7, the concept of 'governmentality' is vital for 'governmentality studies'. There could be no 'social representation community' without the concept of 'social representation'. The editors of *International Journal for Dialogical Science* are giving advance warning that they will treat 'dialogical self' as protected property. Prospective authors know that they will increase the chances of their papers being accepted in these journals if they use these words.

Generally, the editors of journals in the social sciences do not accept papers that are written in ordinary language and that are devoid of specialist terminology (Garbutt, 2009). But the editors will not treat all jargon as equally acceptable. For most journals in the social sciences, there will be some sets of terminology that will identify the author as belonging to an approved approach, discipline or subdiscipline. This means that many journal editors are likely to practise, without conscious intention, a restriction upon free use of language. They will want their published authors to write in ways that their readers feel comfortable with. Some words will have to pass stringent tests before they can gain admittance. Others will be protected currency, circulating untaxed between authors and readers.

A brief example of editorial writing

My argument in this chapter has been that the big trends, affecting higher education globally, have had a series of consequences which have affected the ways that academics earn their living. And this, in turn, affects the way that they write and publish their research. The result, at least as far as the social sciences are concerned, is that the universities now resemble hot-houses in which temperature and humidity have been perfectly adjusted for growing, as far as the eye can see, pot after pot of big words and clunky phrases.

Before passing on, I want to briefly give an example of the sort of clunky writing that I have in mind. This will act as a foretaste of what is to come in subsequent chapters. I have mentioned academic journals, but I have not yet mentioned a much prized feature of most academic journals: the system of peer review. Editors select suitably qualified peers to review anonymously any paper which has been submitted to the journal. In this way, editors will obtain suitably unbiased opinions to help them decide whether the paper should be published. In sending the paper to the reviewers, editors will typically conceal the name of the author. Because reviewers do not know who has written the paper, they should not be influenced by personal considerations. In turn, reviewers know that their identity will not be divulged to the author. Accordingly, they will be able to offer their opinions openly without fear of recrimination.

Defenders of peer reviewing claim that the system improves the quality of published papers. Supporters might add that it helps to improve the style of published writing. Academics rush to send off their submissions, under pressure to produce publications rapidly, but the process of review-ing necessarily slows things down. Editors and their reviewers are likely to ensure that the submitted draft is not the final draft. They will generally insist that the author works further on their paper and they might make specific suggestions to raise the overall style of writing. That, at least, is the theory. But the practice might well be somewhat different. Editors and reviewers will be just as busy as the authors and they will also be authors of academic papers. As such, they are likely to be affected by the conditions that encourage hasty writing, and, more generally, they are likely to support prevailing intellectual and literary standards (Frey, 2003; Souder, 2011). Far from improving standards of writing, they might be average writers themselves.

To illustrate this I have selected an example almost at random. It is taken from an email message sent by two editors who were planning a special issue of a journal specializing in qualitative psychology. I received the message shortly before I started preparing this chapter, and I am using it illustratively because it arrived at a convenient time – not because it is particularly noteworthy. The editors were soliciting contributions for their special issue which was to examine the topic of researchers combining different qualitative methods. They wrote:

This combining of ontologies and epistemologies gives rise to both benefits and creative tensions and provides a focus for inquiry into enhancing awareness of researcher impact.

The aim of this Special Issue is to provide an international forum within which the disparate array of questions that are arising about a pluralistic approach to qualitative research in psychology can be posed and debated. Recognising the potential that this approach offers for accessing the different layers and dimensions of a complex and constructed social reality brings with it both curiosity and questions about its ontology, epistemological tenets, theoretical frameworks and practical applications.

I think that the meaning is decipherable but the passage is not clearly expressed. The third sentence is particularly awkward, with its long grammatical subject and the ambiguous use of 'its', which is well and truly cut off from its referent. The words, especially ones like 'ontologies' and 'epistemologies', as well as phrases such as 'enhancing awareness of researcher impact', seem to have been slapped on without due care, rather like a house painter trying to cover a surface with undercoating as quickly as possible. It is hard to be confident that editors, who can write in this way, will act as guardians of good style.

If I were to continue along these lines, I would, in essence, be developing an aesthetic argument. It is quite true that I do not warm to this style of writing on aesthetic grounds. But, as I hope to argue later, that is beside the point. At root, my argument is not based on aesthetics, but on identifying the linguistic characteristics of much social scientific writing and then trying to show why such characteristics are not best fitted for the social sciences. Having drawn attention to the aesthetics of this extract, I want to pass on to the sort of aspects that I will be discussing in more detail later.

We can note what makes the extract particularly clunky. It is stuffed with big nouns and noun phrases, such as 'ontologies' and 'epistemologies', as well as phrases like 'enhancing awareness of researcher impact'. We can also note that no people appear in this extract: no one is identified as doing anything. If anything is to be done – any action is to be performed – then it will be an abstract concept that does it. The combining of epistemologies and ontologies gives rise to something – with the combiner left in the shadows. People are not identified as recognizing the potential of this combining, but the recognizing itself does something: it brings with itself 'curiosity' and 'questions'. And both these latter two things – curiosity and questions – seem to exist independently from any identifiable people who might be curious and who might be asking questions.

This abstract way of writing – filled with conceptual nouns and emptied of people – is something that we will encounter many times in subsequent chapters. It is a conventional way of writing, but with unfortunate consequences for the social sciences. In analysing this style of writing, I will not entirely abandon all aesthetics. I want to suggest, however, that, once an academic has the requisite big words at their disposal, it is easier to bang out paragraphs of clunky writing, than to try to clarify exactly what one means. Nevertheless, there can be advantages in writing unclearly.

This extract also possesses another characteristic that we shall encounter later and that should not be surprising, given what I have already been suggesting. The authors of the extract are promoting an approach, acting as if they were advertising the unique sales points of their product. The editors are not specifying that the special issue should be based around a problem which they want contributors to discuss and to assess for themselves. Instead, they are suggesting the stance that contributors should take – namely that they should support the combining of different methods. Moreover, the editors are identifying this as 'an approach'. They even give the approach a name – it is 'a pluralistic approach'. And their words convey support for this approach.

They state that the combining of ontologies and epistemologies produces 'both benefits and creative tensions'. They are not asking contributors to discuss whether it does so: they are stating that it does. One would normally expect the word 'costs' to follow the phrase 'both benefits and ...'. But here 'costs' and other bad things are rhetorically excluded. If there are 'benefits and tensions', then these are not just any 'tensions': the tensions provoked by a pluralistic approach are creative ones. The antithesis has ruled out tensions that might not be creative. And who could deny the virtue of a 'creative tension'? In effect, this means that there are 'both benefits and ... even more benefits'. In this way, the authors are implying benefits all the way.

We can know in advance that the special issue is not going to be filled with papers that examine the 'pluralistic approach', only to find it wanting. The special issue will be an opportunity for showcasing 'the potential that this approach offers'. In addition to suggesting the stance that is to be approved, the editors, by their own choice of wording, indicate the sort of concepts that they might expect their contributors to use: words and phrases such as 'epistemologies', 'ontologies', 'constructed social reality' etc. Potential contributors should gain a reasonable idea about what is wanted, both in terms of position and approved rhetoric – they can see what words might be circulated as untaxed currency.

There is one last point. I have been talking about social scientists often feeling the need to declare that they possess 'an approach'. To wander forth into the social sciences without an approach is almost like going naked into a shopping mall. The extract illustrates this nicely. The special

issue could have been about researchers, who, when faced with a complicated research project, use a variety of different sorts of qualitative methods without being committed to any one in particular. However, the
editors of the special issue have an approach to offer. For them, using
different qualitative methods is not just a matter of picking up various
tools where one finds them – doing a bit of this and a bit of that. The
editors are presenting this as 'an approach', as something that is more than
the sum of its parts. Moreover, these editors are advertising the benefits
that their pluralistic approach can bring to consumers. In effect, they are
calling out: 'Use this approach to increase curiosity, awareness and
researcher impact.'

This is something to which I will be returning later – namely that
academics are regularly using the rhetoric of promotion within their
work. In this chapter, I hope to have outlined in general terms some of
the promotional and competitive conditions under which we are working
as academics. Social scientists should not be surprised if the ways that we
earn our living seem to be affecting the ways that we habitually talk and
write. This means that, if we want to understand the social world in which
we live, we should be prepared to examine how we, social scientists, learn
to write in the strange styles that we currently accept as normal.

3   Learning to write badly

No one is born with the ability to produce the convoluted sentences that academic social scientists regularly write. This bad writing is highly educated. Academic social scientists will have typically spent the greater part of their lives in education, passing every possible exam. Accordingly, the problem of writing badly cannot lie in a lack of education, but in the sorts of education that social scientists have received. So, we need to see what literary skills young social scientists are expected to acquire and how these skills, even if they do not aid clear thinking, may help to bring them success in the business of being social scientists.

A number of years ago, the great French sociologist, Pierre Bourdieu, claimed that academic language was 'a dead language', because it was 'no-one's mother tongue, not even that of the children of the cultivated class' (Bourdieu, Passeron and de Saint Martin, 1996, p. 8). We can ask how young apprentice academics take on this dead language, imparting to it some sort of life and, in return, giving their lives to this language. Actually, the phrase 'dead language' is misleading, because, as I hope to show in later chapters, academic language is not quite as dead, or as detached, as Bourdieu imagined. Nor is it actually a language: in order to write academically, one has to use the same grammatical rules, turns of phrase and words, especially verbs, which ordinary people use for non-academic purposes. In the case of academic English – the most widespread of all current academic languages – its apparently dead aspects are parasitic on a language that is very much alive.

Anyone seeking to analyse the conditions for bad social scientific writing is faced with a problem. One has to rely on the studies which academic social scientists have conducted into the matter and which they have published using their own forms of social scientific language. In this chapter, I will be citing the work of social scientists who have examined how undergraduate and postgraduate students acquire the necessary academic skills for writing their essays and theses. In the main, the authors of these studies have made some interesting observations. For example, I will be looking at Bourdieu's classic study of undergraduate essays; his remark about academic language being a dead language comes from this study. The problem is that the academics, who study academic language, usually use academic language to analyse this language. And this can limit their ability to be critical, for they are employing the very tools whose use they are examining.

However, what seems to be a problem can also be an opportunity. In this case, I will do more than just draw upon the studies which Bourdieu and others have produced, for I will also use these works as my case studies. Because these authors are using academic language, their own writings are examples of what the authors are ostensibly writing about. This is true whether or not these authors self-consciously make this connection, and generally they do not make it. By using such studies as my exemplars I will circumvent the temptation to go searching for extreme examples of bad academic writing. Instead I will be following the strategy of taking my examples where I find them.

In following this strategy, I will be treating studies of academic writing as if they convey both intended and unintended messages. The intended messages are the findings and the theoretical ideas that the authors are overtly seeking to communicate to their readers. But in presenting their findings, the authors can use some rather odd turns of phrase and these provide the unintended messages. Sometimes, the unintended messages can be as revealing as the intended ones – and on occasions, far more revealing.

Bourdieu and puffed-up language

Pierre Bourdieu makes a particularly apt starting point: not only was he one of the most eminent sociologists of his generation, but throughout his life he was concerned about the nature of academic writing and the social conditions on which the life of the scholar depends. According to Bourdieu, most academics are incapable of understanding the nature of the life that they lead, for they are like fish that cannot notice the water in which they swim (Bourdieu, 2000). Most of Bourdieu's analyses were conducted before higher education and academic research began to be mass produced to the extent that they are nowadays. As a result, some of his ideas about academic life, as well as his specific analyses of the essays that undergraduates wrote for their professors, can feel a bit dated, but such is Bourdieu's great insight that many social scientists continue to use his ideas and his technical terminology.

One of the basic conditions of academic life was, according to Bourdieu, that academics are required to use the 'dead', academic language. They need to learn that their mother tongue, or naturally acquired way of speaking, is inappropriate for the academic tasks ahead of them. Acquiring this new form of language is particularly difficult for those who, like Bourdieu, come from non-academic, working-class backgrounds. They have to shake off their ordinary, common-sense view of the world. As Bourdieu wrote:

Entry into a scholastic universe presupposes a suspension of the presuppositions of common sense and a *para-doxal* commitment to a more or less radically new set of presuppositions, linked to the discovery of stakes and demands neither known nor understood by ordinary experience. (Bourdieu, 2000, p. 11)

That sentence captures Bourdieu's ambivalent, but ultimately accepting, stance towards academic language. This English translation follows the original French very closely, both grammatically and in terms of its meaning (Bourdieu, 2003, p. 25).

Had he so wished, Bourdieu could have phrased the sentence much more simply, and certainly more personally. As it stands, it is utterly impersonal. It is about abstract things, not people: abstract things, such as 'entry into a scholastic universe', 'suspension of the presuppositions', 'ordinary experience', 'the discovery of stakes', 'a *para-doxal* commitment' etc. One after another, Bourdieu slots these abstract entities into place, and, in so doing, he keeps people from trespassing on the cleanliness of the prose. Grammatically there is no one, no person, who might be entering a scholastic universe, discovering stakes, experiencing the ordinary world, suspending presuppositions. Even ordinary people are not the grammatical subject when Bourdieu describes what they do not know or understand: it is literally a thing – ordinary experience (*l'expérience ordinaire*) – that these other things are neither known nor understood by (or within). Of course, one might say that Bourdieu, like many other social scientists, is seeking to express general laws, rather than describing individual persons. Even so, he could have written generally about a hypothetical person, saying, for instance, that 'anyone entering a scholastic universe must suspend what they had previously supposed to be commonsense . . .'.

We might say that anyone entering the academic world of the social sciences should be prepared to fill their sentences with abstract nouns and to empty them of people, whether real or hypothetical. We shall see much more of this later and try to specify exactly what is going on. It is doubtful that Bourdieu, when writing the above sentence in the original French, deliberately thought to himself 'I must make sure that I don't sound like my parents or grandparents, and the way to do that is to load up the abstract nouns and keep out the people.' Most social scientists, like fishes in water, do not notice what they are doing. They just keep swimming through the density of their own prose.

The sentence, which I have quoted, comes in a passage in which Bourdieu describes his unease with being an academic, who is set apart from the circles in which he grew up. He was writing of his admiration for Pascal, because of the latter's sympathy for ordinary people and impatience with the 'puffed up' words of intellectuals (Bourdieu, 2000, p. 4). Bourdieu certainly knew well what Richard Sennett called the hidden injuries of class (Sennett and Cobb, 1993). Although Bourdieu might sympathize with Pascal and might voice his distrust of puffed up words, he could not resist the academic pressure to puff up his own words. He took on the academic duty to leave simple words and common sense behind. Extra syllables must be added to key words, as if they were badges of scholarly membership. Bourdieu's most famous term – 'habitus' – adds an extra syllable to 'habit'. As Bourdieu wrote, 'habit' is just mechanical, but 'habitus' is more than an environment of habits: it is something that generates how we behave: 'It's a kind of transforming machine that leads us to "reproduce" the social conditions of our own production' (1993, p. 87).

In later chapters, we shall see more writing, in which sociologists and other social scientists postulate machine-like things that supposedly lead people to behave as they do. It is as if these fictional things, which the social scientists have created, have more reality than the people they supposedly control. If, like Bourdieu, social scientists wished to study the academic world and the conditions by which it exists, they would be searching for the 'academic habitus': they are then likely to treat actual academics – their habits and their hopes – as symptoms of the important fictional hidden machine that apparently determines what we all do.

Bourdieu, students and professors

In the 1960s, Bourdieu, in association with co-workers, conducted a study of university teaching and, as part of this research, he examined how well undergraduate students learn the academic language that they hear professors use in their lectures (Bourdieu, Passeron and de Saint Martin, 1996). If students do not become proficient users of this dead language, what exactly are they learning? In posing this question, Bourdieu was deliberately cutting away the academic myths that university professors had encouraged to accumulate. His examination of the practices that hidebound professors used in their teaching may have been radical, but on the issue of academic language, he tended, somewhat conservatively, to side with the professors.

Bourdieu and his fellow researchers looked at essays which French undergraduates in philosophy and sociology had written as part of their courses. They found that the essays did not test what the students knew but whether they could manipulate academic language. The professors, who marked the essays, did not expect their students to understand academic language, let alone criticize it. It was acceptable for them to use this language superficially, for the essays were little more than 'an imposed test of rhetoric' (Bourdieu, Passeron and de Saint Martin, 1996, p. 80). According to Bourdieu, the students' task was to reproduce the words in 'a finite bunch of semantic atoms, chains of mechanically linked words' (p. 14). The students of philosophy would hear their lecturer using words such as 'Descartes', 'methodology' and 'epistemology', and, when writing their essays, they would devise sentences with these words linked together.

Doing this may require a number of literary skills, but it does not demand genuine understanding. You can devise a sentence linking 'Descartes' and 'epistemology' without properly understanding Descartes's philosophy or the concept of epistemology. The students might even take pride in their sentences but that does not mean that they are thinking philosophically. Professors were party to the conspiracy that tolerated students' ignorance. So long as things sounded alright, little else seemed to matter. As Bourdieu and his colleagues put it, both sides were locked into playing a game that was suited 'to hiding ignorance under the cover of mediocrity' (p. 15). In arguing this point, Bourdieu distinguished between a superficial use of academic words and a genuine understanding of those words: student essay writing, he suggested, followed the logic of 'acculturation', rather than the logic of a proper 'cultural apprenticeship' (p. 16).

Both students and their professors were taking for granted that ordinary language was inappropriate for answering the questions posed by the essays. In this context, the use of academic language was 'a given'. Accordingly, the professors and their students were endowing 'a particular set of linguistic requirements with all the objectivity of an institutional fact' (p. 35). This was the safest path for both. Any teacher, who forgoes 'the marvels of professorial language', risks appearing as a primary school teacher (p. 14). Any student, whose essay gives up 'the protections and securities' that come from repeating the lecturer's rhetoric, risks exposing their level of understanding to critical assessment. Such a student 'necessarily pays the price of clarity' and will be likely to receive a poor mark (p. 14). On both sides, then, there are reasons to use professorial words, even at the expense of clarity, or, perhaps, *especially* at the expense of clarity.

At this point Bourdieu could have gone further but did not, for he too accepted 'the given', that the professors must use their special academic language. As such, he assumed there to be a clear division between professors and students. Both have good reasons for avoiding simpler, ordinary language, but he assumed that the professors use academic language properly, while the students use it superficially. Bourdieu acknowledged that his study was limited, because he had only looked at students of philosophy and sociology. He was confident, however, that his findings were more general, because, if students of philosophy and sociology were insensitive to the meaning of academic words, then students in other disciplines were likely to be so much worse. After all, in the disciplines of philosophy and sociology 'academics, as well as students, are professionally trained in the correct and precise management of specialized vocabularies and in the rigorous linking of ideas' (p. 4).

Here Bourdieu shows his basic trust in his own academic world. He believes that sociologists, like himself, are trained in the correct and precise use of their specialized terminology. Bourdieu's contrast between professors and students – between the genuine and the superficial – depends on this assumption. But what if the distance between students and professors is not as great as Bourdieu was imagining? What if the professors themselves do not properly understand the words that they were using? Perhaps they, too, chain together big words, in order to appear suitably professorial in front of colleagues and students.

In the early days of academic disciplines, William James criticized the way that psychologists, especially Wilhelm Wundt and his followers, were using technical terminology. James was particularly irked by the term 'apperception', a particular favourite of the Wundtians. James believed the word to be both unnecessary and imprecise: there were already perfectly adequate words in the English language – such as 'interpretation' 'conception', 'assimilation', 'elaboration' or simply 'thought' (James, 1890, Vol. 2, pp. 107f.). James worried that young people were being too easily overawed by pompous professors. In his *Talks to Teachers*, James wanted to reassure his audience of prospective teachers that using heavy words was not the mark of a heavyweight intellect. When young teachers listen to professors talking of 'apperception', they might assume that the word contains 'a recondite and portentous secret' whereas it actually means 'nothing more than the act of taking a thing into the mind'. In James's view 'psychology itself can easily dispense with the word', especially since its main purpose was to enable professors to appear professorial in front of the impressionable (1899, pp. 156–7).

We can here see a crucial difference between James and Bourdieu. James was hoping to give young people the confidence to see through professorial bombast, while Bourdieu was putting more trust in the professors and their big words. The students, whom Bourdieu studied, may not have been able to use professorial language properly, but they were following the so-called logic of 'acculturation': they were taking on board the culture of the university and of their chosen discipline. This included accepting that, if you were to become a real philosopher or a real sociologist, then you needed to use special, big professorial words (such as 'habitus', 'acculturation' and 'para-doxal commitment'). Such big words were necessary, or so it is said, because the equivalent small ones, that non-professorial speakers might use, were too imprecise and too unacademic – just too plainly ordinary – for the professors.

The glorious ideational metafunction

Much has changed in the universities since Bourdieu analysed those student essays. Students are no longer the privileged minority that they were in Bourdieu's day, nor are professors. It might well have been possible for Bourdieu to imagine that academics were using an old craft skill, when they devised obscure words for the 'para-doxal' tasks that they undertook. William James, of course, was not so easily taken in. Today the scale of innovation is very different, for there is constant mass production of new terminology, as countless academic word processors hum through day and night. And a sense of commerce is never that far away from this continual semantic production.

One thing has not changed: university students in the social sciences still have to learn professorial words if they are to pass their courses. They no longer, however, receive the words, as it were, from on high. At the time when Bourdieu was analysing French students of sociology and philosophy, the conventional procedures for teaching seemed designed to emphasize the distance between professor and student. As Bourdieu noted, even the use of physical space conveyed the difference of status: the professor sat in a formal lecturing chair on a dais, raised above from the audience, who were expected to receive the professorial words in respectful silence.

That kind of distance is no longer acceptable today, as students see themselves as paying customers. The student consumers expect good, prompt service; they certainly do not see themselves as worshippers at the feet of professorial high priests. Teachers must not talk down to their classes, either literally or figuratively, but they are expected to provide instantly accessible 'learning resources', to maintain electronic contact with their students and to make the learning situation as much fun as possible. No longer is grading the prerogative of the professors, but students will officially rate their teachers. The ratings given by the students will be checked by managers, who will be aware that a series of bad ratings for teachers can have adverse economic effects on future admissions. If professors today just sat in their lecturing chairs, intoning their strings of academic words, the students would not admire their superior brilliance. They would complain.

Teachers, nevertheless, have other ways to promote their own status and that of their academic language in the eyes of their students. In the era of mass-produced research, academic teachers are more likely, than those in Bourdieu's day, to be the authors of many academic publications. They can (and, most likely, will) post their own publications as 'learning resources' on the courses for which they are responsible. Their students will then realize that their own teacher possesses the status of a published expert. Although the students will probably not understand their teacher's publications any better than they understand those of other academics, they may well be impressed that this friendly, approachable teacher, whom they know as 'Pam' or 'Dave' or 'Liz', appears to be a figure of some significance.

Because Bourdieu's research belongs to another age, we cannot assume that his findings hold true today. Accordingly, we might repeat the mantra which researchers in the era of mass research frequently utter: 'More research needs to be done.' But, as is often the case, more research has already been done. In particular, some researchers have examined student essays more systematically than Bourdieu and his colleagues did, in order to find out more precisely what might distinguish good student essays from those that are not so good (e.g., Lee, 2010; Knoch, 2007; Tang and Suganthi, 1999; Hyland, 2009, ch. 6). These sorts of studies offer the opportunity to look at intended and unintended meanings – particularly to examine similarities between the ways that students use academic language in their essays and the ways that researchers do so in their papers about students writing their essays. The distance, as we shall see, may not be as great as Bourdieu had imagined.

Undergraduate students may know what is expected of them, when they have to write essays, but they may view their tasks somewhat differently from the professors who have set the tasks for them. By and large students in the social sciences know that they are not expected just to write down their own ideas in their essays but that they must discuss the ideas of established social scientists (Myers, 2006). This means that they must acquire their material from other sources, but it is not straightforward how they gather this material. The students know that they have to copy it from textbooks and other sources, while making superficial alterations for they are aware that their teachers consider 'plagiarism' a major offence – something that perplexes many students (East, 2010). Other academic requirements can be even more perplexing. Teachers expect their students to write essays in styles that are appropriate to the discipline that they are teaching. This can result in students being praised by teachers in one discipline for a style of writing that will receive poor grades from a teacher in a neighbouring discipline (Reynolds, 2010). Students tend to attribute this to the foibles of the individual teachers, rather than to the requirements of different disciplines (Lea and Street, 1998).

Some researchers have tried to identify the features that distinguish a good social science essay from a poor one. Sue Starfield (2004), who teaches academic writing, has examined essays written by first year sociology students from disadvantaged backgrounds at a South African university. Her study is interesting both for her intended messages and for her own style of writing. She interviewed students and their teachers, and she read the students' essays and the comments that the markers wrote on these essays. By and large, she found that the teachers gave higher marks to essays which used conceptual language, particularly 'highly nominalized language' (p. 72). Highly nominalized language is language which contains high numbers of nouns and noun phrases. As I will discuss in later chapters, academic writing in the social and natural sciences tends to contain a higher ratio of nouns and noun phrases than many other forms of writing. In rewarding highly nominalized writing, university teachers are rewarding work which appears to reflect the grammar of academic writing in the social sciences. But, as I will be arguing later, highly nominalized writing can be deeply problematic for the social sciences.

Starfield looked closely at one essay, which particularly impressed the teacher and for which the student, identified as 'Ben', received very high marks. 'Ben' was answering a question about Marx's concept of exploitation and its relation to Marx's 'desired endpoint of socialism'. The teacher had especially liked Ben's introduction to his essay, in which, according to Starfield, the student had clearly linked 'the semantic fields of exploitation and socialism' (p. 71). Starfield does not specify what constitutes a good linking together of 'semantic fields' nor does she attempt to distinguish it from the sort of chaining together about which Bourdieu complained.

Both Starfield and Bourdieu refer to abstract concepts as 'semantic fields' but they do not indicate why they do this. What is to be gained by writing that the student links 'the semantic fields of exploitation and socialism', rather than just writing 'the student links the concepts of exploitation and socialism', or even 'the student links exploitation and socialism'? Why is there the desire, on the part of the academic writer, to link the terms 'exploitation' and 'socialism' with the term 'semantic field'?

One might guess that any student, who writes in their essay about linking 'the semantic fields of exploitation and socialism', would score even better than a student who only writes about linking 'exploitation and socialism'.

If anything is gained by adding the phrase 'semantic fields', it is not necessarily clarity. The phrase does not act as a lens which suddenly makes a fuzzy image appear sharp. A reader would be unlikely to find Starfield's sentence perplexing if she had used 'concepts' rather than 'semantic fields'. In this instance, the lens itself is fuzzy. A lay reader might naively ask 'What is a semantic field?' or 'How do we know where one semantic field stops and another starts?' These questions cannot be answered simply. In any case, such questions are not encouraged by the casual, and unexplained, use of the term. The writer presumes that her readers will understand what is meant by the phrase 'the semantic fields of exploitation and socialism' without knowing what exactly a semantic field might be.

What, then, is gained by using the term 'semantic fields' in this context? This conceptual linking is a form of name-dropping. The academic writer, who drops a conceptual name, is making the reader aware of their knowledge. In effect, they are saying: I don't only know about this student and this essay, but I know about the semantic field of 'semantic fields'.

In the following sentence Starfield makes another linkage and drops some names. She is referring to 'Ben's' linking of semantic fields: 'This use of the ideational metafunction was also found by Prosser and Webb (1994) to be characteristic of successful essays' (pp. 71–2). The author is dropping the name of a previous study 'Prosser and Webb (1994)'. There is another name dropped, the name of a thing: 'the ideational metafunction'. Note the use of the definite article: this is not merely 'an ideational metafunction' but '*the* ideational metafunction'. Starfield does not explain what 'the ideational metafunction' is, any more than she explains what 'a semantic field' is. She does not use 'the ideational metafunction' elsewhere in her essay. Something odd is going on.

Prosser and Webb, whom Starfield cites, also examined essays written by undergraduate students of sociology and these authors sought to identify the linguistic features that distinguish successful from unsuccessful essays. In the previous chapter, I mentioned that many academics in the social sciences believe that they must have an approach. Prosser and Webb claimed to have two approaches: 'phenomenography' and 'systemic functional linguistics'. The concept of 'the ideational metafunction' comes from the latter perspective. Prosser and Webb examine their student essays in relation to two metafunctions: 'the textual metafunction' and 'the ideational metafunction'. They used 'the textual metafunction' to refer to the ways that essay writers provided readers with indications about the structure of their essay – for instance, if the writer mentioned early in the essay which themes they would be discussing later and the order in which they would discuss them. Prosser and Webb found that successful essay writers did this regularly – that is, they used 'the textual metafunction' (or gave pointers to the structure) more than did unsuccessful essay writers.

Then, Prosser and Webb analysed the essays in terms of 'the ideational metafunction'. They explained what they meant by this concept: 'By ideational metafunction, we refer to meaning in the way that it is usually thought of: as content' (Prosser and Webb, 1994, p. 132). So, in analysing the ideational metafunction of the essays, Prosser and Webb were analysing what is usually called the content of the essay. Why not use the usual word? The authors do not claim that the academic concept is more precise than the usual term. After all, they explain the meaning of the posh concept in terms of the workaday one: the ideational metafunction means content. They do not justify using the technical term by claiming that it has a wider or narrower reference than 'content'. It seems that they could just as well have used 'content' as 'the ideational metafunction'. But there is a difference. Had they used 'content', they would have missed the opportunity to name-drop: in this instance, to drop the name of a concept that would link their analyses with systemic functional linguistics (which is one of their two approaches).

This tells us something about the name-dropping in Sue Starfield's article. By referring to 'the ideational metafunction' and to the previous study of Prosser and Webb, the author is not referring the reader to something that the authors of the previous study had analysed more technically. She is not saying: 'Ben's essay shows great use of the ideational metafunction, but I haven't space here to explain what this precise, technical concept means but, if you are interested in finding this out, you should look at Prosser and Webb (1994).' Instead, she is using an apparently technical concept and at the same time dropping the names of authors who explain this concept in terms of a very ordinary word. In consequence, there is a chain of name-dropping that leads us back to the ordinary language concept. On the way, there is no actual analytic gain, which might help us notice something about 'Ben's' essay that we would not have noticed otherwise. There are only some big words being dropped.

Starfield, as well as Prosser and Webb, are doing something similar to those students whom Bourdieu studied. They are chaining together academic terms without demonstrating deeper knowledge. Readers, who are not specialists in systemic functional linguistics, might possibly be impressed by the authors' familiarity with the technical concepts. They might take on trust that the notion of 'the ideational metafunction' leads us to something much more technically precise than do the ordinary words 'content' or 'meaning'. Curiously, if we pursue this linkage, we will find more, not less, imprecision.

The concept of 'the ideational metafunction' comes from the work of the linguist Michael Halliday. However, Halliday did not devise this term to refer precisely to identifiable linguistic features, such as particular parts of speech or grammatical structures, but he used the term to describe the general contexts in which language supposedly evolved. Halliday argues that language evolved in its present forms so that it could be used for broad functions: such as the interpersonal function, to act out interpersonal encounters; the textual function, to create coherent texts; and the ideational function, to connect logic and experience. As Halliday admits, these are very abstract notions about the general functions of language. They do not refer to the particular functions that individual speakers might use their specific utterances to achieve. To distinguish this general sense of function from a more particular sense, Halliday commented with some wryness: 'Since "function" here is being used in a more abstract, theoretical reading, I have found it helpful to give the term the seal of technicality, calling it by the more weighty (if etymologically suspect) term *metafunction*' (2003, p. 18; emphasis in original).

Neither Starfield nor Prosser and Webb used the concept of 'the ideational metafunction' in this abstract, theoretical sense, but they were using it to give their own writing a seal of technicality, as if they were using the phrase to describe something specific in the undergraduate essays that they were examining. Actually, Halliday warns against trying to identify these metafunctions in particular uses of language. He states that, apart from trivial exceptions, 'every act of meaning embodies all three metafunctional components' (2003, p. 18). So, to suggest that an essay writer is making use of the ideational metafunction is either to suggest something trivial or to use 'the ideational metafunction' in a different way from that for which Halliday designed the concept.

Either way, the authors are not using 'the ideational metafunction' to identify something linguistically precise. They are following in the footsteps of Wundt and 'apperception': they are using an impressive concept, not to identify a discovery, but to cover over a lack of discovery. The authors have not actually succeeded in demonstrating what exactly distinguishes the successful sociology essay from the unsuccessful one. Starfield cannot point to a precise linguistic feature to explain why Ben's essay appealed to his marker. 'Semantic fields' and 'ideational metafunctions' seem to be saying more than just 'Ben handles theoretical ideas well'. Without these concepts, the academic analyst might appear little more advanced than the academic teacher who told the researchers in another study 'I know a good essay when I see it but I cannot describe how to write it' (Lea and Street, 1998, p. 163). The term 'ideational meta-function', just like 'the apperceiving mass' in Wundt's writing, conveys depth and understanding without delivering on either.

Any students, who look to these articles as models of how to write in the social sciences, might gather that it is good to link 'semantic fields': this is what academics do and they seem to think it is a practice worth copying. The students might realize that, in order to link semantic fields, you do not need precise arguments or clear concepts: a bit of name-dropping will serve, as well as some big abstract phrases to convey the seal of technicality. By contrast, ordinary terms, however comprehensible they might be, will normally carry no links with sub-fields or theoretical approaches. As Bourdieu implied, ordinary words carry the whiff of the junior school, not the university. They will not create further links, but, worst of all, they might present matters in the sort of awful clarity that academics would wish to avoid: the clarity that exposes that there has been no big discovery.

To judge by the example of 'the ideational metafunction', fellow academics are unlikely to question name-dropping links. Academic journals in the social sciences, especially those with a strong empirical bent, tend to practise a policy of 'onwards and upwards'. Editors prefer to publish new research articles, rather than pieces that pore over the casual wordings of previous articles. Generally in the social sciences, journal editors do not encourage papers that might reveal the superficial rhetoric of their own journal's contents. In defence of current publishing policies, one might say that academic papers are subject to rigorous reviews by experts and that reviewers will weed out superficial references before papers are published. But the review system operates by *peer*-review. If superficial name-dropping is endemic, then the peers, who act as reviewers, are themselves likely to engage in such practices and to see them as standard. The same is true for the editors, who choose the reviewers. The example of 'the ideational metafunction' does not come from an academic author who stands outside the system of academic publishing. Sue Starfield is a co-editor of the journal, *English for Specific Purposes*. This journal specializes in publishing research about the teaching and learning of academic English. She is a distinguished exponent of her field.

A student reader might gain a further tip from the papers discussed here. Writers should seek to locate their work within competing approaches. Generally it is insufficient just to do a piece of work: you should not merely examine a topic, such as student essays, as if you are just looking directly at a slice of the world. You have to say where your work is coming from. This means presenting your work as belonging to something wider – namely, an 'approach', a 'perspective' or a 'theory'. To do this effectively, you should name-drop – whether actual proper names, such as 'Halliday'; or the official name of the approach 'systemic functional linguistics' or 'phenomenography'; or you might name a concept, such as 'the ideational metafunction', and expect your readers to pick up the linkage for themselves. In this way, you will present your work as if it comes with the backing of powerful friends and carries the patronage of impressive technical terminology. The links will be more than links. Through them come opportunities for promoting your work, your approach and your academic self.

This is the grand promotional metafunction, which is very much a part of contemporary academic communication. Prosser and Webb promote the so-called 'phenomenographic approach', which links their work theoretically and methodologically to the 'phenomenography' of Ference Marton (e.g., Marton, 1986 and 1994). According to Prosser and Webb, the phenomenographic approach seeks to go beyond analysing texts (such as student essays), in order to understand the mind of the author of those texts. Proponents not only read students' essays, but they also interview the students about their writing, trying to find out what they might have been thinking when they were actually writing. Doing both things – analysing texts and interviewing their authors – is more than just doing two things: it is an 'approach' and, as such, it merits an impressive name to distinguish it from all other approaches.

'Phenomenography', therefore, is to be presented as possessing unique selling points. Prosser and Webb (1994) admitted that there had not been a great number of previous phenomenographic studies, but these were early days. They wanted to promote this approach, writing in praise of what phenomenography can do. We learn that 'phenomenography favours a dynamic approach' (p. 136); and that 'combining a phenomenographic and a systemic functional perspective . . . provides an opportunity to develop a coherent understanding' (p. 137). Who would not want a dynamic approach or an opportunity to develop a coherent understanding? This sort of claim has more than a passing resemblance to promotional language that boasts the worth of commercial products: this yoghurt improves digestion; this detergent kills all known germs; and this research favours a dynamic approach. Phenomenography might not kill all known ignorance. But, do you want to produce something coherent? Then try Phenomenography right away. Improve your research with new, scientifically tested Phenomenography.

Learning the subdisciplinary language

When undergraduate students write essays, they tend to do them as compulsory tasks over which they have little control. The teacher decrees the subject of the essay and the student complies by reading the recommended texts and then producing the allocated number of words within the permitted time period. That is how it works. The students have hardly any elbow room, for they are boxed in by requirements. In the social sciences, they will know that they should use the special words that their teachers find important and whose meanings the textbooks sometimes explain. Overall, it is little wonder that undergraduate students, as Bourdieu noted, reproduce these words without showing great commitment or insight. These are not the students' own words in any meaningful sense; they are using them briefly and pragmatically.

With postgraduate students, the situation is different. They are engaged in a process of study which many of them hope will lead to their becoming professional academics. At first glance, the life of the doctoral student represents an enviable moment of academic liberty between the prescribed curricula of the undergraduate and the responsibilities of paid employment. In most countries and in most disciplines, doctorates are awarded for a sustained piece of original research. In comparison with the undergraduate, the postgraduate student appears free to study a topic of their choice. We might imagine doctoral students as enjoying the liberty to pursue ideas at will – young enough to challenge the orthodoxies of older academics but mature enough to turn their challenges into creative programmes of original research.

It sounds good in theory. Sometimes it might happen like that in practice. More often something much more conservative occurs, as young academics acquire skills that enable them to fit into the academic world as it is. Foremost amongst these skills is the ability to use the words and literary styles that are appropriate for their small part of the academic universe. Paul Prior, who has studied how postgraduates learn to use academic language, has called this the acquiring of 'disciplinarity' (Prior, 1998). He stresses that learning to use disciplinary language is a major part of developing 'disciplinarity'. What happens, as we shall see, involves something similar to the 'acculturation' that Bourdieu disparaged.

In the age of mass research, it is not good enough merely to think like a sociologist or an anthropologist or a political scientist. To become a fully-fledged member of the discipline in question, and to partake of its identity, one has to be able to write like a proper sociologist or whatever. A central part of any doctoral student's *rite de passage* from student to professional academic is to write an extended thesis that is appropriate for the discipline in which they are studying. In most universities, the regulations for doctoral degrees typically stipulate that the student's thesis should be their own original work and that it should be of 'a publishable standard'. Most young academics nowadays will not obtain their first teaching position without having already successfully written their thesis and possibly even published some papers.

The young academic has to pick up some general, literary skills, as well as ones peculiar to their own discipline. For example, academics generally seem to have a penchant for using phrases that enable them to hedge their bets, by implying more than they actually state (Hyland, 2005 and 2009). Thus, across disciplines academics will tend to use the vaguer 'associated with', rather than the more specific 'caused by' (Flowerdew, 2007) or to say that their results 'indicate', rather than 'show', a particular conclusion (Johns, 2006). The guidebooks for writing academic prose often instruct students how to imply vaguely rather than assert directly. One recent guidebook states that it is often impossible to state that something is or is not the case and so 'there are verbs that allow you "to hedge your bets", by not coming down on one side or another': the authors recommend for such situations phrases such as 'these results *suggest* that . . .' or 'this could be the case' (McMillan and Weyers, 2010, p. 112). Actually these phrases are not neutral, for writers typically use them to favour one side rather than another. The authors of the guidebook, therefore, are educating their readers to write in suitably vague ways, so that, even if it is impossible to state whether something is or is not the case, one can still give the impression that one thing is (or maybe) the case.

Although there might be some turns of phrase that academics in general find useful, nevertheless there are disciplinary and subdisciplinary differences. To write like a sociologist is different from writing like an economist and that is different from writing like a historian and so on (Holmes, 1997, see more generally Bhatia, 1993; Hyland, 2009; Swales, 1990 and 2006). In some disciplines, academic writers might make more, or less, use of certain phrases or types of sentence. Academics, whatever their background, seem to favour conditional sentences which start with 'it' – such as 'it would seem that . . .' or 'it can be argued that . . .' (Hewings and Hewings, 2006). Although academics in general might use these 'it' sentences more than journalists or fiction writers do, some might use them more than others. It would seem that linguists tend to qualify their statements more than economists, or so it could be argued (Dahl, 2008).

All these small and large differences explain why some researchers, who study the subject of academic writing, stress that there is no single 'academic literacy' – no single set of rhetorical and linguistic practices that all academics employ. Instead, the modern university is, in their words, a place of multiple, academic 'literacies' (e.g., Lea and Street, 1998; English, 2002; Lillis and Scott, 2007; Reynolds, 2010). Such researchers underline their point, by calling their approach 'the academic literacies perspective'. The noun 'literacy' does not comfortably take a plural in most other academic circles. For the followers of this perspective, the plural is not merely permissible: it is de rigueur.

Actually 'disciplinarity' is too broad a term to describe what the successful postgraduate needs to achieve. As was discussed in the previous chapter, disciplines today, especially those in the social sciences, are amalgams of different, even opposing, approaches, methodologies, theories, topics and so on. They have the characteristic that Abbott (2001) called 'interstitiality'. That means there is no single way of writing sociology that every aspiring postgraduate must learn, as if they are acquiring an official language through which all educational business must be conducted. Different types of sociology – different sociological approaches – have their own literary styles, favourite concepts, recognized authorities and even ways of arguing. The young sociologist, by writing their doctoral thesis, will be learning how to become a particular sort of sociologist, not how to become a general sociologist. Their linguistic home will not be the whole discipline, but a small sub-part of the discipline. When they write, their choice of words will reveal their intellectual allegiances, just as a speaker's accent can disclose from which part of the country they originate. In this world of subdivided disciplines, no one is expected to lose the accent of their speciality, at least as long as they can keep publishing, obtaining grants and successfully promoting their academic products.

Becoming a native academic

Paul Prior asks a very important question: how do postgraduates in the social sciences learn to use the special language of their academic discipline? When they begin their doctoral studies, they will only have a halting knowledge of this language, gathered principally from listening to undergraduate lectures, downloading learning resources and writing essays that might show promise but will fall well short of professional standards. Yet, by the end of their doctoral study, they should be using their subdisciplinary dialect with all the fluency of a native. How does this change come about?

According to Prior, postgraduates acquire their literary skills by engaging in a variety of different activities. He looked at their written work, interviewed them and observed them engaging in the sorts of activities that postgraduates are encouraged to engage in: such as attending seminars, discussing their work with supervisors and with fellow students, attending conferences, participating in workshops, delivering papers, asking questions, answering questions, reading drafts of others' papers, engaging in argument, and so much more besides. He stresses that there is not one single activity, which on its own is crucial for becoming suitably literate in the academic world. To become a member of a discipline the postgraduate student has to use academic language in a range of different academic contexts over time.

By engaging in these activities, students find themselves being socialized into the academic culture of their subdiscipline. They absorb the concepts and literary practices of the circles which they are entering, copying the linguistic habits of their professors. As such, the whole process possesses a fundamentally conservative element, for the students will be accepting what is already there, taking it up as their own. They will be seeking to join the academic world as it is. Prior, however, is careful to emphasize that the students – or at least the best of them – are not merely copying their professors. He distinguishes between three different levels at which students can use the language of their teachers: 'passing', 'procedural display' and 'deep participation'.

The graduate student, who simply wishes to pass their exams, tries to copy directly the language of their teachers, reproducing the professorially approved words in their written work. Sometimes, their work is tantamount to plagiarism. 'Procedural display' is one step up from 'passing'. The graduate student makes a display of using the approved terminology, often connecting the words of the teacher to the details of their own projects, but doing so in ways that are superficial. 'Deep participation' involves students taking on the concepts of their professors, but using them to develop, rather than adorn, their own investigations and to provide fresh insights. One would like to think that proper academic work requires 'deep participation', whereas 'passing' resembles the sort of superficial copying that Bourdieu found in undergraduate essays and 'procedural display', despite being a small step up from simple copying, still does not represent genuine academic work.

Actually it is not so simple. We have already seen how academics can engage in name-dropping, displaying rhetorical practices that are much closer to what Prior is calling 'procedural display' than to 'deep participation'. In fact, professional academics, who operate highly successfully within their circles, can find it extremely useful to display procedurally their links with big concepts and notable theories. This is clearly an academic skill, which can be used to impress others face-to-face at conferences or in seminar discussions but it can also impress the readers of one's written papers. Young postgraduates can pick up this skill by copying their elders, observing how they name-drop both in person and on the page.

Just like the learning of a foreign language, so the acquiring of academic language occurs gradually over time. By participating in various activities, students find themselves being socialized into the academic culture of their subdiscipline, learning how to speak and write appropriately. Prior has his own way of describing this. He writes that in graduate education, literate activity 'is central to disciplinary enculturation, providing opportunity spaces for (re)socialization of discursive practices, for foregrounding representations of disciplinarity, and for negotiating trajectories of participation in communities of practice' (1998, p. 32; see also p. xiii for a very similar description).

That sentence has more than its share of impressive academic words. It is written by someone who has been well absorbed into the world of academia, and into a part of that world where doing academic work means using this sort of language. Prior is himself demonstrating how postgraduates should write in order to demonstrate their 'disciplinary enculturation' into that part of the academic world which he inhabits. The addition of (re) before 'socialization' conveys that this does not happen all at once. The postgraduate cannot swallow a single pill, or read one special guidebook, and then expect that words and phrases such as '(re)socialization', 'disciplinarity', 'the ideational metafunction', 'trajectories of participation', 'interstitiality' etc, will suddenly pour forth within the appropriate 'opportunity spaces'. It takes time, practice and habit.

What Prior does not say is just as important as what he does. He does not claim to have found that postgraduates develop their terminology because, in the course of doing their work, they have personally confronted the limitations of ordinary language. Postgraduates do not start off by using their normal language – or what Bourdieu implied was their living language – and then find that their research meets an impasse which they can only overcome by seeking out different words and phrases, either because they are confronting new problems, which cannot be expressed in old ways, or because they have been discovering new phenomena, for which there are no existing names. Rather it is the other way round. The need to acquire the new language comes first. In order to do their research in the appropriate ways and to be linked to the worlds of others doing research, the students must learn new sets of words; and they use this odd way of writing and speaking as a sign that they are entering into the world of research, thereby leaving behind their ordinary ways of talking and writing.

Possessing an approach

What most postgraduates acquire from their supervisors is an approach. As was discussed in the previous chapter, academics in the social sciences typically feel that they need to have an approach if they are going to be seen to conduct research successfully. Their approach will tell them what to look for and how to find what they are looking for. Above all, an approach must have a name, so that it can be identified and the researcher can say that they are following the 'phenomenographic approach' or the 'literacies approach' or whatever is the name of their chosen approach. This way, researchers can appear to be following something 'real', something with substance, not just their hunches.

An established social scientist with a suitably labelled approach will be likely to want to recruit others, especially students, to their approach. This is even more likely, if that social scientist is proposing a new approach which they and their colleagues have announced to the world. Size really does matter. An approach with thousands of recruits across the world will be a successful enterprise. And success will bring further success. The adherents of a successful approach are likely to run regular conferences, publish their own journals, attract funding, convene postgraduate workshops, present awards to the founders and so on. An approach without recruits will be a disappointment. 'Phenomenography' did not fail to sparkle because its ideas were drab or its methodology unoriginal – those deficits have not held back other approaches. It failed because its adherents did not attract recruits in sufficient numbers. It never made the big time.

Most approaches provide their followers and their students with more than methodologies or theories, for they also provide them with 'things', or, to be more precise, with technical terminology which stands for 'things'. Most of the special phrases, appearing in the quotations, which I have already cited in this chapter, are nouns or noun phrases. As Sue Starfield wrote, the good student in the social sciences will use highly 'nominalized' language. I will be discussing in later chapters how academic language is packed with big nouns and why this might be intellectually harmful for the social sciences. But for now, we can note how easily academic social scientists, by using their special terminology, can find themselves writing about 'things': disciplinary enculturation, (re)socialization, opportunity spaces, disciplinarity, literacies, semantic fields, etc, etc. In the quotations, all these refer to 'things', which are presumed to exist, to be real.

In consequence, a postgraduate student entering a sub-world in the social sciences is likely to be entering an environment in which they will be provided with names for special things, whose existence is unknown by non-specialists or those with 'ordinary experience'. Again, the words are likely to come first. If students have learnt to speak of 'the ideational metafunction' – and to speak as if they were describing something that actually exists – they will come to take the existence of 'the ideational metafunction' for granted, even when apparently explaining it away as little more than 'content' or 'meaning'. For them, this thing, which supervisors, visiting professors and fellow researchers take seriously, will not be a fiction: it will be real.

In his book *Writing/Disciplinarity*, Paul Prior unintentionally illustrates how this can occur. In the preface, he tells readers that he takes a 'socio-historic approach' in order 'to study the sociogenesis of disciplinarity' (p. xiii). He says that the 'sociohistoric framework' provides a way of seeing writing and disciplinarity 'as situated, distributed and mediated activity' (p. 5); and that the sociohistoric approach views communication and the person as 'concretely situated, plural and historical phenomena' (p. 19). In writing thus, Prior is exemplifying the sort of phraseology of his approach: mediated activity, sociogenesis, situated activity, disciplinarity etc, are all 'things' that are real in the universe of the sociohistoric approach. In addition, Prior suggests that he has a 'practice-oriented approach' (p. x). His practice-oriented approach, however, is not separate from the sociohistoric approach. They are related, for the sociohistoric approach itself takes a practice-based approach to language.

It must be admitted that Prior does not label his approaches snappily in *Writing/Disciplinarity*. More recently, he has described his approach as 'cultural-historical activity theory' (2005, p. 12). This approach stresses the importance of special phenomena such as 'chronotopic lamination', 'heterochronicity' and 'semiotic recirculation'. According to Prior, the approach, by taking the perspective that it does, offers 'perhaps richer ways to investigate and define rhetorical situations' (p. 13). The new label – cultural-historical activity theory – has an invaluable advantage over the old ones. It can be handily condensed into a memorable acronym: CHAT. Thus, it is 'CHAT' that is said to offer richer ways to investigate rhetorical situations. This is branding used in the service of promoting an academic approach.

An approach can be rather like a map, since it can furnish a postgraduate student with a sense of their place in the academic world. They will have the security of knowing that they are properly placed to do the tasks that they learn to wish to do. Actually, I simplified things by saying that every social scientist needs an approach. In fact, the social scientist needs two approaches at the minimum. It is like the old joke that every Jew needs two synagogues – the synagogue you go to and the synagogue you don't go to. All social scientists need two approaches: the approach that you take and the approach that your approach has taken against.

If an approach is like a map, then this map will show the good route that will lead you to your destination and the bad route that will lose you in bogs, sloughs and confusion. Supporters of the 'academic literacies approach' typically contrast their own approach favourably with 'the skills approach' and 'the socialization approach', both of which suffer, or so they contend, from endemic failures (e.g., Lea and Street, 1998; English, 2002). Prior, in *Writing/Disciplinarity*, describes his approach as being a reaction against structuralism: the structuralist approach assumes 'abstraction, uniformity and spacialization' unlike the sociohistoric approach, which does not make these bad mistakes (p. 19).

The postgraduate, who is recruited into a particular approach, is unlikely to arrive equipped with the arguments against competitors. Few will approach a potential CHAT supervisor saying that they do so because, as an undergraduate, they had become increasingly disillusioned with the abstraction, uniformity and spacialization of structuralism. The commitment towards the chosen approach is likely to precede knowing why the competitors fail. Those failures will be part of the environment, into which the recruit is absorbed, just as much as the chosen 'things' and specialist concepts are. As the recruit learns about the strengths of their shared chosen approach, so they will learn about the weaknesses of the neighbours.

Generally speaking, the bigger the enterprise, into which students are recruited, the more they have to take the failures of the rivals on trust. My colleagues at Loughborough University have found this to be the case. Many years ago several of us became disillusioned with the sort of social psychology that we had been taught as undergraduates. In particular, we rebelled against many of the assumptions of cognitive psychology. This led to my colleagues establishing a different type of psychology which they called 'discursive psychology' (e.g., Edwards and Potter, 1993). The enterprise of discursive psychology has grown in the intervening years, becoming well established at least within British social psychology (Edwards, 2012; Potter, 2012). It has even spawned rival brands such as 'critical discursive psychology' and 'the material-discursive approach'. Now, when students wish to study discursive psychology, they have a considerable volume of publications that they must read, as well as new terminology that they need to acquire. The new recruits generally neither have the time nor inclination to read cognitive psychology, as years ago the originators of the approach had to do. Instead, recruits will learn from their fellow discursive psychologists at second hand what the faults of cognitive psychology are. They will pick up the shared view and so will spare themselves the time and trouble of finding out these faults for themselves. In this respect, we will be training our postgraduates to react like readers of popular right-wing newspapers: they will learn what they don't like without having to encounter personally the things or people that they so dislike (see Billig, 2012, for details).

Even when postgraduates have picked up the culture of their chosen approach, they still have to make their way within their wider academic discipline. It is necessary for them to publish – and to publish early – if they are to have an academic career in an institution that encourages research. Publishing can involve fitting into established practices, especially if one's chosen approach is not shared by those who edit the major journals in the field. Bruno Frey (2003) in a brilliant critique has claimed that the system of peer-review makes journals in the social sciences intellectually conservative. Editors tend to be established figures and will pick similar-minded academics to act as their reviewers. The result is that editors, on the basis of reviewers' comments, frequently insist on changes, which make papers less original and more similar to work that has already been published. Frey also points out that editors and reviewers may ensure that their own work is cited as a condition of a paper being accepted for publication. Typically authors do not want to make the changes that editors insist upon but, especially if they are young, they have to comply if they wish to publish in that journal. Frey's examples were taken from economics, but his points are more general. There is evidence that journal editors ask novice authors to revise their papers much more than they ask experienced authors (Hyland, 2009; Swales, 2006). Of course, this might be because young academics have yet to acquire the literary skills for successfully writing journal articles. One of these skills – and it is a skill emphasized by the guidebooks for academic publishing – is to know how to tailor one's article to the preferences of the editor and to the journal to which one is submitting. This is a skill for fitting in, rather than for speaking out. As one analyst has commented, disciplines 'are not games for beginners' (Bazerman, 2006, p. 24).

There is a further point about the academic cultures into which postgraduates in the social sciences become socialized. By and large, postgraduates are entering worlds, or becoming socialized into subdisciplines, which take it for granted that ordinary language is inadequate for their purposes. This assumption is built into these worlds, rather than being something that has to be discovered again and again by the individuals concerned. When postgraduates engage in their various activities, they will be exposed to special words and phrases, whether in published texts, conferences papers or in the supervisory advice offered by their professors. The very practices of academics embody the assumption that these words, or others like them, are necessary. This is why Prior himself, without offering any explicit justifications, can write of 'opportunity spaces', not 'opportunities', or 'trajectories of participation', not 'participating'. He belongs to a world where people write and speak like this.

In learning to become appropriately literate, the young postgraduate may question this or that particular concept, for it is very much part of the social sciences to criticize some concepts as against others. However, recruits are unlikely to criticize the special words en masse and to question whether, in fact, they need technical concepts. Few social scientists will raise an eyebrow if we say that our worlds create 'opportunity spaces' or if we use some other phrase which originates from a particular segment of the social scientific sub-world. It is part of our academic training that we have such phrases at our disposal and, as we deploy them, we demonstrate that we are professional social scientists, rather than ordinary people who happen to have wandered in from the rain. Much may have changed since Bourdieu conducted his study of students and academic language. One thing has not altered: if students and their teachers try to use simple, clear language, rather than big specialized concepts and phrases, then they will risk appearing as if they were inadequate, untrained and, most importantly, as if they did not belong.

Disciplined and never alone

Postgraduates in the social sciences are not just joining a particular sub-discipline or an approach, but they are joining the wider world of contemporary academia, in which their subdiscipline or approach exists. In order to survive, let alone thrive, they must be able to work, and that includes publishing, in the competitive environment that is contemporary academic life. In most universities, which aim to produce large numbers of doctoral students, there are schemes to ensure that postgraduates are not left to their own devices. They are encouraged to meet other postgraduates within their own institution and outside of it. This forms part of modern postgraduate education.

Learning how to write academically is part of a range of social skills that postgraduates are expected to acquire if they are to function as modern, productive academics. It is insufficient merely to be able to do academic work, but, to fit the academic world, it is necessary to network and to promote that work. In the United Kingdom, the state-supported Economic and Social Research Council (ESRC) is one of the main funders of social science postgraduates. The Council expects those institutions, which it funds to train research postgraduates, to ensure that 'the development of communication and networking skills should form an embedded part of their overall programme of research training'; and that 'students should be strongly encouraged to develop skills to communicate their research, promote themselves and build up a network around their research' (ESRC, 2009, p. 21).

Conferences are a big part of the contemporary academic world. Academics do not tend to see travelling for the purpose of attending conferences as a perk of the job – it is a must. The ESRC explicitly states that postgraduates should be given support 'for attendance at conferences' (ESRC, 2009, p. 15). One study of graduate education in Canada estimates that over half the students had attended conferences (Gemme and Gingras, 2009). Students are expected not just to attend conferences but to give papers. For this, they must learn the skills of oral presentation, which can differ from those of writing papers. Accomplished conference presenters will know to begin their papers with a little joke or with praise for the conference organizers (Hood and Forey, 2005; Rowley-Jolivet and Carter-Thomas, 2005). As well as ingratiating themselves with the audience, conference-goers should learn how to question other speakers, not to obtain information, but to draw attention to their own professional skills and importance (Tracy, 1997).

Conferences, so it is said, are ways of discovering about the personal and unwritten aspects of a discipline – about the gossip, the 'hot topics' and the '"in" people', as well as meeting old friends and making new ones (Swales, 2006, p. 197). Much disciplinary and subdisciplinary business is conducted on these occasions. One of the editors of the *Handbook of Scholarly Writing and Publishing* advises that 'networking at conferences' provides a way to 'identify and create writing opportunities'; networking can occur in regular sessions, in hallways, or in preconference gatherings where 'collegial relationships and, in time, real friendships and writing partnerships can develop' (Rocco, 2011, p. 6).

Many national and international conferences in the social sciences go out of their way to encourage postgraduates to attend. Here is an advertisement for the annual conference of the Social Policy Association for 2010 in the United Kingdom. The advertisement specifically invites postgraduates 'to attend the conference and to participate in a range of events', including 'networking events with your peers and established scholars'. The organizers urge postgraduates that this is a way to 'introduce yourself to the social policy community'. It seems so thoughtful of the organizers but there are problematic aspects too. Networking, joining the disciplinary community and self-promotion are all related activities. Writing and publishing will not necessarily bring the young scholar to the notice of senior academics in an age when academics are far too busy to read anything but a tiny fraction of what is published in their discipline.

Face-to-face contact remains important for becoming part of the discipline and for making your way in the academic world. The advertisement for the Social Policy Conference advises postgraduates that 'a drinks reception for all delegates' will enable 'you to meet your peers and more established scholars'; this will offer a chance to 'develop supportive networks and find out about future opportunities'.

Self-promotion is not extrinsic to academic skills, if one considers writing to be an intrinsic academic skill. The would-be academic has to learn to publish and to give papers at conferences. Often academics, particularly young academics, will write a conference paper, in order to obtain funding to attend the conference. More generally, academics do not write first, and then decide to promote what they have written, as if these are two separate activities. As we have seen in the earlier examples, promoting can be ingrained into the writing, as academics promote themselves and their approaches through their writing. The logic of promotion – of selling, branding, marketing – is very much part of modern academic life, affecting our choice of words and the ways we describe our work.

Fitting into a discipline – even fitting into an awkward niche within a discipline, an awkward niche that seems to be in contention with the established parts – is still a fitting in. It is not just a fitting in with the academic world, but a fitting in with an academic world that is itself fitting in with wider trends of management, production and marketing. Did anyone really imagine that travelling to conferences, staying in hotels with expenses paid, attending drinks receptions and attracting the attention of established figures was a good means to develop original, critical thinking? The more academic friends that you make, the longer your list of academics whose work you cannot publicly criticize. It starts so early in the life of an academic. Even before postgraduates have obtained their doctoral qualifications, they will be planning their next conference, their next 'opportunity space' for introducing themselves to their discipline. No one planned all this, but once the round of conferences has been set in motion, few will want to miss the next jamboree. If they do miss it, then there will always be someone else to take their place, to grab the attention, the opportunities and the friendships.

Perhaps it was always like this, with scholars promoting their self-importance through puffed up words and corresponding (networking) with like-minded pedants. Certainly, William James detected elements of this in the newly formed disciplines of his day and he linked the development of professionally minded, academic disciplines with poor writing and conventional thinking. He complained that American philosophy 'is dreadful from a literary point of view': American philosophers were writing in 'technical and semi-technical language', with 'half-clear thought, fluency and no composition!' (James, 1920, Vol. 2, p. 217). But there is a difference of scale between then and now. Today the academic world is vast, compared with the small, cosy, privileged university life that James knew. Yet, James's sense of unease with his times may help us to understand what might be missing in present times and why his own concern with good academic writing was more than aesthetic snobbery. It was a way of resisting orthodoxy.

James would have been appalled by the open bustle of networking and self-promotion. He would have suspected that offers of financial funding for travel, meetings and drinks receptions would dull the critical edge, especially of young people. After receiving an honorary degree from Harvard, James delivered an address, paying tribute to his old university. He spoke of his belief that original thinkers when young 'are almost always very lonely creatures' (1911, p. 354). He would have been thinking of his own youth. Good universities, such as Harvard, should not try to cure young thinkers of their loneliness. The good university should nurture and encourage them, providing a 'climate so propitious that they can be happy in their solitude' (p. 355). Only by being alone – by resisting the blandishments to become part of the crowd – can the young thinker develop to think independently.

The academic world today operates to eradicate that loneliness before the solitary student can turn their sense of aloneness into independent thinking. 'Discipline' is an appropriately double-edged word, as if to become a member of a discipline means finding one's thinking disciplined. The networking, the language of the subdiscipline, the loyalty to the approach, the need for self-promotion – all these are factors to prevent the aloneness that James was praising. The academic world, in the form of disciplines and subdisciplines, beckons the postgraduate with a friendly wave, offering the promise of rewards, success and friendship. 'Come in, speak like us, write like us, and make yourself at home at our conferences' it smiles in welcome.

James ended his address by declaring that 'our undisciplinables are our proudest product'. Let us agree, he concluded, 'in hoping that the output of them will never cease' (p. 355). Today, university managers have a different understanding of the words 'product' and 'output'. They are now proud of products and outputs which are financially accountable and which, in consequence, are highly disciplinable.

4   Jargon, nouns and acronyms

First, a small example, which in itself is utterly irrelevant to my topic but which stands for something wider. Cricket is a game which often appears old fashioned in its laws, dress and codes; most of its followers derive great enjoyment from their sense of the game's history. Like other major sports today, the game is also a huge commercial enterprise and its administrators, who wish to maximize streams of income, cannot be sentimental about history. Traditionally, cricketers have accepted the decisions of umpires without displays of dissent on the field of play, but, with television providing almost instant replays, the umpires can now be speedily shown to be wrong. Recently, the administrators of international cricket have reacted to changing times by amending the game's laws (and traditionally cricket has had 'laws' not 'rules'), so that players can, under closely regulated circumstances, request that an umpire's decision be checked against specified forms of technological evidence. This process has become known as the Umpire Decision Referral System (UDRS).

I do not imagine that many readers of this book will be interested in the intricacies of cricket's laws or in the new technological advances for improving umpiring decisions – except possibly in relation to one aspect. C. L. R. James, the great cricket writer, literary critic, and Marxist philosopher, used to say that the history of cricket reflected the wider historical forces of the world (James, 1963). The new system for appealing against the decision of an umpire belongs to an age of technology and finance, and culturally to a time which is at ease with questioning official authority. These are not my concerns here, for they do not relate to academic writing. But one aspect does: the new system needed a name. As C. L. R. James would have recognized, it is not haphazard how people choose to name new things, regulations or procedures. We can ask why these procedures for questioning umpiring decisions in major matches have come to be known by a sequence of four capitalized nouns – Umpire Decision Referral System. The Victorians, who formulated cricket's old laws, would never have used such a syntactic sequence. So why do the legislators of today's game take it as entirely normal to use this sort of wording, as do the commercial enterprises that market the technology on which the system depends? And why, just as naturally, has this sequence of nouns so quickly become shortened into abbreviations – either UDRS or DRS?

Cricket's legislators, players and writers are not generally known for being linguistic innovators. In this case, those who have named the new procedures are not the revolutionaries who overthrew the grammatical rules (not laws) that their Victorian forefathers would have held in great respect. As in most sports, cricket's administrators are inherently conservative, even when they are engaged in radically changing their own sports. In naming their new system for questioning the decisions of umpires, the legislators were following linguistic practices that have now become common-place. Many academic social scientists, when they have something new to name, follow the same principles. If you want your new name to sound formal, official and substantial, then you should think of linking together some nouns, especially if the nouns include abstract concepts such as 'decision', 'referral' or 'system'.

The managers of my own university followed these same linguistic principles when they instituted a new way for tutors to record on a central database their meetings (and non-meetings) with tutees. They gave their innovation the grand title: 'Co-Tutor Student Management Relationship System'. This 'system' possesses one noun more than the Umpire Decision Referral System, and like the latter it does not contain a single preposition to link its nouns together. It is not merely administrators, whether sporting, academic or other, that follow this style of naming. Academics, including social scientists, will use the same principles to name their inventions, especially if they have devised systems, which they hope practitioners will use in their professional lives. For example, there is the Behaviour Exchange Systems Training (Blyth, Bamberg and Toumbourou, 2000), for helping parents deal with adolescent children who might be abusing substances; or the Picture Exchange Communication System to be used in the treatment of autism (Bondy and Frost, 2001). The devisors of these systems have been careful to order their nouns so that they produce easily pronounceable acronyms: BEST and PECS. This is a sensible ploy when promoting a system to the world.

This style of naming is not confined to academics who want their creations to be used in the non-academic world. Academics often come up with similar sorts of names for intrinsically academic theories and approaches. In the previous chapter, we came across CHAT as the name of a social scientific approach (although in this case only two of the initials stand for nouns). There is no shortage of similar names in the non-applied parts of the social sciences: Speech Exchange System, Politeness System Theory, Phrase Structure Grammar, Leadership Categorization Theory, etc and etc. In this and subsequent chapters, we will come across further examples. For the present, I will mainly be following the strategy, which I adopted in the previous chapter, of taking my examples where I find them, rather than going out of my way to search out especially choice cases.

My aim is to show the prevalence of nouns in the technical concepts that contemporary social scientists devise. Also acronyms are particularly visible in modern academic writing and these tend to be used for noun phrases. I will be outlining the evidence from those linguists who suggest that noun phrases, comprising solely nouns, represent one of the most important linguistic developments in modern English and that they are prominent in academic writing. But it is not sufficient merely to show that this has occurred and that it is affecting academics as well as cricketing and university administrators. I will need also to show why this nouny writing might be such a problem in the social sciences.

In this chapter, I will be suggesting why the prevalence of nouns means that the problem of pompous or starchy writing in the social sciences is not adequately understood as being simply a problem of 'jargon'. To be sure, academic social scientists like to make up big words, and critics can easily pounce on these big words as being unnecessary 'jargon'. We have already come across some nominal whoppers such as 'massification', 'the ideational metafunction' and these will not be the last that we shall encounter. But even if we removed the worst of these whoppers, there would still be serious problems. The noun-based names and acronyms, which I have just mentioned, do not rely on big confected words. Ordinary nouns can be strung together, without intervening prepositions. 'Picture', 'exchange', 'communication' and 'system' are all non-technical words in common usage, just as 'umpire', 'decision' and 'referral' are. A sense of technicality can also come from the way that such words are combined, and not just from the individual elements of that combination.

As well as looking at the predominance of nouns in social scientific jargon, I will also discuss some of the implications of this for those who might defend or criticize the use of technical concepts in the social sciences. By and large, both the critics and the defenders overlook the prevalence of nouns, not grasping why it might be significant that so many of the concepts, which offend the critics and which the defenders believe to improve on common language, are nouns or noun phrases. If we ignore this aspect, we will be unable to pinpoint what is going wrong with social scientific writing.

As I hope to show in this and the following chapter, the real problem is not that social scientists invent too many big words, although that is a problem; but the real difficulty is that the big words tend to be nouns, not verbs. This means that general denunciations of social scientific writing for containing 'too much jargon' do not get to the heart of the matter. It is because social scientists, when trying to describe and explain what people do, fill their prose with nouns that they end up writing both awkwardly and imprecisely.

The case against jargon

It is tempting to phrase the case against bad writing in the social sciences as a case against jargon. A generation ago, the sociologist Stanislav Andreski let rip against his fellow social scientists for using 'obfuscating jargon' to conceal a lack of anything to say (1971, p. 216). Anton Zijderveld, another distinguished sociologist, suggested that sociologists may be more prone to use jargon than the members of any other discipline, with the possible exception of psychology. According to Zijderveld, sociologists use technical words 'which may be semantically poor but which the specialists keep repeating, like sorcerers repetitively reciting their sacred formulas' (1979, p. 73). Although Zijderveld was arguing that using clichés was an invaluable part of social life, he did feel that sociologists could cut back on theirs. Today, there are journalists, such as Francis Wheen (2004) and John Murray (2008), who take up the fight against jargon, often directing much of their ire against specialists in management studies, as well as post-structuralist theorists.

In the argument between Wilhelm Wundt and William James about the former's concept of 'apperception' and whether it represented a useful contribution to knowledge or was just an empty piece of bombast, my sympathies are with James. It would be easy, then, for me to say that 'apperception' is a typically nasty bit of jargon. However, the word 'jargon' usually bears too strong a critical tone and too weak an analytic force to be entirely satisfactory. As Walter Nash remarked at the beginning of his book *Jargon* (1994), no one has a good word for jargon: the problem is that people always use 'jargon' to refer to the words that others use, and we consider our own technical concepts to be entirely justified and, therefore, not jargon.

Linguists tend to describe 'jargon' as being technical language which is linked with 'a specific area of work or interest' (Yule, 2010, p. 259). The lexicographer, Julie Coleman, claims that we associate jargon with 'well-defined occupational or interest groups, such as doctors, computer-programmers or model train enthusiasts' (2009, p. 314). She might have added 'management consultants', 'academics' and 'lexicographers' to her list. Of course, technical concepts, in themselves, can be innocuous, for particular groups and professions might need specialist terminology to refer to arcane aspects of their specialism, which have little interest to outsiders. This does not make their words 'jargon', as the term is commonly used. The charge against jargon is that groups or professions sometimes use their technical language for extra-linguistic purposes such as promoting group solidarity or baffling outsiders who do not understand the words (Allan, 2001, p. 172). The terminology then becomes a badge of belonging or a means of excluding outsiders, rather than just being an invaluable term by which lexicographers might name an unusual type of word or model train enthusiasts a particular type of miniature piston rod.

Jargon can also provide handy euphemisms, so that the speaker is able to use a technical term which appears to make objectionable meanings less objectionable (Hudson, 1999, pp. 418–19). This can be useful for members of a profession who regularly engage in morally problematic behaviour. According to one observer, management consultants have invented 'a whole new lexicon of management jargon' in order to 'camouflage their actions', so that 'the contracting out of work became "outsourcing", the removal of levels of management became "delayering", cutting jobs became "downsizing"' and so on (Nichols, 2005, p.186). What makes these terms 'jargon' is not their intrinsic meaning but the uses to which they are put. In these cases, managers, by using technical terminology, can avoid thinking about the consequences of their decisions to sack members of their staff.

When William James criticized Wundt for his use of 'apperception', he did not imagine that the German psychologist was using a euphemism because he was too fastidious to talk directly about the human mind. He was accusing Wundt of using a grand word in order to make himself appear grand. When critics accuse academics of using 'jargon', they normally have this sort of illegitimate function in mind. Management consultants also face the same accusation. One example, which linguists have cited but which may possibly be apocryphal, is managers in the hamburger industry coining the term 'autocondimentation' to refer to customers putting sauce on their own hamburgers. The word adds nothing to our understanding of what is going on, but, by using such an official-sounding, multi-syllabic word, the managers are said to confer dignity upon themselves and upon their industry (Allan, 2001; Allan and Burridge, 2006). Those, who accuse social scientists of using unnecessarily big words, suspect that academics regularly have their 'autocondimentation' moments. In the previous chapter, we saw how an academic was using 'the ideational metafunction' in this sort of way. An unnecessary word or phrase is rolled out to convey one's own knowledge, just as James accused Wundt of using a word that was intellectually empty but rhetorically weighty.

Look again at these examples of jargon: 'the ideational metafunction', 'autocondimentation', 'apperception'. They are all nouns or noun phrases. In Chapters 2 and 3, other words and phrases were mentioned: 'massification', 'chronotopic lamination', 'semiotic recirculation'. Those last three could all possibly be used as verbs: 'to massify', 'to chronotopically laminate', 'to semiotically recirculate'. However, social scientists rarely use them in this way. The managers in the hamburger industry could have talked about customers 'autocondimenting' their meals. But it was the abstract, or general, concept – the turning of the commonplace action into a philosophical sort of thing – that seems to convey the big status.

Now, we can see the problem with using 'jargon' as our critical concept: the word is grammatically indiscriminate. The verbal phrase 'to chronotopically laminate' is no less jargon than 'chronotopic lamination'. However, if the noun phrase is used much more frequently than the former, then we need to be aware of this and to try to understand why this might be so. This is crucial if, as I will argue later, the frequent use of noun phrases is particularly problematic in the social sciences. Just seeking out instances of 'jargon', and then denouncing the academic writers in question for being portentous, might be fun, especially when the denunciation is delivered with the wit of a William James. But after a while the fun will pall, as it does in the case of Andreski, if it is backed by bitterness rather than by analysis.

The defence of jargon

Social scientists will sometimes defend themselves against the accusation of using 'jargon', by arguing that their technical concepts are necessary for the development of social scientific understanding. By and large, they overlook how nouny social scientific jargon tends to be. This applies to three main sorts of defender. First, there are those who claim that jargon is necessary simply because it is integral to the social sciences. Then, there are those who argue that, regrettable though jargon might on occasions be, it can offer greater clarity than ordinary language. A third sort of defender claims that radical social scientists must extract themselves from the grip of ordinary language by inventing new terms. I will consider this third type of defence towards the end of this chapter.

Only after I have presented some of my main arguments, will I be in a position to deal adequately with it.

Zina O'Leary's *The Social Science Jargon Buster* (2007) offers an example of the first sort of defence. Her book has a catchy title, as if it promises to debunk and expose unnecessary jargon, but it is not that sort of book. The subtitle gives a clue to the nature of the book: *The Key Terms You Need to Know*. The potential reader is a student in the social sciences, who is worried by the technical terminology that they are expected to acquire. The author, in her introduction, concedes that there may appear to be a lot of jargon in the social sciences. From the outside 'it might seem like social science terms are somewhat vague, abstract, pretentious or even meaningless' but, she reassures the reader, 'such "jargon" does have a function' (O'Leary, 2007, p. ix). She says that it is tempting simply to 'apply everyday understandings to key social science terms' but that is not good enough: 'engaging "jargon" is actually central to our understanding', because it represents 'key constructs, fundamental concepts, critical theories and influential schools of thought' (p. ix). In short, O'Leary is denying that the 'jargon' really is jargon.

O'Leary's book encapsulates the assumption, which, according to Bourdieu, underwrote the social sciences and which was discussed in the previous chapter: the students are being told to accept that ordinary language is not good enough for the scholarly work of the social sciences. The author warns students to resist the temptation to use ordinary terms because they need to engage with 'jargon'. In effect, the students are being informed that, if they wish to complete their courses successfully, they need to learn the special terms. The author's justification for jargon is not an actual justification: she does not point out why particular terms should be preferred to 'everyday understandings'. She is telling students that the terms, which she is including, are 'key', 'fundamental' and 'influential'. At root her justification is authoritarian, despite the chumminess of her tone: these are the sorts of terms that you must learn if you are to pass your examinations, because these *are* the key, fundamental and influential terms.

The social psychologist Daryl Bem tackles the issue of jargon in his chapter in the edited book *The Compleat Academic* (1987). The book has done well commercially since its first edition and it now is being published by the American Psychological Association. Originally a practical guide for 'beginning social scientists', the book is now offered as a 'career guide' for psychologists. Bem concedes that technical words, or jargon, can give rise to problems and he advises his readers to try to 'write in English prose, not psychological jargon' (p. 176). Insiders may be at ease with technical terms, but the same words can disorientate outsiders: 'Much of our jargon has become second-nature to us and serves only to muddy our prose for the general reader' (p. 196). He does not discuss the possibility that jargon may also be muddying prose for specialists.

Although we should try to avoid jargon, nevertheless, according to Bem, it cannot always be avoided because jargon serves 'a number of legitimate functions in scientific communication' (p. 196). A specialized term may be 'more precise or freer of surplus meaning than any natural language equivalent' (p. 196). Bem gives the examples of 'attitude' and 'reinforcement': both, he suggests, are more precise and freer from surplus meaning than the equivalent ordinary language terms, 'disposition' and 'reward'. These terms show that technical language can make important conceptual distinctions 'not apprehended by the layperson's vocabulary' (p. 196).

The idea that specialists need a vocabulary, which is free from the surplus meaning of ordinary language, is interesting, but it does not match the usual practice of social scientists, including psychologists. Almost always when social scientists feel the need to invent new terms, they construct them out of ordinary language concepts, as Bourdieu's 'habitus' builds on 'habit' and 'massification' on 'mass'. As Valsiner and van der Veer (2000) point out, social scientists, unlike many natural scientists, do not create wholly neutral concepts, freed from associations with ordinary language. Valsiner and van der Veer give the example of 'attachment', which many social and developmental psychologists use as a technical concept. This term retains connections with ordinary language and with ordinary life (such as a mother feeling attached to her child). It carries what Bem might term surplus meaning, but then so do both 'attitude' and 'reinforcement'. When social scientists devise technical concepts, they make sure that they bear the echoes of messy, ordinary life and its ordinary messy concepts. Yet, even as they do this, they seem to justify their special concepts, by claiming them to be more precise, and having fewer associations, than the concepts of ordinary language.

Those, who accuse social scientists of creating jargon for jargon's sake, suspect them of aggrandizing themselves through their big words. Certainly academics, in general, have a particular fondness for using longer words than journalists or fiction writers (Biber, 1988). Nothing illustrates the love of social scientists for extra syllables than the history of the word 'methodology'. In the early nineteenth century, the word was used to describe the study of methods, especially scientific methods. Works about methodology, at that time, would be expected to discuss different ways of collecting evidence and arranging classifications. In the past fifty years, the word has been used to describe the particular methods that researchers might use. In this sense, the term is used as a synonym for 'method': when researchers discuss their 'methodology', they are typically describing their 'method'. We see here (and in other instances) the reverse of what often occurs in non-technical discourse. In ordinary language, lengthy terms, which are commonly used, tend to be abbreviated – 'bicycle' becomes 'bike', 'refrigerator' becomes 'fridge' and 'television' becomes 'TV'. In the academic world, as the example 'methodology' shows, commonly used short words can sprout surplus, largely decorative syllables. Status is involved in these escalating syllables: ordinary people only have methods, but academics have methodologies.

One further point is the predominance of nouns amongst the technical concepts of social scientists: attachment, attitudes, reinforcement and methodology are all nouns. None of them are verbs: Bem is not talking about 'attaching', 'reinforcing' or 'attitudinizing' as being technical concepts. He seems to take it for granted that the technical concepts, as nouns, will be standing for 'things'. This is so taken for granted – so obvious – that it does not require special comment. But, of course, the things that we take for granted as being obvious are often the most interesting aspects of the social world.

One standard defence for the use of jargon is that social scientists define their concepts, but ordinary speakers do not, as if definitions are the vital ingredient for being precise. However, the existence of definitions is no guarantee that technical concepts are going to be used consistently, or even in accord with their definition. Sometimes, the definitions seem to be largely ritualistic, providing a display of precision rather than its actual practice. As we have seen, academics have used 'the ideational metafunction' very differently to the way that it was originally defined (which itself was hardly rigorously). Similarly, specialists have used 'massification' in different, mutually inconsistent ways. What percentage of a nation's young people need to receive tertiary education before social scientists will say that 'massification' has taken place? It depends which social scientists you are asking. Some experts have argued that massification refers to conditions where between fifteen per cent and fifty per cent of a country's population acquire tertiary education; and that if the figure is more than fifty per cent, then this indicates the 'universalization', not the 'massification', of tertiary education. Other investigators have used 'massification' to refer to countries such as Norway and Finland where many more than fifty per cent of young people receive tertiary education (even reaching above ninety per cent in the case of Finland). On the other hand, researchers have talked about 'massification' in sub-Saharan Africa where the figures are around six per cent (for examples of such widely varying uses of 'massification', see: Becher and Trowler, 2001; Kivinen, Hedman and Kaipainen, 2007; Mohamedbhai, 2008; Smeby, 2003; Trow, 2000 and 2005).

The technical term is no guarantee of precision and agreement. Quite the contrary, where there is a piece of technical terminology in the social sciences, one might expect to find diverging uses and disagreement about its meaning.

Specialists may find a technical term handy, but that does not mean that it adds anything that ordinary words would not. Suppose I wanted to talk about the way that a social scientist might invent a particular technical term and might offer a seemingly rigorous definition for this new word. And then other academics take up the term, as they investigate the same topic. And as the term spreads so it becomes used in increasingly more diffuse, even contradictory, ways. The result may be that semantic anarchy follows from the spread of a seemingly rigorous concept. I might decide to invent some technical terminology of my own to describe these sorts of processes. First there is a process of 'rigorization', as the original social scientist and their colleagues build an ordinary word (such as 'habit', 'mass' or 'rigour') into a technical concept: habitus, massification and rigorization. They do this in the interests of appearing rigorous and they will offer official definitions for their key concept. When they are successful in recruiting others to use their concept, then the process of rigorization will be followed by the opposing process of 'de-rigorization', as the key term becomes diffusely used. Sometimes the two processes may overlap. But, generally, the more the concept is used, the more diverse its meanings become. I might see a general trend here, which, using four suitable nouns, I will propose to call: the Rigorization De-Rigorization Exchange System (RDRES).

Perhaps I will recruit some followers to study the four-noun phenomenon of RDRES. We could arrange several symposia, successfully attract funding and recruit postgraduate students to our projects. Our combined efforts might ensure a modicum of success for RDRES (or 'redress' as we are likely to call it, when chatting informally amongst ourselves). However, the formal title, Rigorization De-Rigorization Exchange System, which I introduced in the preceding paragraph, adds nothing new to the ordinary language descriptions which I also put into that paragraph. The formal title might sound more impressive than those ordinary descriptions, but it is parasitic on them. If the ordinary descriptions had not been comprehensible, then the basic notion of RDRES would have appeared obscure. What the formal title and its acronym add is not an original idea, but they offer a means for encapsulating and marketing the idea.

There is nothing new in questioning whether the technical terminology of scholars improves on the supposed faults of ordinary language. In the eighteenth century, Abraham Tucker, the sadly neglected English philosopher, whose analysis of the mind prefigured in many ways that of William James, doubted the worth of inventing new words. In the introduction to his great work, *The Light of Nature Pursued*, he wrote that scholars often employ 'technical terms, hoping thereby to escape the confusion incident to the language of the vulgar'; the technical terms, Tucker noted, are derived from ordinary words and, in consequence, 'partake in some measure of the slippery and changeable quality of their primitives'. Moreover, Tucker observed that scholars cannot 'always agree with one another or maintain a consistency with themselves in the application of their terms' (Tucker, 1768, p. xlii). If Tucker could only see the world of scholarship today, he would be unsurprised to find that, despite all the advances in science and technology, scholars had still failed to find a way to overcome these same basic problems with technical terms.

Nouns and more nouns

I need to present a bit more evidence to show that nouns predominate in social scientific jargon. Inventing my own imaginary label proves nothing, except that it seems to follow a recognizable style, but that is not good enough. So, let me first turn back to *The Social Science Jargon Buster* to see what sorts of concepts it presents as necessary jargon; and then I shall look at several other guides to technical concepts in the social sciences.

The *Jargon Buster* explains 147 terms in alphabetical order; 110 of these items are single nouns, such as 'epistemology', 'fundamentalism' and 'reification'. A further thirty-two are noun phrases like 'game theory', 'research credibility' and 'socio-economic status'. These noun phrases come in two sorts. Some like 'socio-economic status', 'social movements' or 'developed countries' consist of an adjective qualifying a noun. Most of the noun phrases, which O'Leary listed, are of this type. However, there were others which were comprised of two nouns, with the first noun qualifying the second: for instance, 'game theory', 'research credibility', 'risk society' and 'systems theory'. Only five of O'Leary's 147 items were neither nouns nor noun phrases. Four of these were adjectives like 'collective' or 'post-industrial' and there was one adverbial/adjectival phrase 'a posteriori/a priori'. There were no verbs.

This basic pattern can be found in other books of key terms in the social sciences: it is nouns and noun phrases all the way. In *Sociology: The Key Concepts* (2006), John Scott lists sixty-eight entries, fifty-seven of which are single nouns and the other eleven are noun phrases. *Key Concepts in Politics* has sixty-eight nouns, fifteen noun phrases and one lone adjectival entry (Heywood, 2006). Schaffer's *Key Concepts in*

Developmental Psychology (2006) only has nouns and noun phrases. Taken together, in these books more than ninety-eight per cent of the items are nouns or noun phrases. Collectively their authors list no verbs.

Sometimes the nouns seem to colonize other parts of speech, especially adjectives. David Jary's (1997) 'A Brief Guide to "Difficult" Sociological Jargon' shows how this can be done. It contains one pair of words that are prima facie adjectives: emic/etic, appear as adjectives in phrases such as 'emic methods' and 'etic methods'. But in the text, Jary refers to 'the emic' and 'the etic' thereby converting the adjectives into nouns by means of the definite article (p. 177). In *Social and Cultural Anthropology: The Key Concepts* (2006), Rapport and Overing include 'unhomely' as a basic concept, but list it with the definite article. None of the obvious nouns is similarly accompanied by 'the'. In this way, the authors ensure that 'the unhomely', a grand conceptual noun, is not confused with homely adjectival 'unhomely'.

Transforming adjectives into nouns by means of 'the' has become a common trope in social scientific writing today. Writers will refer to 'the imaginary', 'the comic' or 'the feminine' and so on. The general concept stands for all the various things that might be described as being imaginary, comic or feminine. Instead of talking about particulars, the theorist can theorize in general about the imaginary, the comic, the unhomely, etc. Shortly before writing this passage, I received an email, inviting me to participate in a workshop which aimed to examine how 'we research and generate knowledge "beyond the sensory", into more ethereal and intangible domains'. The organizers were not content to let the topic for the proposed workshop rest in an adjectival form (as in 'ethereal domains'). The workshop was about 'Researching Ethereality' and 'Researching the Ethereal'.

The workshop, according to the organizers, would 'involve presentations from researchers who have explored various aspects of the ethereal in their research and writing, including: ghosts, hauntings and the supernatural; angels; spirituality in everyday life'. The grammatical form presumes that there is such a thing as 'the ethereal' (or 'ethereality'): if it did not exist, it could not be researched. At the same time, the writers are not presuming that ethereal elements (namely, the ghosts, angels, spirit world) might themselves exist. The authors have created their own fictional thing ('the ethereal'), which takes precedence over the particulars and whose reality is assumed. One can achieve this momentous feat with the tiny word 'the'.

In such grammatical moves, one can see the value which contemporary social scientists place upon creating abstract nouns. It is insufficient to be looking at comic, ethereal or imaginary things in all their variety: it appears better to look at *the* comic, *the* imaginary, *the* ethereal. Moreover, in the advertisement we can see the promotional context in which this can operate. The workshop was not being presented as if it were pulling together a vast amount of research, which had already been conducted, nor was it being proposed to see if there was such a thing as 'the ethereal', for that was being taken for granted. It aimed to create a topic and to form a network to aid research into that topic. The proposers were aiming to shift the research agenda from 'the sensory' to something 'beyond the sensory'. 'The ethereal', as a title, is much snappier than 'ethereal domains' or 'ethereal topics'. It also carries a hint of intellectual profundity.

It should be pointed out that there is nothing new in this grammatical move of transforming adjectives into abstract nouns in the cause of promoting intellectual products. In the eighteenth century, much fuss was made about 'the sublime'. Samuel Johnson, as might be expected from a defender of plain English, took against the concept, complaining that some of his contemporaries were being 'dazzled in a bazaar of facile systems' (Hitchings, 2005, p. 170). No prizes for guessing what he might have thought about today's academic systems.

Verbs as servants

In the big houses of the eighteenth century, the great families displayed their wealth and social standing as they lavishly entertained guests. Heavy plates of food would be carried to great tables; glasses would be filled with yet more drink; tea and coffee would be poured into fine china cups; and all the while the hosts and their guests would continue their polite, elevating conversations. They would barely pause to see who was bearing the salvers of food, decanters of wine or pots of coffee. So it is linguistically with the writings of the social sciences today. The great nouns are assembled, sometimes bedecked with elegant modifiers and sometimes aloof in isolated importance. No one notices the great burden carried by the humble verbs, as they bear the weight of the grandly gathered clusters of nouns in sentence after sentence.

Often in the social sciences, it is insufficient only to notice what is present; one has to be aware of absences. In the distribution of key concepts, we can see nouns, noun phrases and occasional adjectives. Verbs are the great absentees. In none of the works cited is a verb listed as a key or basic concept. Yet, all social scientists must write their sentences with verbs.

Occasionally a verb is almost listed in the compendia of key concepts. Rapport and Overing (2006) include 'Reading' and 'Writing' as basic anthropological concepts. Grammatically, 'reading' and 'writing' are participles and, as such, they are ambiguous. They can be used as parts of verbs ('the children are reading') or as nouns ('reading improves the mind'). It is clear from the text that the authors are treating 'Reading' and 'Writing' as nouns. Introducing the entry on 'Reading', they declare: 'An anthropology of reading explores the diversity of reading traditions in the world, treats these as historically, culturally and socially situated practices, and examines the consequences of their use' (2006, p. 310). Reading, thus, is an entity, or practice, and the authors are not using the word here as a verb.

As Rapport and Overing expand on their topic, 'reading', as a noun, appears as the subject of verbs: 'Talking, writing and reading are significantly implicated in one another; reading is a "kinetic art"' (p. 311); 'it is not only in terms of historico-socio-cultural milieus that reading attains to particularity' (p. 312); 'reading is an event' (p. 313); and so on. Reading has become a 'thing' that can do or attain other things. In these statements, humble verbs ('is', 'explores', 'are', 'attains', etc.) bring the meaty meanings (big conceptual nouns like 'kinetic art', 'particularity', 'historico-socio-cultural milieus', etc.) to the table.

Perhaps verbs are only absent from these lists of conceptual key words because compilers, in the process of making their lists, concentrate unduly on nouns. If so, the absence of technical verbs might reflect the practices of the list-makers, rather than the nature of academic writing. However, lists of non-academic jargon are not so verb-free in their entries. Tony Thorne's *Shoot the Puppy* is a lively and sympathetic guide to what its subtitle calls *the curious jargon of modern life*. The main title comes from a verb phrase, which Thorne includes and which he defines as 'to dare to do the unthinkable' (2006, p. ix). The book contains plenty of other verbs and verbal phrases ('to add value', 'to action', 'to de-locate'), as well as adverbial phrases ('al desko'), adjectival past participles ('Dilberted') and expressions of assent ('okey-dokey, artichokey!').

Shoot the Puppy certainly does not give the impression that the new, informal jargon of contemporary life revolves around nouns and noun phrases. But there may be a difference between the official phrases of management experts, which can be heavily influenced by academic terminology, and the insubordinate words of office life. *Shoot the Puppy* gives us official terms, such as 'performance-enhancement', 'visibility-providing infrastructure', 'user-behaviour management', 'hyperindividualization' – all academic-type nouns and noun phrases. 'Okey-dokey, artichokey' and 'al desko' are not quite so formal.

The rise of nouns in academic writing

'Corpus linguists' have provided some of the best evidence that academic writing is being filled with nouns. These linguists take very large stocks (or corpora) of written texts and spoken conversations; and then, with the aid of sophisticated computer programs, they trawl through these stocks noting the frequencies of particular grammatical structures, parts of speech and individual words. They can then note linguistic changes over time, as well as observing exactly how different forms of spoken and written language differ from each other. The work of Douglas Biber on the grammatical features of academic writing is particularly significant for our purposes.

Basically, Biber has shown the 'nouniness' of academic writing. 'Nouniness' is a word that Biber has invented albeit semi-humorously, but this word, despite not being part of 'high' linguistic theory, nevertheless captures an important meaning. Biber and his colleagues have examined the ratio of nouns to verbs in academic writing in English, comparing it with the ratio in fictional writing and in conversations. The overall pattern of the results is clear: academic writing contains almost double the ratio of nouns to verbs than do the other two forms (Biber, Conrad and Reppen, 1998). One feature which is particularly common in academic prose is the noun-filled noun phrase, in which the word or words modifying the major noun are other nouns (Biber and Conrad, 2009; Leech et al., 2009). It is much less common in fiction. A novelist, who writes about 'patient behaviour', is likely to be describing how a character is waiting without complaining. An academic, using the same phrase, will probably be referring to the behaviour of those attending medical clinics.

In the eighteenth century, medical and fictional writings in English were grammatically very similar to each other (Biber and Conrad, 2009). In neither was the noun-only phrase very common. Biber has commented that the growth of this type of phrase has been 'one of the most dramatic areas of historical change in English over the past three centuries' (Biber and Conrad, 2009, p. 167). We might add, in passing, that in the eighteenth century, this sort of phrase was quite common in slang, being especially used in terms of abuse. In his *Classical Dictionary of the Vulgar Tongue* (1785/1963), Francis Grose listed terms such as 'moon curser', 'crab lanthorn', 'Cheshire cat' and many other double-noun insults. In polite literature, including scientific writing, the double noun, let alone triple noun, was much less common. Any eighteenth-century writer, even a writer of medical matters, who mentioned 'patient behaviour', would have been describing someone patiently awaiting their fate.

Throughout the nineteenth century, new words and phrases, comprising nouns modifying or qualifying other nouns, were emerging in English: such as 'cricket bat', 'railway', 'railway station', 'timetable' and even 'railway station timetable'. However, the real spurt in the multi-noun phrase within academic English came during the twentieth century and especially the latter half of the twentieth century. As Biber and Gray (2010) document, this constituted an enormous change in the way that academic prose was written, so that scientific writing today is grammatically very different from what it was 200 years ago. Biber and Gray write that 'virtually every sentence in a present-day written academic text illustrates the use of complex noun phrase constructions' (2010, p. 17), subtly proving their own point by sneaking in without ado the triple noun, preposition-free 'noun phrase constructions'.

It might be thought that academics have been the pioneers of this grammatical construction which has so changed the face of modern English. But we should not boost our own importance, for the real drivers behind the growth of the multi-noun phrase were journalists (Biber, 2003; Leech et al., 2009). Newspapers had long increased their ratio of nouns to other parts of speech, before academics had begun their dramatic spurt. In fact, newspapers have hardly increased their ratio during the past fifty years, simply because, when academics started catching up, newspapers had, in the words of Leech et al., already reached their 'noun saturation point' (p. 209). The rise of nouns in newspapers has been accompanied by a decline in the use of prepositions, the two processes being linked because of the growth of multi-noun, preposition-free phrases (Leech et al., 2009).

The reason why newspapers led this grammatical revolution is obvious: newspaper editors wanted to pack in as much information as possible in as little space as possible. They could save space by increasing the number of nouns and omitting the prepositions, using phrases such as 'government approval', 'business empire', 'air disaster', or 'baggage inspection procedures' that pack information densely (Biber, 2003). Generally, newspapers use different sorts of multi-noun phrases than do academics. Newspapers use them in headlines to encapsulate events: 'Pig Transport Offences Man Fined'; 'Government Scandal Crisis Talks'. Journalists frequently string nouns together, when describing people and their positions: 'San Francisco Redevelopment Agency Executive Director Edward Helfeld' (Leech et al., 2009, p. 215). That is eight nouns in a row, which seems to be about the maximum number to be found.

Academics rarely use such strings of nouns to describe people in this way. In the social sciences, academics will use strings of nouns to create general concepts, which stand for things, ideas or for processes occurring in the social world. 'Noun saturation point' would be one such string which bears the mark of academia rather than the world of journalism. There are, of course, many others in the social sciences: 'language acquis-ition device', 'gene-environment correlation', 'user-behaviour manage-ment' and so on. As we shall see in Chapter 6, academics are particularly prone to constructing nouns from other parts of speech, especially verbs, in order to describe processes; linguists sometimes refer to these types of nouns as 'nominalizations' (Biber, 1988; Biber, Conrad and Reppen, 1998).

If newspapers were driven to create their noun-filled phrases out of a desire to save space, then we might wonder whether academics were motivated by a desire for clarity. As we have seen, the defenders of academic jargon typically claim that academics have to create their own terms because normal words are insufficiently precise. Given that many technical terms are strings of nouns, it might be thought that a phrase such as 'noun saturation point' offers the sort of precision that might be lost if prepositions intruded between the nouns. Douglas Biber, however, argues persuasively that the opposite is the case. When academics string together nouns, they do not specify the relationship between those nouns. Although a variety of different relationships may be possible, academic writers will assume that their readers know what relationship they intend to convey. The phrases, however, are intrinsically less clear than they would be if they contained the preposi-tions and this indicates that the complexity of academic writing is not necessarily produced by a desire to state meaning precisely (Biber and Gray, 2010).

Let us consider the terms 'infant perception' and 'object perception', both of which are common to psychologists. Both terms consist of the noun 'perception' being modified by another noun with no linking prep-osition. Despite their similarity, these two phrases express different rela-tionships between their two nouns. 'Object perception' refers to the perception *of* objects, whereas 'infant perception' refers to perception *by* infants, although grammatically it could refer to the perception *of* infants. Psychologists know this but this knowledge is not derived from the intrin-sic meaning of their terminology but from their general knowledge of psychology. Sometimes matters can be unclear. Amongst social psychol-ogists the term 'group stereotype' can refer to stereotypes *of* groups, or stereotypes held *by* groups, or stereotypes *of* groups *by* groups. Often social psychologists do not clarify exactly what they mean when they use the concept. In Chapter 8, I will suggest that social psychologists routinely use their technical terminology in less than clear ways, for it spares them the trouble (and even embarrassment) of being precise. Social psychologists are by no means unique amongst social scientists in finding it useful to deploy ambiguous terminology.

My charge is not that academic social scientists happen on occasions to use technical terminology in less than desirably clear ways, as if sometimes they unguardedly let standards slip. The charge is stronger: academic social scientists have explicitly created terminology that is inherently ambiguous. John Bellquist was for many years employed by the American Psychological Association to work as a copy-editor for the association's leading journals. He was disturbed that some of the academic writers, whose articles he had copy-edited over the years, could write so poorly. So, after many years of correcting grammatical infelicities, Bellquist wrote a style manual, which he intended primarily for experimental psychologists but which he hoped would also assist other academic authors (Bellquist, 1993).

One of the grammatical habits, which Bellquist warned against, was what he called 'nominalization'. Actually, he used 'nominalization' differently to the way that Biber uses the term but that is no problem: as I shall discuss in Chapter 6, linguists use this technical term in a variety of very different and contradictory ways. Bellquist used 'nominalization' to refer to the increasing use of nouns, especially in phrases which link together nouns without prepositions. Clearly he disliked this mode of expression, finding it ugly and frequently unnecessary. Bellquist preferred authors to write 'rats were presented with a novel solution' rather than using a phrase such as 'novel-solution-presented rats' (1993, p. 127).

Bellquist was not just concerned that noun phrases without prepositions could be aesthetically unattractive. Like Biber, he argued that the absence of prepositions makes for unclear writing, despite the outward appearance of technicality. As an example he discussed the phrase 'process differences', showing that it can mean 'different processes', 'differences in processes' and 'differences between processes' (see Chapter 8 for comments about the ambiguity of the term 'categorization processes'). Bellquist commented that one should never 'force a reader to sift through several diverging semantic alternatives, unless ambiguity is actually part of one's purpose' (p. 128). Regarding the growth of 'nominalization', Bellquist offered several reasons why authors might choose this style. It showed, he suggested, an admiration for the abstract at the expense of the concrete; also, he commented, 'the excessive use of abstract nouns confers a false air of prestige and knowledgeability' (p. 130).

In short, academic authors can benefit from using this way of writing, but what they gain tends to be prestige and a sense of technical proficiency rather than intellectual lucidity. They can sound as if they are being technically precise without having to specify exactly what they mean.

This way of writing is not something peripheral in the social sciences, but it is linked to the major grammatical development in modern academic prose.

The rise of acronyms

Another major grammatical development in modern English writing has been the use of acronyms. We have already seen some examples of academic acronyms, and, as I shall suggest in this section, the rise of academic acronyms is connected with the dominance of nouns in academic writing. Today academics live in a world of acronyms. We work in research centres and in university schools, which will be conventionally known by their acronyms. The committees, on which we sit, will be known by the first letters of their official titles, as will the research funding bodies and the professional organizations for our disciplines. And, as I will suggest, acronyms can be particularly useful as we seek to promote our work and our approaches.

In England most sociologists will belong to the BSA (British Sociological Association) and will apply for grants from the ESRC (Economic and Social Research Council), especially if they want to improve their standing in what was formerly known as the RAE (Research Assessment Exercise) but now is termed the REF (Research Excellence Framework). Good performance in these auditing exercises will increase the funding to their department provided by HEFCE (Higher Education Funding Council for England). Few academics, when talking amongst themselves about these organizations, will refer to them by their full names. They are conventionally and conveniently known by their initials.

Neil Mercer (1996) has analysed a recording of two university managers talking on the telephone, discussing a research centre and a teaching programme, both of which they identify by three-letter acronyms. They were doing something very conventional, for, according to Mercer, three-letter acronyms have become a common feature of 'business English' and they represent a 'normal feature of the English language being used efficiently as a specialized tool of work' (p. 97). Mercer's analysis shows that it is not just speakers of business English who use acronyms. He uses the three-letter acronym 'TLA' to refer to three-letter acronyms. He also cites the work of conversation analysts who shows how a speaker can hold the floor in a conversation by continuing to speak past 'what is called a "transition relevance place" (TRP)' (p. 95; I will discuss this concept at more length in Chapter 7). Here, in this small example, Mercer demonstrates that the use of acronyms is not confined to the management of academic business but is also to be found in the business of academic work.

Since 1961, in English academic writing there has been, according to Leech et al. (2009), an increase of roughly 200 per cent in the use of acronyms. Acronyms are particularly used in the natural and medical sciences. Rather than repeating long scientific terminology, authors can abbreviate their major terms into acronyms. Editors of scientific and medical journals sometimes write editorials justifying the use of acronyms, while regretting that they have become so necessary (e.g., Reider, 2008). Predictably the common justification is that acronyms save precious space in the journals.

Like the use of noun-filled noun phrases, acronyms make demands on readers because their meaning may not be immediately apparent. There are genuine worries that their proliferation might be leading to misunderstandings and some observers worry that doctors do not have sufficient knowledge of the acronyms that medical specialists commonly use (Parakh, Hindy and Fruthcher, 2011). Editors of scientific and medical journals will often provide updated glossaries to assist readers and potential contributors. One editor, in providing a list, commented that his journal seemed to have at least one acronym per line (Fisher, 1991). Academics are likely to struggle with acronyms if they read journals outside their specialist areas, for they may be unfamiliar with the abbreviations that other specialists take for granted. When I was doing the background reading for this book, I looked at journals which specialized in research about academic writing. In one journal, I came across an article whose full title was simply: 'EAP or TEAP?' (Todd, 2003). The author and the editor, who accepted the piece, must have presumed that all prospective readers would be insiders, familiar with these acronyms.

Even when editors worry about the profusion of acronyms, they usually accept that they are necessary evils. Some acronyms may be specific to particular articles. For example, an author might describe the various experimental treatments of their study, using cumbersome phrases, such as 'novel-solution-presented rats', as compared with 'repeated-solution-presented rats'. Instead of using each phrase in full throughout the paper, the author might abbreviate the former condition to NSPR and the latter to RSPR. These acronyms would be explained the first time that they were used in the paper and the authors would not expect these acronyms to be recognized outside the particular paper. In this respect, they would differ from EAP and TEAP, whose meaning all specialist readers were expected instantly to recognize without any accompanying explanation.

To say that academic acronyms exist only, or even principally, to save space is to overlook their role in promoting concepts and approaches, especially in the social sciences. A clue is given in one article, which outlines a means for obtaining acronyms and their definitions from the web (Sánchez and Isern, 2011). The authors, who are very much in favour of acronyms, provide three justifications for using them. Predictably, they claim that acronyms enable authors to avoid using lengthy descriptions of concepts and entities. This, however, is only their second justification. Their third is that acronyms offer easy ways to remember concepts and entities – a curious bonus, one might think, for serious academic specialists. Their first justification is that acronyms can be used to 'stress the importance' of entities and concepts (p. 311). Here, we can see a connection between the usefulness of acronyms as a means for authors to promote their academic products, by encouraging readers to remember concepts and to accept their importance.

There are other signs that academic acronyms are not merely, or even principally, devices for saving space. In academic writing, they almost exclusively stand for noun phrases – to describe ideas, things, processes and approaches. If academics simply used acronyms as abbreviations to save space in journals, then we might expect academic English to resemble texting, tweeting and blogging, where all manner of words and phrases are abbreviated: 'cu' (see you), '4' (for), 'IMHO' (in my humble opinion), 'lol' (laugh out loud), 'SMH' (shaking my head) and so on. There are no equivalents in contemporary academic English. Academic writers have certain standard phrases (or what Douglas Biber has called 'prose bundles') which they use frequently in their writing, such as 'it is important to' or 'it is necessary to', 'on the one hand', etc. (Biber, Conrad and Cortes, 2004). None of these commonly used bundles have been abbreviated but academics have to type out (and read) in full 'it is important to' again and again. When offering conjectures in their papers, they cannot use 'IMHO'. There is no academic acronym MRNTBD: 'more research needs to be done'. If there were, space would indeed be saved.

Curiously, acronyms and abbreviations for Latin phrases and clauses have long been acceptable in academic prose: 'n.b.', 'i.e.', 'e.g.', 'op cit'. However, no analogous new abbreviations are seeping into academic English, even at a time when acronyms are generally multiplying in academic writing and when new abbreviations for phrases are being developed popularly. This shows that the growing use of acronyms in academic writing cannot purely be a response to the need for efficiency and space saving. Today's acronyms, therefore, must also serve other purposes. QED.

Often, social scientists will describe their approach by an acronym. In the previous chapter, we came across CHAT, standing for 'cultural-historical activity theory'. Here are two linguists writing on the second page of a book about political language which they are editing: 'It can be said, in a nutshell, that critical scholarship (whether under the label of CL, SFL or CDA), provides PL/APD with important insights' (Okulska and Cap, 2010, p. 4). Early into the book, initials are being mobilized to set the agenda. The first three acronyms stand for approaches to linguistics: Critical Linguistics, Systemic Functional Linguistics and Critical Discourse Analysis. The second pair of acronyms (PL and APD) stands for a topic (Political Language) and for an approach to a topic (the Analysis of Political Discourse). In a footnote, the authors justify using 'APD' in preference to 'PDA', in order to avoid confusion with the entirely different 'PDA' of 'positive discourse analysis' (p. 3n). It is as if the authors are organizing their academic landscape into familiar acronyms, thereby taming a potentially wild territory.

Of course, no one has the copyright on an academic label. Two different camps may claim the label 'PDA' but neither could establish a legal ownership, just as academics cannot impose their preferred meaning on a technical concept which is being used in different ways. Often the existence of two identical, but different, acronyms signals that there are two separate academic communities with virtually no overlap between them. TRPs, as mentioned above, are to be found in the research of those who analyse the details of spoken talk, using Conversation Analysis or CA. This CA differs from the CA of those who conduct the quantitative Content Analysis of media content. Each group is likely to refer to 'CA', as if theirs is the only CA in the whole world.

Amongst the acronyms, which the editors of the volume about political language mention, is 'CDA'. For specialists in the study of language, 'CDA' means 'Critical Discourse Analysis' (which I will be discussing further in Chapter 6). Such is the vastness of the modern academic world that there are many other CDAs. To illustrate this, I checked the titles of articles in academic journals within a two-month period in late 2010 to see what other CDAs there might be. In a social policy journal, there was an article about CDA, or Child Development Accounts; an electronics specialist wrote about correlated double amplification (CDA) as a technique for amplifying low voltages; there was an article about CDA 510, a particular phosphate bronze, and another about CDA, or Clinical Document Architecture, for exchanging medical information; a dental specialist wrote about CDA or Children's Dental Anxiety. Psychiatrists were using this same acronym to refer to anti-psychotropic drugs or Conventional Depot Antipsychotics. A CDA gene featured in the title of another publication; and a medical specialist reported that he had compiled a CDA, or Combined Damage Assessment index, for measuring vascular damage. And, yes, there was one article – just one – that referred to CDA as critical discourse analysis.

It is humbling to realize how many other academics are utterly unaware of one's own taken-for-granted acronyms, but that is not really the point. All these authors were using 'CDA' in the titles of their articles, where the use of the acronym could not have been seriously saving space. Moreover, all these CDAs stand for noun phrases; there were no verbal clauses. They refer to 'things', albeit very different sorts of things. The articles in the natural sciences tend to refer to physical things, such as a phosphate, a gene or a drug. There are also topics (children's dental anxiety), research techniques (amplifying voltages, sharing documents, indices for measuring damage), approaches (analysing discourse critically) and so on. By and large, these were 'things' that the authors were promoting in some sense: a technique, an approach, an index, a topic. There were no 'baddy' CDAs in these titles – no acronymized things (or approaches or techniques) that an article was seeking to overcome, refute or get rid of (not even children's dental anxiety, which was being promoted as an important topic to study).

Using an acronym provides solidity to the 'thing' that the academic is writing about, especially if that thing is an approach. Systemic Functional Linguistics (SFL), Critical Discourse Analysis and CHAT, through their initials, appear as approaches, which are solidly established. A sole professor, who has failed to attract recruits, does not need to acronymize the creations of their own making. But the existence of a capitalized acronym announces that the world is taking seriously an approach or topic to such an extent that they need to shorten its official name. So, the acronym bears witness to its own success – to the need for people to shorten something that is familiar to them.

An official-sounding, nouny label, such as 'Children's Dental Anxiety', can imply a more thing-like, established topic than the phrase 'children being anxious about dentists', just as 'patient behaviour' sounds more official than the behaviour of a patient. A further step is taken when such a title is compressed into initials: it suggests that a sufficient mass of others recognize the status of Children's Dental Anxiety as a proper topic for research. Similarly, acronyms for research tools (such as the 'CDA' for the Combined Damage Assessment index) aid in presenting the instrument as being recognized, authenticated and semi-official. Widespread academic success need not have actually been achieved, for authors can confer the status of an acronym upon the entities that they themselves have created. In so doing, they will be conveying that this thing is so important that it needs to be an acronym, with its capitalized components standing above rows of lower case letters. An abbreviation does not need to be capitalized, but an acronym with its densely packed big letters acts as a sign, self-importantly drawing attention to itself in its upper case regalia.

Pierre Bourdieu's argument against ordinary language

Now that I have presented my arguments about the nouny nature of current academic writing and about the growing importance of acronyms, it is time to turn to an important defence of technical writing in the social sciences. I have already criticized the argument that social scientists need specialist words because those of ordinary language are too imprecise. But I delayed examining another argument until after looking at the grammatical nature of contemporary academic writing. This argument for using specialist terminology concentrates on the inadequacies of ordinary language because it is ordinary. If analysts try to use ordinary language to examine ordinary language, then they will be trapped in the meanings and ideology of ordinary life – the very meanings and ideology from which they need to escape if they are to analyse them. Literary theorists often produce variants of this argument. Some of the contributors to the book *Just Being Difficult?* justify the difficulty of literary theory on these grounds (Culler and Lamb, 2003a). If what literary theorists wrote was easy, then it would be common sense. And if it were common sense, then it would be conservative and non-intellectual. So, literary theory has to be difficult.

Social scientists, rather than difficult literary theorists, are my concern here. Accordingly, I will not be doing any more than making passing references to literary theorists. Instead, I wish to examine Pierre Bourdieu's sociological version of the argument against using ordinary language. We have already seen, in the previous chapter, Bourdieu's discomfort with the puffed-up language of intellectuals, but his discomfort did not stop him from using such language. In *Sociology in Question* Bourdieu claimed that the need to 'resort to an *artificial language*' was greater for sociology than for 'any other science' (1993, p. 21, emphasis in original). The reason lay in the conventional nature of 'ordinary language'.

In Bourdieu's view, sociology has to speak 'against the received ideas that are carried along in ordinary language' (p. 20). If sociologists were to speak in ordinary language, they would 'accept unwittingly a whole social philosophy' (p. 20). One cannot use ordinary language to expose this philosophy, because the words, which one would be using, would be expressing that very philosophy. In order to 'break with the social philosophy that runs through ordinary words', the sociologist has no choice but to invent new words. By rejecting ordinary, commonplace words, sociologists are able to 'express things that ordinary language cannot express' (p. 21). Bourdieu warns that this 'rigorous and controlled use of language' will rarely lead to 'clarity', for what is clear is usually either self-evident common-sense or plain fanaticism (p. 21).

This is a seductive argument, which dignifies the job of creating technical concepts in the social sciences. And it seems to offer social scientists a good reason not to try to write simply. The simpler their writing, the less intellectual and more conservative it will be: to be radical one has to escape from simple, clear writing. The defence dangles the prospect of obtaining superior knowledge through the very technical concepts (or jargon) that mystify (or irritate) ordinary people. The argument offers the moral high ground for difficult prose, condemning clarity to low boggy grounds. Indeed, Jonathan Culler offers the possibility that literary theory may not be too difficult but not difficult enough (Culler and Lamb, 2003b, p. 9).

Bourdieu, it should be noted, does not specify what that 'whole social philosophy' is that apparently is contained in the words of ordinary language. In assuming that the words of a language contain a whole social philosophy, he is taking a rather restricted view of language, especially 'ordinary language'. He seems to be considering language to be a thing, an object, possessing definite characteristics and expressing certain views. Significantly, Bourdieu talks about 'ordinary language', not ordinary speakers. However, there can be no language unless there are people who use the language. 'Language', in the sense that Bourdieu is using the term, is an abstraction which is derived from all the things that people do when conversing (and writing). Significantly, Culler and his contributors also talk about language as if it were a thing. Culler writes that 'theory takes language as an object of critical inquiry' (Culler and Lamb, 2003a, p. 5). The assumption is that there is such a thing as 'language', rather than people using language, and that this thing must be criticized from outside.

This sounds as if the radical critic should avoid using ordinary language in the way that others use it. However, there is a problem, if we take 'language' to be an academic abstraction, at least in the way that sociologists and literary theorists are liable to use the term. Bourdieu's argument, for example, would sound very different, if he changed his remarks about 'ordinary language' to remarks about ordinary speakers or ordinary people. For instance, if he claimed: ordinary people, when they speak, unwittingly accept a whole social philosophy; they can only repeat received ideas with the words that they are able to use; unless they accept the words that we sociologists have created – unless they study our rigorous works – they will not be able to understand their own lives; they will just be saying ordinary, commonplace things with their ordinary, commonplace words. And so on.

It does not sound good. Rather than talking about people, sociologists often seem to be more at ease talking about abstract things – especially abstract things which supposedly can only be described in their own invented terminology. This is something that I will be discussing in more detail later. But for now, a particular function of social scientific jargon can be noted. It can give the insider confidence to claim superior, radical knowledge without appearing to downgrade others; and also to claim that attacks on jargon indicate just how ignorant and conservative the attackers are. In this way, the jargon-user can act elitist while speaking radical – a handy skill in the contemporary world.

Bourdieu's argument (and that of others) has a weak spot, right at its centre: this is its concept of language. How can a whole social philosophy be written into the words of ordinary language? The very notion seems to envisage 'language' as a thing with a precise nature, not as an abstraction which simplifies an infinitely varied set of complex human activities. In this thing, the words press down to form the minds of the users, rather like a machine for making sticks of sugared rock, through whose length the name of a seaside resort (or a set of commonplace beliefs) has been inscribed in red sugar.

This is not how people use language. Speakers habitually use words (and gestures) for rhetorical purposes. This means that they engage in the activity of arguing in the broad sense: they justify, they criticize, they disagree and they agree (Billig, 1991 and 1996). To do this, they have to use a crucial linguistic element that is found in every known human language: they use the grammar of negating, of saying no. No animal system of communication provides the means for negating and for justifying that negating; and just as significantly, all human languages do. Negating and arguing enable us to be what we are. We habitually justify and criticize, and when we do, we frequently find ourselves disputing the meanings of words. In short, we can use ordinary words to explore, contradict and reject the meaning of ordinary words. This is all part of ordinary, everyday activities. It does not require superior, artificial sets of words.

This means that an ordinary language – and for the moment, let us assume that such an abstraction exists – cannot contain merely one single philosophy. As Antonio Gramsci wrote in his *Prison Notebooks* (1971), most languages contain bits and pieces, picked up through the ages. Moreover, the competent speaker will know how to challenge what other speakers say – to enable them to oppose thesis with anti-thesis, one opinion with an opposing opinion, one bit of common sense with another bit. Even in times, when the majority of a given population believed in God, and when common everyday phrases contained godly meanings (such as 'God willing', 'please God', 'how angelic!'), it was still rhetorically possible for anyone to declare, using the most ordinary of ordinary words: 'God does not exist! Anyone, who says that He does, is lying.' The language itself cannot forbid the use of its rhetorical possibilities. And atheists did not have to wait for sociologists to devise big new words before they could challenge common-sense, religious orthodoxies. Similarly, the poor can complain of the injustice of their poverty, and the oppressed of their oppression, without the aid of technical terms. Historically, it has been those who are wealthy and privileged, who have tended to use complicated words to justify wealth and privilege and to tell the poor that they were 'really', philosophically or theologically fortunate for convoluted reasons that they, the poor, found hard to understand.

We can note that sociologists, who wish to argue for the superiority of their own trade-language, have to use ordinary language to do so. When Bourdieu was outlining his views about the supposed conservatism of ordinary language, he was, for the most part, using everyday words. Regarding ordinary language, he claimed that 'the dictionary is charged with a political mythology' (p. 20), but he did not have to invent new terms to say that. He was using ordinary words – the very type of words that he was accusing of carrying a political philosophy – to make the point. He did not explain how this was possible.

As we have seen, the specialist language of the social sciences largely comprises nouns and noun phrases. Social scientists still take most of their verbs from ordinary language. If ordinary language carries a conservative philosophy, then why do the academics presume that this is spread through the nouns and not through the verbs? Are we to assume that the verbs are good, honest servants, who will do our bidding, while the nouns of ordinary language are so untrustworthy that they must be replaced? It seems silly to assume that the different parts of speech have their own politics.

Bourdieu's distinction between the linguistic creativity of sociologists and the linguistic staidness of everyone else is overdrawn. In his autobiography, Roland Barthes recalled his pleasure as a young man in using 'intellectualist jargon' – a pleasure enhanced by the fact that the ordinary public (and especially his maiden aunts) seemed affronted by his fancy words. Because he used intellectual language, Barthes felt himself discriminated against, as if he were 'the object of a kind of racism' (Barthes, 1995, p. 103). Perhaps Barthes was describing conditions that were common in provincial France when he and Bourdieu were young. The defenders of good, solid ordinary words attacked the show-off intellectuals, who were usually, but not invariably, left-wing radicals.

But these are not the conditions of today. We live in a world of continual linguistic change, where big new words and phrases are being mass produced. When academics create their new nouns, noun phrases and TLAs, they are not resisting a fixed, dominant common sense but grammatically they are flowing alongside commercial trends. If I wanted simultaneously to analyse and to resist current trends of academic and commercial language, I would not be best advised to establish in genuine earnest my RDRS framework. The Rigorization De-Rigorization System would exemplify just what I should be critically examining. It could hardly provide special insight except perhaps as an ironic gesture. And then I would need to be careful not to make serious claims about the value of 'the Ironic'.

I am suggesting that, if we wish to stand outside the trends that are dominant in contemporary academic life, now might be the time for simpler language. Our standard social scientific forms of expression today resemble those of commerce too closely for us to assume that they will provide a satisfactory sense of detachment. This resemblance is not conveyed by the meaning of individual terms, but by the grammatical similarities between academic and commercial forms. This is why the Umpire Decision Referral System is, despite its topic, ultimately relevant. There is also an interesting implication. If we want to understand, resist and, maybe, change how people are doing things in the academic world and elsewhere, then we will have to dream that we can do things differently. We might take note of the verbs – to understand, to resist, to change and to dream – and we might hope, but not expect, to find ways to set these old linguistic servants free on our pages.

5   Turning people into things

Social scientists in their writings often give pride of place to the sorts of theoretical things that they create, especially if these theoretical things are big words ending with 'ization' or 'ification'. In the race for status, using smaller words to describe what people do comes a long way down the field. Grammatically this difference in status is reflected in the way that nouns seem to take precedence over verbs. Stylistically this is reflected in a tendency to produce unpopulated, rather than populated, writing. This does not mean that all pieces of writing are either completely unpopulated or completely populated, either filled with theoretical things or filled with depictions of people. Much social scientific writing will be mixed, containing populated and unpopulated passages and sentences. The higher status of unpopulated writing can be seen within texts where writers will use descriptions of people in order to serve the theoretical things that they value. As I will suggest in this chapter, the movement tends to be one way, as writers seem to move from people to things – from verbs to technical nouns.

There are also writings where people hardly get a look in at all. Sometimes, social scientific writing seems to resemble jigsaw puzzles. The writers have slotted their theoretical things together, fitting one concept into another with little reference to actual people and their lives. I will be giving some examples of this jigsaw writing. By and large, one might say that such writers reify the social world, by turning the actual world of people into a world of theoretical things, albeit neatly arranged theoretical things. In the social sciences there is a long-established tradition of writers warning about the dangers of turning people into things, often using the concept of 'reification' to flag up their warning. As I will suggest, in constructing their warnings against reification, social scientists can turn people into things even as they are delivering their warnings. So strong is the preference for things over people that some notable social scientists, as they warn about reification, give the noun 'reification' – the theoretical thing – pride of place over the verb 'to reify', which by comparison they treat rather shabbily.

This chapter comes with a cautionary message: Beware of long words ending in 'ization' or 'ification'. They promise much to we social scientists, as if, by using them, we can solve our intellectual problems. Certainly the big words can provide the means to academic success in the social sciences, for it is professionally advantageous to be an expert in a particular ization or ification – and better still to be known as the inventor of an ization or ification. Yet, like cigarettes and alcohol, these big words should come with warnings. If one looks closely at them – more closely than most social scientists normally do, especially those who are regular users – they can flatter to deceive. Often our social scientific izations and ifications provide only the appearance of technical advance and precision. We should remember that all that glitters is not the product of aurification.

In the nineteenth century, Thomas de Quincey ridiculed the pretentious, over-scholarly style of Samuel Parr, thought by many to be the next Dr Johnson. Describing Parr's endeavours, de Quincey scoffed: 'There was labour, indeed, and effort enough, preparation without end, and most tortuous circumgyration of periods; but from all this sonorous smithery of hard words in *osity* and *ation*, nothing emerged – no massy product – but simply a voluminous smoke' (1863, p. 33). 'No massy product' – now there's a phrase that deserves to be remembered when considering the izations, ifications and other hard words of today.

Freud: two ways of writing

The status for things over people, and for nouns over verbs, is nothing new in academic work. Sigmund Freud, one of the greatest of all social scientific writers and a writer who continues to influence many social scientists today, alluded to it. As an author, Freud was a supreme exponent of both populated and unpopulated ways of writing. He was capable of producing vibrantly populated writing, as well as highly theoretical writing, full of theoretical things that he had imaginatively created.

Freud's case histories are wonderful accounts of people's lives, and in writing about 'Dora' or 'the Rat Man' or 'Little Hans', he does more than bring an individual to life. He places that person in their family and portrays a whole milieu in its messy humanity. We can understand the person's fears and hopes, their insecurities and the ills that have been done to them. He presents the life as if it were a mystery story. The problem is not a dead body that has been discovered in a locked library, but a very much living body. He asks why a particular person is behaving so strangely. Little clues, red herrings, suspicious characters, who might be guilty perpetrators, are pursued energetically and, by the end, the author, like a master detective, presents his account of what might really have happened.

But there is a difference between Freud and Poirot. When the fictional detective solves the mystery, the story is finished and its hold over the reader is broken, for there was nothing else to the story but the artificial puzzle. This is not the case with Freud's great case histories. Freud's solution is not *the* solution, but, as he always recognized, other interpretations are possible and further sub-themes should be explored. He cannot say, with the certainly of a Monsieur Poirot or a Miss Marple, that the id did it and it did it in just this way and for this one particular reason – and that all other interpretations are henceforth redundant. Such is the brilliance of Freud's writing that we can return again and again to his accounts of the young woman Dora or to the rather sad life of the little boy Hans; and we can notice further clues that the great psychoanalytic detective may have overlooked. This is only possible because Freud presents their lives with such warm humanity and with so many details that resist being constrained into a single explanation. Whatever Freud's preferred solution to the problem – whether it is an Oedipus complex or a hidden, shameful love – there is always much more that cannot be packed into that single explanatory bag.

Because of the richness of Freud's writing and the narrative power that he uses to tell the stories, later analysts have returned to the case histories again and again, claiming to discover new secrets about the patients, about Freud and about the nature of psychoanalysis. None of this would have been possible had the case histories resembled the sort of short diagnoses and descriptions of treatment that came to characterize many subsequent case histories after psychoanalysis became well established (Meehl, 1990). Later case histories are like medical reports but Freud's case histories have the enduring quality of great literature.

Amongst Freud's extensive oeuvre, there are far fewer case histories than those who might be unfamiliar with his work might have supposed. Although Freud continued to see patients regularly, even after he had become a famous figure, he wrote up very few of his cases for publication. Much more of his writing was theoretical, or what he called his 'meta-psychology'. Here, Freud often wrote about psychological things, rather than people and their lives. We can read about the big mechanisms of the mind – the ego, the id and the superego – and the things that these mental mechanisms create: such as complexes, abreactions, cathexes, defence mechanisms, primal repression etc. Freud will give us medical-sounding terms for the complexes: castration complex, anxiety neurosis, obsessional neurosis etc. These are all formal things, marked by formal names. If anyone doubts the power of nouns in this sort of writing, they should look at *The Language of Psycho-Analysis* written by two distinguished French psychoanalysts, Laplanche and Pontalis (1983). It is a book which lists the main concepts in psychoanalysis and bears one feature in common with the guidebooks of sociology and anthropology, which I discussed in the previous chapter: it is nouns and noun phrases all the way.

A number of years ago, Roy Schafer produced an important, but somewhat overlooked book, *A New Language for Psychoanalysis* (1976). Schafer, who was himself a psychoanalyst, was worried by the extent to which his colleagues would use medical-type language rather than a more humane way of writing about patients. He traced the problem to Freud, who in his view had two very different styles of writing. First, there was Freud, the great writer, who used, what Schafer terms, 'action' language to great effect. Freud wrote about people and what they did, usually avoiding technical terminology as he did so. In Freud's passages of 'action' language, his long dead patients still live on as characters with their enduring problems. This is the Freud whose writing Schafer unequivocally loved.

Then there was another Freud, who wrote about psychoanalytic things and mechanisms. In his metapsychological writings, Freud used what Schafer called a 'reified' language. Here Freud was turning the dilemmas of people into a world of things, in which objects like the ego, the id, complexes, cathexes and defence mechanisms were the actors, not the people themselves. We can read about what the id or superego does. Sure Freud would mention case histories, and he would devise brilliant metaphors to explain his complicated theories in simple terms, but he was using the human examples and the metaphorical images to illuminate the theoretical statements that he was making. These theoretical statements generally describe the actions of mental mechanisms which supposedly lie behind our thoughts and desires. The movement in Freud's theoretical writings, thus, was from the lives of people to the objects of his theory, or, to put it crudely, from the psychology of people to the metapsychology of psychoanalytic things.

Schafer was arguing that psychoanalysts, both as practitioners and theorists, should get back to the Freud of 'action' language, rather than the Freud of 'reified' language. As far as Freud's influence on contemporary social scientists, particularly in areas such as cultural studies and film studies, this is somewhat of a vain hope. So many psychoanalytically influenced social scientists seem to raid Freud's writings for the big concepts – the big psychoanalytic things – which they can use to augment their theories of social processes. They do not tie such concepts down to the doings of people but they give priority to the things over the people.

I do not intend to give examples here, but I have written elsewhere about this in relation to the writings of Lacan and his followers (Billig, 2006).

Repression and repressing

Most people would assume that the basic concept in Freud's work was 'the unconscious' for psychoanalysis as both a theory and a therapy was devoted to exposing the hidden role of the unconscious in the lives of people. However, when Freud came to write a history of the psycho-analytic movement, he described the theory of repression as 'the corner-stone on which the whole structure of psychoanalysis rests' (1914/1993, p. 73). The importance that he gave to repression is easy to understand, for without repression there could be no unconscious. In Freud's theory, the unconscious comprises that which has been repressed or pushed from conscious awareness. Unless a troubling thought or desire has been repressed, the individual would be consciously aware of that thought or desire. They would not then need a psychoanalyst to help them recover this forgotten element of their mental life. This means that whatever is unconscious must have been repressed. Accordingly, the notion of the unconscious, and thereby the whole theory of psychoanalysis, rests upon people's ability to push troubling thoughts from their minds.

Freud first used both the notions of repression and the unconscious in his first book, *Studies on Hysteria*, which he wrote jointly with his older colleague Josef Breuer. Because this book, which appeared in 1895, introduced Freud's ideas on repression to the world, some commentators have seen it as containing the basic ideas of psychoanalysis (e.g., Grubrich-Simitis, 1997; Grünbaum, 1998). Freud was to be more ambiv-alent about this early work, as he made clear in his preface to the second edition of *Studies*. When he wrote *Studies*, he had not yet developed his theory of infant sexuality and therefore in that work he did not link repression specifically with the forgetting of childish sexual desires. But, for my purposes here, *Studies* is particularly significant because, as well as introducing his key term of 'repression', Freud also commented on his own style of writing and why it might appear to lack status in the eyes of scientists.

Studies is not a univocal work, quite apart from the obvious fact of its having two authors. Only the first theoretical section was jointly written by the two. The other sections were attributed clearly to one or the other author. In another respect, and more importantly for my present argu-ment, *Studies* is multi-vocal for it contains Freud's two styles of writing. The book has theoretical sections, describing the mental operations underlying hysteria, and in these the 'reified' style of writing predominates. In addition, the book comprises five case histories – one written by Breuer and the other four by Freud. Freud, in writing these chapters, used his 'action' style, while Breuer's case history, by contrast, is noticeably wooden.

In the final case history of *Studies*, Freud presented the case of the young woman, Elisabeth von R. She suffered from a series of neurotic ailments: she reported episodes of blindness, pains, numbness, and other medical complaints all of which rested on psychological, rather than physiological, factors. Freud was to link these ailments with her unconscious, and strongly denied, love for her late sister's husband. It was a dramatic story, vividly told by Freud. After outlining the story, Freud commented on his own style, mentioning that he had not always been a psychotherapist but had originally trained as a neuropathologist: 'It still strikes me as strange that the case histories I write should read like short stories and that, as one might say, they lack the serious stamp of science' (1895/1991, p. 231). He added, both modestly and defensively, that 'the nature of the subject is evidently responsible for this, rather than any preference of my own' (p. 231).

If Freud was conscious that his style of writing might be seen to lack the serious stamp of science, he was keen to correct the impression that he might be just a storyteller and not a scientist. That is why, when he mentions his style, he goes out of his way also to point out his credentials as a neurologist and, thereby, as a proper scientist. Psychoanalysis, in his view, was serious science and he wanted to convince readers that his explanations were properly scientific and that he was not explaining the behaviour of his characters as a novelist might.

In Freud's view, the concept of repression was a scientific concept and he wanted readers of *Studies* to grasp this. The book illustrates how quickly Freud moved grammatically from the verb 'to repress' to the noun 'repression'. Significantly the first mention of repressing comes with an active verb in the opening section, which both authors wrote jointly. Here the authors are discussing the traumas which might underlie neuroses: 'It was a question of things which the person wished to forget, and therefore intentionally repressed from his conscious thought' (1895/1991, p. 61; 1895/1952, p. 89). In this passage, the authors do not use the noun 'repression' (*Verdrängung*), but use the verb to indicate an action that a person performs: the person has to push aside or repress (*verdrängte*) thoughts and this is something that they do intentionally (*absichtlich*).

In the case history of Elisabeth von R., we see the young woman struggling to dispel from her own mind the shameful thought that she desired her sister's husband and may have even secretly felt pleasure as her sister lay dying. Her symptoms are a way of distracting herself from these thoughts and from the memory of the shameful feelings towards her sister. Each time that she suspects these thoughts to be creeping up on her, she has yet another symptom. When Freud raises his suspicions with her, she suddenly has a full-scale attack, necessitating the end of that session and, thereby, stopping Freud from continuing to make his accusations. Repressing, here, is an all-too-human action, which we can see a patient undertaking and which protects her from thinking about something that she would rather not think about.

'Repression', as the noun derived from the verb *verdrängen* (to push aside), makes its appearance later in the case history of Lucy R., of which Freud was the sole author. Freud was considering whether Lucy R.'s symptoms, such as her loss of smell, might owe their origins to her having repressed certain desires such as love for her employer. Freud cites the reasons for his suspicion and these relate to his analyses of similar cases. He does not specifically refer to these previous cases, but he writes in general, theoretical terms:

[A]n idea must be *intentionally repressed from consciousness* and excluded from associative modification. In my view, the intentional repression is also the basis for the conversion, whether total or partial, of the sum of excitation. The sum of excitation, being cut off from psychical association, finds its way all the more easily along the wrong path to a somatic innervation (1895/1991, p. 180, emphasis in English translation but not in original German text: 1895/1952, p. 174).

In this passage, Freud begins by using the word 'repress' as a verb, and again with the adverb 'intentionally' (*absichtlich*), but this time he uses the verb in the passive voice. Instead of writing that a person intentionally represses an idea, he writes of an idea being intentionally repressed (*verdrängt*), thereby omitting the human agent, who might be doing the repressing. Then, Freud moves from passive verb to the noun 'repression' (*Verdrängung*), which he uses here for the first time in his writing. 'Repression' is the subject of the sentence, which includes two other abstract nouns, both denoting processes – 'conversion' (*Konversion*) and 'excitation' (*Erregungssumme*: or excitation-sum). In the next sentence Freud describes how 'the sum of excitation' does something – namely, 'finding its way' along a path to a 'somatic innervation' (*körperlichen Innervation*).

Freud has made a move from 'action' language, using 'repress' as an active verb to highly reified, noun-based language. No person appears in the quotation about 'repression'. The actor now, who does things, is not a person but a process – a supposed, but unspecified, process of excitation. The description contains features that we will encounter in unpopulated sociological writings: there are no persons present; if verbs describing actions are used, then they are used in the passive voice without any human actors being identified; the subjects of active verbs are not people but are abstract concepts or theoretical things. Thus, we can see Freud in *Studies on Hysteria* moving from using 'repressing' as an active verb to describe a person doing something, through to using it in the passive voice and then finally to the noun 'repression'. When we get to that point, we read about things, not people.

This is certainly not the language of short stories but it carries the valuable stamp of serious medical language. We might expect, in consequence, that Freud has moved from imprecise ordinary language to more precise, scientific language. However, the opposite is true. Despite the technical quality of Freud's language at this point, his descriptions are utterly vague, far vaguer than his comments about what his patients have done. He leaves unclear what things are being converted, excited and innervated, and how they are being so affected. What exactly is this 'sum of excitation'? It is described as being cut off from 'psychical association' (*psychische Assoziation*), as if it could be associated with psychical, non-material entities, but it is also described as finding its way to something material or bodily (*körperlichen*). Is this a neurological phenomenon? If so, how is it to be identified? How does a sum of excitation go about 'finding its way'? Freud does not say, nor could he say with any degree of precision.

The paradox is that when it comes to describing human actions ordinary language can be quite specific, whereas technical, scientific-sounding language by contrast can be imprecise. There is a theoretical cost when Freud moves towards the reified language and away from the type of language that ostensibly lacks the serious stamp of science. Using the reified language of scientific things, Freud posits 'repression' as if it were a thing that performs hidden bodily tasks, creates unconscious thoughts and has effects on the psychological health of the person. Repression, therefore, is the great hidden object in psychoanalytic theory – an object that seems to do so much harm to people.

In their first use of the word, Freud and Breuer were talking about the person willingly pushing thoughts from their mind. While repressing was being seen in these terms, it is natural to ask how people might push away troubling thoughts. What sorts of skills do they need to acquire, if they are to keep secrets from themselves? How do they distract themselves when they feel that the troublesome thought might be on the verge of breaking back into awareness? However, when the act of willingly repressing is transformed into the thing 'repression', then the theorist can push these difficult questions from their own mind. Repression is something that happens, like a machine being set in motion, subject to hydraulic pressures. What psychoanalytic theorists, then, seem to care about are the causes and effects of repression, rather than how people actually go about repressing.

In consequence, there is a large gap right at the heart of Freud's theorizing (Billig, 1999). He does not specify what people need to do in order to be able to repress thoughts and what actions they need to take in order to keep those repressed thoughts from seeping back into conscious awareness. In Freud's developmental theory, it is as if the biological engine of repression automatically starts up when the child is at the Oedipal stage: as if repression just happens to take place. Even in his case history of Little Hans, Freud does not observe how the parents are teaching the child that ideas should be pushed from his mind, and that by their own actions they are demonstrating to Hans how this might be done; in this regard Freud does not see how 'Oepidal' parents are creating their Oedipal child (Billig, 1999, ch. 5).

Much of this repressing cannot be consciously intentional, as Freud and Breuer might have implied in their early comments, but must be subtly habitual. We learn habits of talking to others and, from that, habits for talking to ourselves in ways that we can use to redirect our own attention from troublesome to less troublesome matters. Freud, in his metapsychological writings does not say how we might learn these habits of repressing. Piling up more abstract concepts and creating more psychoanalytic things would not provide answers. If we want to understand more about this key concept of psychoanalytic theory, then we need to go back to observing the actions that people take when they are engaged in pushing away thoughts and desires. And if we want to write about what we observe, then we should be using the sort of language that is appropriate for describing human actions, not the motions of machines.

Reification and turning people into things

When Roy Schafer claimed that Freud and later psychoanalysts tended to use 'reified' language, he was using a concept that has been extremely important in the social sciences. Generally, social scientists use the concept of 'reification' to indicate the process by which people come to treat other people and human actions as if they were things. Freud might be said to have reified what his patients were doing, when he treated 'repression' as if it were a mechanism, which somehow just happens to be set in motion, rather than as an action that people have to perform. Grammatically, Freud's tendency to reify was illustrated by using the noun 'repression', in preference to using the verb 'to repress' in the active voice.

In the previous chapter, I discussed Zina O'Leary's *The Social Science Jargon Buster* (2007), a book, which aims to guide students through the difficult terminology which they must understand if they are to study the social sciences successfully. O'Leary lists the noun 'reification' in her book as one of the important concepts of the social sciences. O'Leary describes 'reification' as 'the process by which abstract concepts are treated as if they're real material things' (O'Leary, 2007, p. 224). We might notice how, in this statement, she uses the passive voice: she does not say who might be treating abstract concepts as if they were material things. In her entry on 'reification' she does not use the verb 'to reify' at all.

When she outlines what 'reification' might be, it is as if she is writing in a reified way. She begins her entry by saying that 'taking the abstract and treating it as if real is actually something we come across every day' (p. 224). We might notice her use of 'we': she says that 'we' come across reification every day, not that 'we' might actually engage in reification ourselves. Again, she does not say who might be treating the abstract as if it is real, but she is not accusing 'us' of doing so. It is as if 'reification' is something that others bring about or that just seems to happen. Her description of 'reification' underlines an important aspect of the concept. She is writing about 'reification' as if it is something that might closely be connected with intellectual work: social theorists and intellectuals work with abstract concepts and, in consequence, they might be uniquely placed to treat abstract concepts in reified ways. As we have seen, academic social scientists are particularly prone to believing in the reality of their abstract concepts.

There is an awkward possibility that I want to raise at this point. What if the concept of 'reification' is the sort of abstract concept which can erroneously be treated as if it were a material thing? And do social theorists run the risk of treating this abstract concept as if it were real by not tying 'reification' closely to the activity of 'reifying'? If theorists allow the abstract noun to slip free of the verb, they might be reifying their own concept, even if they are trying to use that concept to explain and to expose the reality of 'reification'. I want to consider this first in relation to the concept of 'reification' and then, more generally, in relation to the general class of concepts, to which 'reification' belongs – namely the sort of concepts which end with the suffixes 'ification' or 'ization' and which social scientists use to describe social processes without linking them closely to particular sorts of actions performed by people.

Compared with most izations and ifications that social scientists are using today, the word 'reification' is not particularly recent. The *Oxford English Dictionary* records that both the noun 'reification' and the verb 'reify' were first used in English around the mid-nineteenth century. One of the first appearances of both the noun and verb came in an anonymous article published in 1854 in *Fraser's Magazine*, a publication aimed at intellectually minded British women. The article in question was about ancient Greek mythology. According to the author, the ancient Greeks originally 'deified' their physical world. This meant that they imagined physical objects, such as rocks, trees, rivers etc, to be living gods. The author described 'reification' as 'the conscious conversion of what had hitherto been regarded as living beings into impersonal substances' (pp. 74–5). In this sense, 'reification' was the counterpart to 'deification': whereas deification meant transforming things to make them appear as if they were living gods, reification involved treating things as things. Deification, thus, was the error and reification the correction of that error.

This early use of 'reification' differed crucially from later sociological uses of the word: the anonymous author was treating 'reification' as a sign of scientific progress, rather than an indicator of error and social misfortune. When social scientists began using 'reification', they used it to denote the error of treating people and their actions as if they were things. Marx used the concept of *Verdinglichung* (or 'thingification') in the third volume of *Capital* (1894/1959, ch. 48), when discussing how, in capitalist society, people see commodities as possessing intrinsic, objective value, thereby ignoring that these commodities had gained their value from a series of exploitative relations between humans. Marx argued that, as commodities become fetishized, so there is a mystification of the capitalist mode of production, with social relations being treated as if they were things.

Marx's English translators of *Capital* did not render *Verdinglichung* as 'reification' until the interwar years of the twentieth century. Until then, the translators tended to use the phrase 'the conversion of social relations into things' rather than 'the reification of social relations'. In the interwar years, a number of Marxist theorists, particularly George Lukács, started to develop Marx's notion of *Verdinglichung*, seeing 'reification' as something that occurs both in practice and in theory. It occurs in practice, as capitalists treat their workers as things not people and in theory, as capitalist economists produce 'rational', mathematical accounts of 'work-processes'; both the theory and the practice of capitalism combine to destroy the older 'organic' relation between the producer and the product (see, for instance, Lukács, 1923/1971, especially pp. 83ff.; and also

Bewes, 2002). Importantly, both Marx and later Marxists saw intellectuals as playing a key role in distorting the nature of capitalism, for intellectuals produce ideas and theoretical concepts which transform the real, exploitative world of people into an artificial, abstract world of things in which real relations are distorted.

The sociologists Peter Berger and Thomas Luckmann widened the concept of 'reification', so that it ceased to be a Marxist concept that critically described the conditions of capitalism. In their classic book *The Social Construction of Reality* (1967), Berger and Luckmann suggested that 'reification', far from being confined to capitalist societies, could be found in all societies. They defined reification as 'the apprehension of human phenomena as if they were things' (p. 106). Everywhere people treat the creations of their society as if they were objective things, and, in so doing, they forget that these 'things' have been produced by human actions.

In the previous paragraph, I indicated that *The Social Construction of Reality* was first published in 1967. In writing that sentence, I was assuming that there was an actual year of '1967'. I did not write that Berger and Luckmann's book was published during the period of 365 days that we moderns have arbitrarily chosen to label as '1967'. Like most others, I do not treat our code for labelling time as arbitrary and I write as if I have forgotten that this code had to be created historically by human social actions. I certainly push out of my mind the religious meaning of this dating. When mentioning the year '1967', I did not offer to translate that year into the corresponding numbers by which alternative calendars label it. In short, I have treated this date, and other dates, as if they were objective things, reifying them as I forget the history of this arbitrary system which I habitually and unthinkingly use. Berger and Luckmann saw collective forgetting as being a crucial part of reification and they write that reification 'implies that man is capable of forgetting his own authorship of the human world' (1967, p. 106).

Many sociologists have followed Berger and Luckmann in using 'reification' in this wider sense, stretching (and softening) Marx's insights about capitalism to cover all forms of society. They have retained the sense that 'reification' refers to an error, which needs to be corrected and which, in their view, can be corrected by sociological insight. Certainly Berger and Luckmann believed that an important feature of sociological analysis was to remember what is conventionally forgotten during the process of reification. For them, the sociological study of reification had a wider purpose: if the reified world is 'a dehumanized world', then sociological understanding becomes a means of re-humanizing the world (1967, p. 106).

This aspiration is admirable, but there is a problem in practice. The means to re-humanize the world is to expose reification and to remind people of what they habitually forget. But the concept of 'reification' is itself a conceptual 'thing' which has been created by humans and which sociologists treat as something real. More generally, it is hard to see how sociologists can succeed in re-humanizing the world if they write in unpopulated ways, particularly if they assume that they should analyse the social world by using izations and ifications, including 'reification'.

How to reify with reification

To see how social scientists might reify with reification, we need to examine how they use language when discussing the problems of reification, especially how they prefer the abstract noun 'reification' to the verb 'to reify'. We can see this fondness for abstract nouns in *The Social Construction of Reality*, where Berger and Luckmann described 'reification' as 'the apprehension of human phenomena as if they were things'. In this definition, the authors explain one abstract noun in terms of another: 'reification' is an 'apprehension'. Berger and Luckmann do not explain people reifying in terms of their apprehending. The authors are fitting conceptual things together as if they were arranging the pieces of a jigsaw puzzle.

This is not a passing aberration, occurring in one sentence, but it represents something much more general. This can be seen in a classic article which Peter Berger published together with Stanley Pullman, just before *The Social Construction of Reality* appeared (Berger and Pullman, 1965). This article is a major piece of work, examining the concept of reification and its place in sociological thinking. Berger and Pullman discuss when reification might occur and, significantly, what it supposedly does. They write that reification 'operates in a society by bestowing ontological status on roles and institutions' (p. 206); also reification 'converts quality into quantity' and it 'converts action into process' (p. 208). In such statements, reification appears as the actor who does things. Incidentally, Zina O'Leary, in her presentation of what 'reification' is, claims that statements, which impute actions and motives to human creations, rather than to humans themselves, are examples of 'reification'. She offers the example of the statement: 'Religion tries to repress sexuality.' Religion, she comments, is 'a human-made belief system and, as such, can't "try" to do anything' (2007, p. 224).

Whereas Berger and Pullman devote much space in their article to discussing the noun 'reification', and what it might do, they hardly use the verb 'to reify' at all. In fact, they only use the verb in two sentences. In one of these sentences, the authors compare a twentieth-century person, 'who reifies himself as "a representative of the corporation"', with a twelfth-century person, who reifies himself as a lord and gentleman (p. 208). Both types of 'reifier' can be presumed to be very different from the sociological authors of the article and their academic readers, who are unlikely to think of themselves as representatives of corporations. In this way, the authors are presenting 'reification' as something that others do. Berger and Luckmann do not discuss the sort of modern person who might reify themself as a 'sociologist', and who might think of themself as a representative of an academic discipline or a sociological approach; nor do they think of someone who might reify themself by bestowing 'ontological status' on the concept of reification. When it comes to bestowing 'ontological status', the authors describe a thing, namely reification, rather than persons, such as sociologists, as performing this act (and 'ontological status' – the thing that is bestowed – is, of course, yet another abstract thing). In this way, the authors seem to produce examples of the very thing that they are critically examining.

More jigsaw work comes with Axel Honneth's recent book *Reification: A New Look at an Old Idea* (2008). Honneth was a student of Jürgen Habermas and, thus, a third-generation member of the Frankfurt School. Like earlier members of the Frankfurt School, Honneth's intellectual interests span across conventional academic disciplines, including social sciences, psychoanalysis and, above all, philosophy. In *Reification* he seeks to revive the concept of reification, giving it contemporary meaning and significance while building on the ideas of Lukács. As Honneth writes, Lukács used the concept to designate 'a cognitive occurrence in which something that doesn't possess thing-like characteristics in itself (e.g. something human) comes to be regarded as a thing' (2008, p. 21). We can note some familiar features: the abstraction of the statement, its lack of people, the passive voice ('comes to be regarded') and human acts being described by abstract nouns rather than by active verbs ('cognitive occurrence'). Generally, Honneth is concerned about the thing 'reification', not the activity of 'reifying' – and throughout he uses the noun rather than the verb.

Basically Honneth operates at a high level of abstraction, in which he links abstract concepts together. The two big jigsaw pieces that he slots together are 'reification' and 'antecedent recognition', claiming that the former is the product of forgetting the latter: 'forgetting our antecedent recognition, which I take to be the core of all forms of reification, indeed corresponds to the result produced by a perceptive reification of the world' (2008, p. 58). This forgetting occurs through the influence of other big concepts which seem to affect things: 'habitualization has the power ... to disable the antecedent stance of recognition' (p. 157).

The concept of 'antecedent recognition' has played a key role in Honneth's work. He derives the idea from the work of several psychoanalysts, most notably Donald Winnicott. Honneth relates the concept of 'antecedent recognition' to a series of other concepts in order to describe what he means. 'Antecedent recognition' takes place when the mother has shown 'adaptation' to the child but this stage of closeness cannot last. As Honneth argued in his book *The Struggle for Recognition* (1995), 'de-adaptation' has to follow 'adaptation' especially if such processes as 'individuation' are to occur: 'Corresponding to the mother's graduated de-adaptation, there is an intellectual development in which the expansion of conditioned reflexes is accompanied by the capacity for cognitive differentiation between self and environment' (1995, p. 100). This set of processes seems to happen universally, for Honneth claims that 'in every epoch, individual, particular anticipation of expanded recognition relations accumulate into a system of normative demands' (p. 84).

So, Honneth arranges his abstract nouns in their places, but it would be an exaggeration to say that his writing is completely unpopulated. When he discusses 'de-adaptation' and the forgetting of 'antecedent recognition', he quotes from psychoanalysts who describe in simpler language what mothers and their babies might be doing. These quotations tend to be general statements about what a hypothetical mother or a baby might be doing, rather than statements about a particular mother or baby. Moreover, these statements do not come with the rich narrative of a Freudian case history. Honneth uses such quotations to serve his big concepts, rather than using the big concepts in the service of understanding the little actions of everyday life. He is constantly advancing towards a theoretical position, in which abstract concepts are set in their respective places. As Honneth analyses the problem of reification (and not the problem of 'reifying'), he does not seem to consider that his abstract style of doing academic work might result in his reifying the world by turning people into thing-like conceptual entities, whose reality he accepts and whose unreality he forgets.

It is as if this type of intellectual inquiry consists of finding the right pieces to complete the jigsaw, so that the analyst, after much struggle, can fit the last piece – the final abstract concept – in its place. Having pieced together the bits to form an elegant view, the analyst can stand back, satisfied that the work is done. No matter how long it takes to complete a jigsaw and no matter how much effort we have put into the task, we will then run the risk of reifying what we have done, if we mistake the composite picture that we have formed for the real world of people.

Mediatization and other izations

Both 'repression' and 'reification' are similar as general concepts, in that each is linked to a verb. We can talk about someone repressing or reifying and when we do, we are referring to some sort of action that the person is doing. Of course, the fact that we can use the verbs, which correspond to the general concept, does not mean that analysts take advantage of the possibility. As I have argued, all too often analysts do not avail themselves of this opportunity but will pass over the verbs in favour of the nouns. However, some general concepts, which social scientists use, do not have corresponding verbs and, in consequence, are not linked to actions that individuals might perform. Some of the big izations and ifications are of this type. 'Massification' cannot be said to exist because people 'massify'; similarly, we do not say globalization is happening, whenever we see someone 'globalizing'. In this regard, both 'massification' and 'globalization' resemble the concept which I will be considering next: 'mediatization'. No one is said to mediatize. The concept of 'mediatization', as we shall see, is far removed from individual actions: it is a concept built on other concepts, an abstraction of abstractions.

I have not chosen to look at 'mediatization' because the concept is, at present, enormously important in the social sciences, although a number of experts in media studies take it seriously. It is part of my general strategy of taking examples where I find them – a strategy that I followed better in previous chapters than in the present one. Most social scientists use izations and ifications without commenting on their nature as concepts. However, Winfried Schulz (2004), a distinguished professor of Mass Communication and Political Science, began a paper on 'mediatization' with some remarks on izations in general. His paper presents a good example of how such concepts – especially when they are abstractions of abstractions without corresponding verbs – can be highly imprecise and also how academic social scientists do not just use such concepts but they can seek to promote them.

Schulz began: 'Mediatization and other "izations", such as globalization, commercialization and individualization, have a critical and expressive function' (Schulz, 2004, p. 87). Such words have a critical function, Schulz continued, because they were 'instrumental in critical assessments of social change with the latent function of expressing a certain attitudinal or political position'. Although such words might be useful for social critics, they lack, in Schulz's opinion, the precision necessary for 'scientific analysis' and therefore it is necessary for scholars to 'clarify their meaning and to specify their analytical usability' (pp. 87–8). Schulz was aiming to clarify 'mediatization'.

I will leave aside Schulz's comments about the political functions of izations, except to agree with Orwell that waffly words will lead to waffly politics. Accordingly, even those, who wish to use izations for their political function, rather than scientifically, should be concerned that these words are as clear as possible. The basic idea of 'mediatization' is that the influence of the media is spreading throughout the world and that most other institutions are finding that they have to adapt to 'the logic of the media'. This broad idea is basically impersonal: it deals with trends in institutions rather than individual behaviour. Above all, as we shall see, it posits 'the media' as agents of change and holders of power – rather than particular individuals or social groups.

In some respects, Schulz attempts to specify the analytic 'usability' of 'mediatization' by setting out the pieces of his conceptual jigsaw, linking his key concept with four other processes, in which the media are said to play a key role. These four processes are extension, substitution, amalgamation and accommodation, and these, Schulz says, constitute 'a description of mediatization' (Schulz, 2004, p. 90). Again, these processes are not linked to specific sorts of actions. Schulz is not saying that we know mediatization occurs when we see people substituting and amalgamating. Not only does he stick to nouns, when describing his four processes, but these nouns summarize complex patterns of social processes, linked to other processes, rather than to individual actions.

Schulz might not write about individuals amalgamating or mediatizing, but he portrays the media almost as if they were a person, capable of performing actions. For example, when he discusses three of the four processes of change, which he claims to represent the basis of mediatization, he describes them as things that the media do: such as the media 'extend' human capabilities, 'substitute' social activities, 'amalgamate' with various non-media activities (p. 98). In Schulz's formal description of the fourth process – that of accommodation – 'actors' appear: 'Actors and organizations of all sectors of society accommodate to the media logic' (p. 98). Actors are only seen to act by accommodating to 'media logic'; they are not being seen to create, impose and protect that logic.

Quite what 'media logic' comprises is left unclear. Nor does Schulz specify what is involved in 'accommodating' to such logic. There is no extended example of someone, or some group, displaying the sort of behaviour which constitutes accommodating to the logic, so that we can specify the key features and be clear exactly what such accommodating might involve and what it does not. The statement that actors and organizations in all sectors of society display this behaviour is itself vague. It does not specify what percentage of actors and organizations might be expected to do so and how often. Is Schulz implying that some actors and organizations do so regularly? Or that most do so often? Or all do so occasionally? It is quite vague – certainly vaguer than would be acceptable for a natural scientist specifying a physical process such as oxidization or calcification.

Generally when Schulz mentions people in relation to the four processes, he tends to depict them as the objects of actions, which are supposedly taken by the media. Thus, when Schulz writes about 'extension', he claims that 'as the media extend the communicative and perceptive capabilities of humans, they impose media-specific constraints on the messages shaping the communication process in a way that the users can hardly control' (2004, p. 91). The sentence describes what the media do: it is the media that extend human capabilities and impose constraints, not humans extending their own capabilities through the media. The media are the subject and the humans are the object. In writing like this, Schulz has constructed a statement that assumes an antithesis between humans and the media: the humans, in this case, are being controlled and shaped by the media. This is the storyline of science fiction being presented as usable science.

None of Schulz's four processes is actually an ization, but other theorists have explicitly linked mediatization with a variety of other izations. For example, Knut Lundby quotes with approval an analyst who sees mediatization as one of the main processes behind modernity 'together with individualization, commercialization and globalization' (Lundby, 2009, p. 10). Lundby mentions another expert who connects mediatization with individualization and deterritorialization (p. 15). When Lundby writes about these connections, he does not, and could not, illustrate them with any descriptions of humans individualizing or deterritorializing. It is more things spinning around other things.

It is no surprise that, despite his best efforts, Schulz has been unsuccessful in laying down how other media experts should use the term 'mediatization' (e.g., Couldry, 2008; Deacon, 2012). This is entirely predictable because social scientists are resistant to following those of their number who stipulate how they should, and should not, use the big concepts of their field. In addition, Schulz does not help his case by writing in such an abstracted, unpopulated manner. Whatever actions that people may have performed seem to fade from sight when the big linguistic ships – the mediatizations and the deterritorializations – are launched down the slipway into the oceans of theory. There, these great liners sail on and on, miles from the ports that teem with human life. They seem to be curiously deserted: no captain can be seen at the helm, no crew members swabbing down the decks, no passengers sunning themselves. Yet, on they massively go.

Promoting big concepts

I have used the metaphor of the jigsaw puzzle to describe the sort of abstract writing where the social scientist seems to be concerned, above all else, to fit concepts together. Actually, the metaphor, as I have been using it, is inadequate because all the pieces of an actual jigsaw puzzle are equally important: normally there is no one piece, on whose correct positioning all the other pieces depend. That is not the case with jigsaw writing in the social sciences, for the writer usually has a central concept, around which they are arranging their other concepts. We can see this in Honneth's writings, where 'recognition' is his key concept – even in his book on reification. Similarly, Schulz is fitting 'accommodation', 'extension' etc. around his key concept of 'mediatization'. It is as if the completed jigsaw depicts a picture of 'mediatization' or 'antecedent recognition' or whatever. All the little pieces are being used to create this big picture and to show off this big conceptual thing.

This is important because sometimes the social scientific compilers of jigsaws often have a central concept to promote. Schulz, for example, was using his article to promote the value and 'usability' of 'mediatization'. He was not just saying to his readers 'this is an interesting concept', but 'with my refinements, you should be using this concept'. The theorists of mediatization have clearly invested much in the term 'mediatization', while, on the other hand, rival theorists believe it to be equally important not to use 'mediatization'. For example, Couldry (2008) advocates 'mediation' over 'mediatization'; both Cauldry and Schulz prefer their respective terms to John Thompson's 'mediazation' (Thompson, 1995). As the rivals line up to support their word of preference, they agree that it matters having the right ization in place. These words function as more than summaries of complex social processes, involving the role of the media in modern life, for the words have become commodities in themselves, with social scientists using the ization to label approaches that are to be championed or to be rejected.

The rival theorists describe the productive powers of their favoured words and the limitations of rival concepts. Schulz writes about the value of the concept of mediatization 'if it precisely defines the role of the mass media in a transforming society and if it stimulates an adequate analysis of the transformation processes' (p. 98). It is as if the concept of mediatization is capable of doing all this, unmediated by its own media and by the social scientists that must produce the analyses. Couldry writes critically that '"mediatization" encourages us to look for common patterns', while 'mediation', by contrast, does not encourage us to be so narrowly focussed (2008, p. 377). Again people (namely, 'us') are the objects, and things (namely the words 'mediatization' and 'mediation') are the subjects, the actors who are capable of encouraging and stimulating us.

Knut Lundby, in the introduction to an edited work on 'mediatization', writes approvingly of the powers possessed by the concept of 'mediatization', which he identifies as a key concept for media studies. Lundby suggests that mediatization 'gives media scholars a different agenda and a different set of priorities'; and that it also 'addresses a key role for the media in larger processes of social change' (2009, p. 9). Again, we find out what 'mediatization' can do, rather than what academics might do with the concept; and, in this instance, we don't hear so much about what 'mediatization' cannot do. For its supporters, the extra 'tiza' in 'mediatization' gives the word added powers over 'mediation'. For the rivals, those extra four letters block the analyst's view of the world: they must be removed so that we can see things more clearly. 'Mediatization' here is more than a word that denotes, rather loosely, large-scale social processes. It is an academic term that functions as a brand label for an approach. This is why the academics can invest so much in their debates about words.

After listing the powers of 'mediatization', Lundby adds a further comment: 'This should be also of interest to other scholars and students in the social sciences and humanities' (p. 9). What sort of language do these comments echo? It is the world of advertising, where products are capable of doing amazingly desirable things. 'It should be of interest to ...' is the sort of statement that publishers have for many years been putting on the covers of non-fiction books, in order to attract purchasers: 'This book should be of interest to all students of sociology' or 'to all readers interested in the media'. Now the statement is put between the covers to attract recruits to a way of doing the social sciences. In this instance, a social scientist is describing the so-called logic of the media, while apparently following 'the logic' of advertising and promotion.

The supporters of 'mediatization' are telling potential customers or users: 'Put a Sparkle into your Research with Mediatization' or 'Look what Mediatization, with enhanced Scientific Usability, can do for you'. As the proponents of mediatization do battle with those supporting mediation, they resemble the Coca-Cola Corporation, fending off the challenge from Pepsi Cola, with the claim that its product is 'the real thing'. But that is the problem. Social scientists feel pressures to create and defend their izations and ifications, treating them seriously as if they were the real thing. That is how we have learnt to do the social sciences.

6   How to avoid saying who did it

I have been arguing that social scientists, who write in ways that transform people into things, tend to write imprecisely. When it comes to describing human actions, ordinary verbs have the edge on the big izations and ifications. In the previous chapter, I offered a number of examples to support this view but in the present chapter, I want to go further: I want to give technical reasons why this should be the case. In order to sustain my points, I will have to take a number of twisty turns. Principally I will be drawing on ideas from linguists to show what sorts of grammatical moves authors make when they write in unpopulated ways and then I will need to argue why such moves might be problematic for social scientists.

This will not be straightforward, because I will need to use and also to hold at a distance some linguistic izations, such as 'nominalization' and 'passivization'. I was faced with a similar problem in the previous chapter, when I needed to use and to criticize the concept of 'reification'. I will be suggesting that even critical linguists, who see ideological problems with 'nominalization' and 'passivization', fail to heed their own warnings when it comes to their own writing. My preference is to use the verb forms – 'to nominalize' and 'to passivize' – but this will not always be possible, especially when I follow the arguments of those who use the nouns. There might also be times when I could have avoided using the izations myself, but use them regardless: it can sometimes be hard to climb out of the pit in which we are accustomed to play.

I will be discussing how social scientists, natural scientists and ideological writers all tend to use the grammatical constructions of nominalization and passivization, but for different reasons. The ideologists do so because it is often expedient for them to absent themselves from their own texts and to delete agents from their descriptions of the world. The natural scientists derive other benefits from writing in impersonal, depopulated ways. However, it has been a mistake, in my view, for social scientists to try to follow the same path as the ideologists and the natural scientists. My argument will require a deviation into the history of scientific writing, but this will be necessary if I am to argue why social scientists should write differently from natural scientists.

In making my points, I will be summarizing some arguments that I have presented elsewhere in greater detail (Billig, 2008b and 2008c). In those publications, I discussed how critical discourse analysts often use the same grammatical constructions that they claim to have identified as being ideologically problematic. Some critical linguists responded to my arguments and they made their critical points in good spirit (see, Fairclough, 2008a and 2008b; van Dijk, 2008; see also Martin, 2008). I do not have space here either to reproduce my own arguments, at least in full, or to discuss the objections to them.

Whereas natural scientists need to avoid personifying the physical world, social scientists should try to avoid reifying the social world. Nevertheless, they can derive conventional benefits from using reified language. I will be suggesting that, with their noun-based language of things, social scientists can appear to be technically proficient, but by using technical nouns they can spare themselves the trouble of being precise. After my twists through linguistics and the history of scientific writing, I will be returning, at the end of this chapter, to a familiar theme. Social scientists, writing in ways that omit the agents of particular actions, not only resemble ideologists and natural scientists, but their turns of grammar can also resemble those used by advertisers. The style of contemporary writing in the social sciences is not always far removed from the writing styles of promotion and advertising.

Grammar of ideology

How do authorities use language to exert control over others? This was the question that a group of radical linguists asked in an important book, *Language and Control*. Roger Fowler and his colleagues wanted to discover whether ideological discourse, especially that used by powerful authorities, contained particular linguistic features that might distinguish it from other sorts of discourses (Fowler et al., 1979). Their project was inspired by George Orwell and his vision of Newspeak as a language which a totalitarian government invented in order to control the thoughts of its subjects. In the appendix to his novel *Nineteen Eighty-Four* (1949/2008), Orwell had discussed the principles of Newspeak. Its vocabulary would diminish, not expand; the authorities would invent new words that would express the official philosophy; nouns and verbs would be interchangeable. Fowler and his colleagues believed that Orwell was basically correct to suppose that authorities could maintain their authority through exploiting particular grammatical features, but they questioned whether Orwell had identified the correct features. They also rejected Orwell's assumption that authorities would have to create a virtually new language to exert control. They thought that those in power could adapt any language, including Orwell's beloved English, to their purposes, by using certain grammatical formulations and avoiding others.

There were two linguistic constructions in particular that Fowler et al. concentrated upon: 'nominalization', or the creating of nouns out of verbs, and 'passivization', which is the turning of active sentences into passive ones. Fowler and his colleagues claimed that these two constructions feature heavily in official language and later research has tended to confirm this. It has also confirmed that discourses, which are rich with nominalization, also tend to be rich with passivization and vice versa (Biber, 2007). That would not have surprised Fowler and his colleagues for they suggested that both constructions can be used for similar purposes. By nominalizing and passivizing, authorities can produce formal documents which describe actions and present orders as agentless things, thereby achieving what Fowler et al. called 'agent-deletion' (p. 33).

For example, authorities often phrase orders in the passive voice – 'You are requested not to walk on the grass'; 'Students are informed that essays should be submitted before 17.00'. When authorities use the passive, they can obscure themselves as the authors of these orders and they present their commands as if they were objective necessities of the world. It is the same if authorities express the submitting of essays in terms of a noun or noun phrase: 'Essay-submission deadline: 17.00'. Authorities will often favour these grammatical constructions because they allow 'the details of the exercise of the mechanisms of control to be obscured, mystified' (Fowler et al., 1979, p. 41).

Fowler and his colleagues also believed that Orwell was basically correct in supposing that the coining of new words was vital to maintaining control over the thoughts of others. As they wrote in relation to a club, which they studied, an obstinate individual might resist being manipulated on a personal level, but the same person would find it difficult to evade the control exercised by the new terminology which those in charge of running the club were introducing. Thus, the inventing of new words – or what Fowler et al. called 'relexicalization' – could be central to the exercise of control, especially when it came to nouns being formed from verbs by means of nominalization. As Fowler et al. wrote, 'nominalization facilitates lexicalization' and the invented nouns can be 'spotted by their ending in –ion, -ition, -ation, -ience, -ness, -ment' (1979, p. 40).

Orwell may not have been correct in supposing that authorities exercise control best through contracting the vocabulary of a language. After all, nominalization involves creating new terminology and thereby expanding the vocabulary. Nevertheless, Fowler and his colleagues believed that both nominalization and passivization led to one vital form of linguistic contraction. They write that nominalization is a 'process of syntactic reduction' (p. 41); it contracts meaning because it 'reduces a whole clause to its nucleus, the verb, and turns that into a noun' (p. 39).

Roger Fowler was to illustrate this 'syntactic reduction' in his book *Language in the News* (1991). He looked at the headlines of newspapers, to see how the headline writers reported an event in which police had attacked unarmed protestors. It tended to be the left-wing papers that used active verbs with subjects in their headlines: 'Police Attack Protestors'. Right-wing newspapers, which basically supported the police, tended to omit the police in their headlines. They would, for example, describe the event in the passive voice: 'Protestors Attacked'. Or they would nominalize the event by using the noun 'attack' rather than the corresponding verb: 'Attack on Protestors'.

In English, if one uses a verb such as 'attack' in the active voice, then one has to indicate the grammatical subject – namely, the agent who performs the action. By choosing to use the passive voice or by nominal-izing the event, the headline writers could avoid identifying who did the attacking. We can see how nominalizing or passivizing leads to a reduction of information. In using the passive voice – 'Protestors Attacked' – the writer omits the agent but still uses a verb which puts the action in the past. Even this information is lost in the nominalized 'Attack on Protestors' – the noun does not indicate when the action might have happened or even if it occurred at all.

Fowler referred to one of the important general conclusions of *Language and Control*, when he wrote that 'we claimed that nominalization was, inherently, potentially mystificatory' (1991, p. 80). He went on to link nominalization with reification:

If *mystification* is one potential with nominalization, another is *reification*. Processes and qualities assume the status of *things*: impersonal, inanimate, capable of being amassed and counted like capital, paraded like possessions (Fowler, 1991, p. 80, emphasis in original).

In this way, Fowler saw the studies, which he and his colleagues had conducted, as successfully demonstrating how ideology and reification worked through the use of language. When speakers and writers nomi-nalized, the end result was not just the hiding of agents but the turning of human actions into things. No wonder these linguists viewed nominaliza-tion with suspicion.

However, there is a problem that Fowler and his colleagues did not confront: nominalization and passivization, also feature heavily in academic, especially scientific, discourse (Biber and Conrad, 2009; Biber and Gray, 2010). This raises the conundrum: why should scientists and ideologists favour the same sorts of grammatical constructions? If the former are revealing the structure of the world and the latter are hiding it, one would expect them to use language in very different ways. As the discussion of 'reification' in the previous chapter suggested, social scientists also like to use big, nominalized nouns. Does this mean that their writing is potentially 'mystificatory' or that nominalization is not inherently problematic?

The key to the answer lies in recognizing that, when it comes to describing human actions, the constructions, produced through nominalizing and passivizing, transmit less information than simple sentences with active verbs. The right-wing headline writers, who concealed the identity of the attackers, were not doing anything extraordinary. Any competent user of English should be able to transform an active sentence into a passive one. Also, they should be able to transform a verb into a noun or noun phrase. You just have to understand the rules of grammar and the customs for turning verbs into nouns, even if it means constructing a new noun by means of suffixes such as 'ification' and 'ization'.

However, these transformations are generally not reversible, for, while one can always create passive sentences out of active ones with an object, one cannot always transform sentences the other way round. From the statement 'police attacked protestors', a competent user of English should be able to construct the sentence 'protestors were attacked'. However, if one is faced with the passive sentence 'protestors were attacked', one cannot generate an active sentence unless supplied with further information about the nature of the attackers (for example, if the passive sentence identifies the agents by specifying 'protestors were attacked *by police*'). The phrase 'attack on protestors' provides even less information for transforming it into a sentence with an active verb. There is no indication whether the attack has taken place, is taking place or might take place in the future. We, therefore, do not know the tense or modality for our verb. But it does not matter: we cannot in any case create a sentence with an active verb because we do not know the grammatical subject.

I might appear to be emphasizing some very elementary points of grammar, which school children might be expected to learn, but I have a reason. If academic social scientists tend to favour nouns and passives in their writing, then they are not merely using grammatical forms that are useful to those who seek to reify the world: they are using forms which contain less information than sentences with verbs in the active voice. This means that we cannot readily transform statements about abstract things, such as 'reification' or 'mediatization', into sentences with human actors as their grammatical subjects. Social scientists, in creating their izations, will have lost key information on the way. It is then little wonder that their big nouns appear to be imprecisely linked to human actions. We will see this later, when we look in detail at the concept of 'nominalization' itself. What is strange is that social scientists accord higher status to grammatical forms that contain less information.

Repeating the problem of nominalization

The work of Fowler and his colleagues has been extremely influential, for amongst other things, it formed the basis of what has become known as critical discourse analysis, an approach whose abbreviation 'CDA' I discussed in Chapter 4. Critical discourse analysts have systematically developed the project that Fowler and his colleagues initiated (see, for example, Fairclough, 1992; Fairclough, Mulderig and Wodak, 2011; van Dijk, 2003 and 2010; Wodak, 2006; Wodak and Meyer, 2010). By and large, critical discourse analysts have continued where Fowler and his colleagues left off. They still treat 'nominalization' and 'passivization' with suspicion, considering these to be among the key means for constructing ideological messages and for hiding the identity of powerful agents. For example, one critical discourse analyst writes that 'syntactic transformations, particularly those labelled "passivization" and "nominalization" can be considered ideologically problematic because they may obscure agency – who did what to whom' (Schroder, 2002, p. 105).

But look at that sentence: its principal verb is in the passive voice ('can be considered'). The sentence accuses 'nominalization' and 'passivization' of obscuring agency, but it identifies no agents. It is as if these syntactic transformations do things by themselves without human help. Somewhere along the line, the actions of people have been transformed (by whom?) into things such as 'syntactic transformation', 'passivization' and 'nominalization'. These things have then theoretically become the agents who carry out the business of obscuring agency. The writer seems unaware that he is using the very forms of language that he is claiming to find ideologically problematic.

But maybe it is not so odd, for the signs were there all along in the writings of Fowler and his colleagues. They were warning against the dangers of using language in ways that suppressed the agency of people. Yet, they themselves were using nouns such as 'passivization' and 'nominalization', rather than taking care to formulate sentences with verbs such as 'nominalize' and 'passivize' in the active voice with human agents as subjects. Even when specifically warning how authorities maintained control by inventing new words, they did not stick with old words, using a phrase like 'inventing new words', but they used the noun 'relexicalization'. When they warned of writers deleting agents from their sentences, they then formulated a new noun phrase – 'agent-deletion'. They could use this phrase without specifying who was deleting the agents. It was the same for the idea that nominalizing and passivizing sentences would reduce meaning: this became the thing 'syntactic reduction'.

What Fowler and his colleagues were doing seems to fit Fowler's own glorious description of reification. They were creating technical terminology for 'processes and qualities' and their nouns and noun phrases 'assume the status of *things*' which could be 'amassed and counted like capital, paraded like possessions'. We can note the structure of Fowler's own description: it too is devoid of people, as he writes about 'reification' as a thing, not an activity. Those who might be doing the counting, amassing and parading are absent visitors. In the description, the only actors are processes and qualities that supposedly assume the status of things.

This is not just a metaphorical turn of phrase which authors are using to capture dramatically an underlying idea. In more prosaic passages Fowler and his colleagues also make their abstract things act in various ways. As we have seen, nominalization is said to 'facilitate' relexicalization – one thing paving the way for another thing without humans in the way. Nominalization has other talents – the authors write that 'nominalization can depersonalize, depopulate' (1979, p. 43). That statement too is unpopulated and impersonal: the agent, who performs the acts of depersonalizing and depopulating, is the thing 'nominalization'. The authors could have written that writers and speakers depersonalize and depopulate by nominalizing, but they do not. In the next sentence, they repeat the linguistic construction, claiming that 'it [nominalization] can also drain the language of actional vitality' (p. 43). They once more present nominalization as an active doer, while introducing yet another thing – 'actional vitality'.

I think that I have given sufficient examples to show that these creative writers did not apply their message to their own writing. They warned against creating nouns from verbs in ways that enable writers to avoid specifying who does what. Yet, they seemed unaware that they were using this very type of noun. It is as if they could not stop themselves amassing and parading their own izations. They may have been reacting against many academic conventions – and they were certainly rebelling against the intellectual narrowness of much mainstream work in linguistics – but their prose still bears the customary marks of today's academic writing.

With the development of critical discourse analysis, there is now much more than a small group of rebellious scholars who are studying the grammatical characteristics of ideology. The critical approach to analysing discourse has become a recognized approach, practised and taught across the world. It is identified by its own acronym and supported by specialist journals, postgraduate courses, conferences etc. Students, who wish to study CDA, have much terminology to acquire, if they want to publish in the specialist journals. There are books and articles to assist them in their endeavour.

One such article is by Theo van Leeuwen (2010), in his contribution to a methods textbook on critical discourse analysis, which is aimed primarily at students. Van Leeuwen is an important figure in critical discourse analysis and has worked with Gunther Kress, one of the original co-authors of *Language and Control* (van Leeuwen and Kress, 2011). Subsequently, van Leeuwen has imaginatively applied some of the techniques of linguistic analysis to the study of visual materials and to music. Van Leeuwen's chapter is of particular interest here, because he deals with the topic of nominalization and he discusses how, by using this and other grammatical constructions, writers can omit agents from their descriptions of the world. Van Leeuwen is instructing students how to recognize these constructions and, just as importantly, he is giving students official names for such constructions. However, as he does this, he uses the same constructions, and his prose becomes, as it were, a parade of amassed official things.

In two subsections, respectively entitled 'Objectivation and Descriptivization' and 'De-agentialization', van Leeuwen discusses how writers turn actions into agentless things (van Leeuwen, 2010, pp. 156–7). These are not the only big words for thing-like processes in his chapter. He begins the section on 'Objectivation and Descriptivization' with a distinction: actions, he writes, can be '*activated*'; that is, represented as actions, or they can be '*de-activated*' or 'represented in a static way, as though they are entities or qualities rather than actions' (p. 156, emphasis in the original). Note his wording: van Leeuwen writes in the passive voice and his sentence does not mention any actors doing the representing. If the technical terms, which he is introducing, seem to be the passive participles of verbs (*activated* and *de-activated*), then van Leeuwen uses these words adjectivally in a noun phrase, rather than as verbs, when he refers to 'de-activated representations'.

Van Leeuwen's focus is upon the de-activated representations, rather than on the activated ones. He describes how de-activated representations might be '*objectivated* or *descriptivized*'. Again this is an agentless passive. However, van Leeuwen soon moves from verb to noun: 'In the case of objectivation, actions or reactions are represented as ... things, for instance by means of nominalization or process nouns' (p. 156). Again he has used an agentless passive sentence. He then introduces two more process nouns to indicate two further types of 'objectivation' – namely *temporalization* and *spatialization* (p. 156).

According to van Leeuwen, all these are forms of '*de-agentialization*', which represent human actions as if they are not actions but are things. Van Leeuwen does not then give examples of the way that writers or speakers 'de-agentialize' or 'agentialize' actions. As a writer he has moved from verb to noun – from de-agentialize to de-agentialization – and he is not about to shift back again to the verbs. Instead, he mentions three different types of 'de-agentialization', each of which he describes in agentless, passive sentences, writing of the way an action or reaction 'is represented'. These three types are named with more nominalized process nouns: *eventuation, existentialization* and *naturalization* (p. 157, emphasis in original). There is more of the same in the next section, whose name is 'Generalization and Abstraction'.

Van Leeuwen is scattering theoretical things around him as he goes on his way. In the course of a single page, he has produced eight theoretical things (and a ninth, if you count the old friend 'nominalization'). He does this in a section in which he is describing how actions are turned into other things, with the act of 'de-agentializing' itself becoming a thing – 'de-agentialization'. Van Leeuwen does not connect his own choice of words and his rhetorical style to the topic about which he is writing, but he uses his own terminology as if it were entirely natural.

In this essay, van Leeuwen, is not just providing terminology for students, but he is constructing a set of fictional things out of a series of processes. In effect, he is saying to students, you should be able to spot this sort of thing and that sort of thing: you should be able to distinguish an existentialization from a temporalization and you will need these words if you're going to do your research properly. As such, he is engaging in what Fowler et al. (1979) called 'relexicalization' (itself an example of relexicalixing) and which they identified as a particularly effective way of exerting control over others.

Van Leeuwen is assisting students by equipping them with a guide for translating the messy things that people actually write (and say) into a cleaner set of inter-locking theoretical things. The paradox is that his big nouns seem to refer to the sorts of thing that he is doing by producing these big words. He is writing like the theorists of 'reification', whom I discussed in the previous chapter and whose own words seemed to turn the act of reifying into a thing. It is as if such social scientists are always looking outwards to others, rather than contemplating whether their arguments contain messages for themselves, particularly about the ways that they should be writing.

The problem is that by using the big words, the analyst – whether expert or apprentice – will not be getting near to describing the action of producing big words. Instead, analysts seem to transport themselves away from the bustle of the world, where humans act, speak and write, into a fictional warehouse where the big words are neatly stacked, packaged and ready for distribution. It is then the job of analysts to teach students how to fetch the requisite packages from the warehouse and to deliver them onto their own pages.

Things and processes

I expect that most social scientists will reject my criticisms about izations and they will make an obvious rejoinder. They will say that when social scientists use such terminology they are neither being ideological nor failing to be self-critical. They are simply being scientific, for social scientists, like natural scientists, cannot stick to describing particular phenomena but must formulate theoretical statements. It is no good saying 'Look, there's a fellow, who's reifying the world, and there's another one who's confidently issuing orders in a formal, agentless manner.' The social scientist needs to construct theories that say something about how reification or de-agentialization might work in general. To create general theories, they require abstract nouns.

There is nothing remarkable about this, for natural scientists do exactly the same, when they formulate theories of oxidization or calcification. How could Darwin have written *Origin of Species* without the concepts of 'evolution' or 'natural selection'? He might have described this or that species changing, but he required general concepts to pull things together. So what is wrong with social scientists writing like scientists and using grammatical forms such as 'nominalization' and 'passivization'? That surely is how progress is to be made and any recommendations to avoid such terminology would only send things backward.

Certainly, there is a strong case to be made that natural scientists need to label processes with nouns and that nominalizing has proved to be invaluable for this. In saying why, I will draw upon the arguments of Michael Halliday, the linguist whose work inspired early critical discourse analysts, including Roger Fowler and his colleagues. I want to outline some of Halliday's arguments about the development of science, for his arguments can help us to understand why there might be crucial differences between the natural and the social sciences – and, in particular, why we need to be careful not to treat human actions linguistically as if they are physical processes. I should point out that many of Halliday's followers will not approve of the way that I will be adapting his ideas for my own purposes.

We have already encountered Michael Halliday, in earlier chapters, as the inventor of 'the ideological metafunction', which I used to illustrate the sort of technical phrasing that some academics cannot resist using. It must be said that Halliday has a fondness for devising new technical terminology but he cannot be blamed for the ways that others might misuse his concepts. His continual use of neologisms can be hard going for outsiders; even fellow linguists can find it off-putting (e.g., Leech, 2006). As much as possible, I will try to avoid using Halliday's terminology, even at the risk of simplifying his thoughts.

Halliday argues that the great scientists of the early modern period had to be grammatical revolutionaries, for science would not otherwise have developed. In the days before science, according to Halliday, people tended to refer to things and processes in different ways. Speakers would use nouns to denote entities such as material things or people – 'the rock', 'Moses', 'God'. When it came to describing processes, or events occurring over time, speakers would use verbal clauses. They would say: 'the trees grew tall', 'the rock rolled down the mountain', 'God created the heavens and the earth' etc. These ideas could not be expressed by a single word. Whether the processes were natural events ('it rained for forty nights'), or were human actions ('Moses killed the Egyptian') it required a whole clause to describe them.

Thus, in the early days of language, speakers would use one grammatical form for referring to things and another for processes. Halliday referred to this as the 'congruent' pattern, claiming that it was 'historically prior' in the history of language (Halliday, 2006, p. 107). He also notes that young children, when learning to speak, use this pattern first with passive verbs and nouns denoting events coming later. One might say that the congruent pattern appears to be the natural pattern, for it always seems to come first, regardless of culture or historical epoch, but Halliday resists using the word 'natural', preferring to use the term 'congruent'.

Having distinguished between the early ways of describing things and processes, Michael Halliday then makes a bold claim: if language users had stuck with the original, congruent pattern, then scientific thinking would have been impossible. The pioneers of modern science discovered new processes for which they invented new names. Grammatically, this was far more revolutionary in its impact than devising names for newly discovered things. Coining names for new species of plants, which had been found in tropical forests, or for microorganisms, which could only be seen under powerful microscopes, was not in itself a revolutionary act. However, the naming of processes was a different story. The scientific writers of the early modern period used existing grammatical mechanisms to create new nouns for processes by using the verbal participle or, as became increasingly common, by turning verbs into nouns by means of suffixes such as 'ization' or 'ification'. Halliday claims that 'the device of nominalising ... is an essential resource for constructing scientific discourse' (Halliday, 2006, p. 149). Historically it was the physical scientists, rather than biological scientists, who led the way, and the movement coincided with the rise of scientists writing in their own vernacular languages rather than in Latin (Banks, 2003; Pahta and Taavitsainen, 2004).

When Newton described processes in his book *Opticks*, he tended initially to use clauses with nouns and verbs. But then he would often move to a noun, or noun phrase, which would capture the meaning of that sentence. At one point, Newton was writing about the humours of the eye decaying in old age. He commented that when this happens 'light will not be refracted enough' (quoted, Halliday, 2006, p. 68). Here Newton was explaining the idea clausally. Then, Newton quickly proceeds to sum up the idea of light being refracted by using the single word 'refraction', writing of 'the want of a sufficient Refraction' in old age (p. 68). This sort of move occurs again and again in Newton's scientific writings.

Joseph Priestley did something similar in *Theory of Positive and Negative Electricity*, where he formulated theories about the 'repulsion' and 'equilibrium' of particles. Priestley started by writing clausally about particles being attracted towards, and repelled by, one another. He then moved to writing about the 'mutual repulsion' and 'mutual attraction' of particles, as well as their 'equilibrium' (Halliday and Martin, 1993). Again, the move is from verbs to nouns, and from using more but shorter words to using fewer but longer ones, although, as Halliday (2006) has pointed out, nominalized constructions are often not noticeably shorter than more clausal ones 'despite a common belief' to the contrary (p. 156).

By turning verbs and clauses into nouns, Newton, Priestley and other scientists of the time were creating new types of things, constructing science, in the words of Halliday and Martin, as 'an edifice of things' (1993, p. 17). Particles repelling one another had become 'mutual repulsion' and, by this grammatical move, the process of repelling 'has been reworded to look like an object: repulsion' (1993, p. 63). Newton and Priestley were not writing completely like twentieth-century scientists, for they did not use noun phrases, comprising only nouns. It would take a while for phrases such as 'particle repulsion' and 'particle attraction' to become commonplace (Biber and Gray, 2010).

Natural scientists continue to find nominalizing useful today. Halliday (2006) offers the example of a modern physicist writing about the way that the 'indistinguishability' of electrons 'gives rise to' an extra 'attractive force' between them (p. 73). An abstract quality – indistinguishability – becomes the cause of a process, which is, in its turn, depicted as another thing, namely the attractive force. In this way, it is not the physical objects themselves, namely the electrons, which are the agents of the action but abstract qualities and processes, which the scientist is depicting as if things.

As Halliday has stressed, scientists gain a number of advantages from writing like this. By nominalizing their descriptions of processes, they are saved the trouble of repeating themselves: instead of endlessly using clauses that depict particles repelling one another, the author can shorten this all to one word – repulsion. More than this, the single word can be used to sum up what has come before and what the scientist has claimed to have established. Thus, Priestley builds up an argument with the word 'repulsion', just as Newton did with 'refraction', for they use such nouns as if they stand for established, discovered things. Both authors, as it were, can move forward argumentatively, without having, all the time, to refer back to earlier clausal statements. Importantly, this means that they can proceed to devise theories about processes, such as 'refraction' and 'repulsion'. Unless they had named these processes as if they were things, the scientists would have been unable to formulate theories about them.

This language of things was important in another respect because by writing in this way the early modern scientists could avoid the danger of unintentionally personifying the physical world. Newton and Priestley did not wish to depict physical entities as possessing god-like, or human-like, powers, for they were propounding scientific laws for the physical world. If Priestley continued to depict particles attracting, or repulsing, one another, he would have been using verbs that are typically used about humans. The particles might then seem to resemble humans attracting or repelling potential lovers; or worse still, they might resemble god-like beings. By using concepts of 'attraction' and 'repulsion' Priestley would minimize the danger of personifying the physical things about which he was writing. It was as if the thing-like 'attraction' or the thing-like 'repulsion' were causing the observed movements, not the inner powers or intentions of the individual particles.

Similarly, by using the noun 'indistinguishability', the modern scientist avoids suggesting that the particles might possess the power to distinguish different entities. In this way, the writer puts the thing 'indistiguishability', not the act of distinguishing (or not distinguishing), at the heart of things. Similarly, scientists can find it useful to put verbs in the passive voice, for the writer then does not have to specify that an agent is doing something. Instead, light *is* refracted or particles *are* repulsed, without any agent appearing to be engaged in carrying out the refracting or repulsing. It is no surprise, then, that corpus linguists have found that both 'nominalization' and 'passivization' frequently occur in scientific writing (Biber, 1988; Biber and Conrad, 2009).

Scientists might benefit from writing in these ways, but, as Halliday points out, there are also downsides. Scientists treat their newly named processes 'as if they were some kind of abstract entity or thing' (Halliday, 2006, p. 20). Halliday refers to these scientific entities, created by nominalizing verbs and clauses, as 'virtual phenomena' – virtual entities, virtual processes – which exist solely 'on the semiotic plane' (2006, p. 123). In this regard, they resemble what Hans Vaihinger called, in his unjustly neglected book *The Philosophy of 'As If'* (1924/2009), the made-up fictions, which scientists often use in their theoretical thinking and which can cause problems when scientists treat their fictional things as real things. The problem, according to Halliday, is that this edifice of things tends to convey a static view of the world, which is out of line with modern physical theories that emphasize fluidity, movement and change rather than thing-like stability.

The issue here is not whether this way of writing has drawbacks for natural scientists, but whether it does for social scientists. We can see why natural scientists might wish to avoid personifying the physical world, by treating things linguistically as if they were persons. Social scientists face the opposite problem of reifying the social world, by treating humans and their actions as if they were things. This is the problem with treating human processes, such as 'mediatization', 'reification' and 'nominalization', as if they were things. If social scientists remove people from the social world, they will run the risk of writing imprecisely, just as natural scientists will risk producing poor science if they populate the world. This is why it is important to examine how social scientists use passives and turn verbs into nouns.

Scientific writing and the passive voice

By using the passive voice, scientific writers can clear the stage of human actors, permitting the chosen fictional things to be the stars of the show. Formulaic phrases using 'it', followed by a verb in the passive voice, can be particularly useful: 'it can be seen that …', 'it has been demonstrated that …', 'it is argued that …', 'it will be shown that …', and so on (Hewings and Hewings, 2006). Whoever is doing the showing, demonstrating or arguing slips into the background. The object of the showing, demonstrating and the arguing stands there in the rhetorical spotlight in full objective glory, ready to take the applause.

Modern scientists are particularly likely to use passive verbs in the results and methods sections of their research papers (Biber and Conrad, 2009). Scientific writers did not always write in this way. When Isaac Newton described what he did in his various experimental investigations, he had no hesitation in using the first person singular. In his *Opticks*, Newton described how *I* held the prism, how *I* looked through it, how *I* observed the image etc. (Halliday, 2006, pp. 145f.). Nowadays, a scientific writer is unlikely to write quite like this, but will learn to use agentless passive verbs: an image *was* observed, the prism *was* positioned, chemicals *were* refined etc.

When it comes to describing results, modern researchers are also unlikely to be as personal as Newton was. If a research team is publishing their results – and many scientific papers these days are multi-authored – they are unlikely to indicate who precisely did what. Team leaders will not use their positions of command to write: 'My statistician/research assistant/postgraduate student found significant results.' The person, who ran the statistical tests, will remain rhetorically absent: 'Significant results were found . . .'

This is not just a matter of convention but there is a philosophical gain to be made from presenting less information. By writing about things being done – and not about people doing those things – scientists can present their methods and their findings as being independent of the identity of the researcher. It does not matter, who injected the rats or who ran the statistical tests, for the results should have been just the same. This is conveyed by the passive voice: 'the rats were injected', 'the substance was oxidized' or 'analyses of variance were computed'. The more that is revealed about those who did the work, the more readers might take this information as relevant. 'My nice, friendly research assistant ran the experiment' might imply that the results depended on subjective factors such as niceness and friendliness. Imagine what could be read into the statement: 'Our Italian statistician found significant results'. Are the writers subtly alluding to a national stereotype whether Italians might be thought to be good at statistics or might be bad at them? If there is no allusion to a stereotype, why mention the statistician's nationality at all? By using the passive voice, authors avoid all these problems. They are implying that anyone, who followed the research procedures and who was suitably trained, would have found identical results, whatever their personality, appearance or nationality.

The use of passives remains high within the social sciences although in recent years the first person singular has been making a comeback, largely as a result of feminist academics challenging the impersonal, masculine style of writing. However, Biber and his colleagues have pointed out that, in numerical terms, this has not had a massive effect on academic texts as the number of times that academic writers are using the first person singular is small compared with the overall number of passives and nominalized nouns that they use (Biber and Conrad, 2009; Biber and Gray, 2010).

Using passives when describing procedures need not always be problematic for social scientists. Biber and Gray (2010), in their analysis of academic writing and its grammar, have a section describing the corpus of materials, which they selected, and the grammatical features, which they examined. In the first two paragraphs, they use active sentences with 'we' as the subject: 'We collected texts from three 20-year intervals … we consider these as a single group' etc. (p. 4). In the fourth paragraph, they switch to passives, when describing the *Longmans Spoken and Written Corpus*, which they were using: 'The corpora were grammatically annotated … more specialized computer programmes were developed' (p. 4). The identity of those who did the annotating and who developed the programs was not relevant so long as the research workers did their tasks appropriately: and the writers convey this by choosing to put their verbs in the passive voice. Of course, it might also be the case that the writers did not know who had conducted these tasks, while still trusting that the anonymous workers had performed suitably. By using the passive, the writers can avoid naming, or admitting that they cannot name, the hired hands.

Many linguists deal with written texts and, since they are not actually interacting with anybody, it does not matter greatly, when describing their procedures, if they write: 'I collected seventeen newspapers' or 'seventeen newspapers were collected'. Who gathered up the newspapers, so that they landed on the analyst's desk, is not a matter of great import. However, things may be complicated when social scientists are directly dealing with people rather than with bits of paper. Whether interviewing respondents, tape recording conversations or conducting experiments, they will be interacting in some way with those whom they are studying. In these cases, it may not be so suitable to use the grammar of the natural sciences. My example will come from outside linguistics.

Experimental social psychologists pride themselves on being scientific, and they typically copy the styles of natural scientists. I will be discussing their linguistic habits in greater detail in Chapter 8, but for now I want to consider what social scientists can lose by following the rhetoric of natural scientists. Here is the methods section from an experimental study which was investigating the attitudes of white Australians towards aboriginal Australians. The researchers were aiming to find out whether white Australians, who had aboriginal Australians as friends, would be more willing to meet a hypothetical aboriginal Australian than would white Australians without aboriginal friends. The authors describe their procedure:

Participants were recruited for a study entitled 'Being Australian' and completed the questionnaire in supervised groups of 10–12, and were compensated for their time with course credit. They were informed verbally and in writing that their anonymity was protected. Completed questionnaires were placed in an opaque drop box, and participants were debriefed and given the opportunity to request a summary of the results of the study (Barlow, Louis and Hewstone, 2009, p. 394).

Of the eight verbs in these three sentences, seven are in the passive voice: 'were recruited', 'were compensated for', 'were informed', etc. In none of these seven instances do the authors specify who performed the various actions. The sole active verb refers to an action taken by the participants: they 'completed the questionnaire'. The researchers, by contrast, are grammatically absent from the methods section. We have to assume that it is the researchers who recruit the participants, protect their anonymity, do the debriefing etc. One of the passive verbs is particularly ambiguous. The writers state that the completed questionnaires 'were placed in an opaque drop box'. It could have been the participants or the researchers who did the placing. Probably it was the former but the syntax, linking three passive verbs by two 'ands', would suggest that the unnamed agents might well have been the same for all three actions. Here is an instance of something more general. The rhetorical conventions of scientific writing are often less precise than standard ways of writing, at least when it comes to describing actions (see Billig, 2011 for more details).

The authors are writing like physical scientists describing the oxidizing of substances or the injecting of animals. Whatever might be the skin colour, nationality, gender etc. of the researcher, it is presumed to be irrelevant when they oxidize substances or inject animals. However, a social psychological experiment is very different from one in the natural sciences. We would have good grounds for suspecting that the identity, or social persona, of the experimenters might very well affect how the participants behaved. If the persons doing the recruiting, protecting, debriefing etc. were aboriginal Australians (or even if they were Australians of African or Maori descent), then the white Australian participants might have reacted differently, especially when indicating whether they were willing or not to meet aboriginal Australians.

The general point is that the researchers were not examining something entirely separate from the social character of the experimenters. Basically, social psychologists are interested in social relations and when they study their topics experimentally, they set up social situations – namely, experiments – that involve social relations. The investigators, as they interact with the participants, are part of these social relations. As a result, there is no clear separation between the procedures of investigation and the topic under investigation. This is so different from the experiments that physicists or chemists typically conduct: what they are examining is theoretically distinct from the person doing the examining.

If the authors of the experimental report had used active voices, when describing their procedures, they would have had to describe the agents of the experiment. They could have used terms such as 'we', 'the researchers', 'our researchers' etc., or even possibly 'the white Australian researchers'. The latter term would have conveyed most information, but, at the same time, it would have suggested that this extra information – about nationality and skin colour – might be relevant to the processes that the authors were investigating (Billig, 1994). It would have underlined that the social persona of the experimenters might well have been relevant and might have affected the experimental findings. By not mentioning the researchers, the writers can avoid the dilemma of choosing how to describe the researchers and also they can avoid implying that the persona of the experimenter might have affected the results. The resulting rhetoric conveys 'objectivity' and 'scientific procedure', but it accomplishes this by being vague.

The writer is following convention by describing the processes of the research in ways that reify them: it is as if the procedures just happen. The readers know perfectly well that this cannot have been the case, but there is a tacit conspiracy between journal editor, writer and readers to pretend that it is. It might seem strange that social scientists, especially those who pride themselves on being scientific, should systematically describe what has happened in uninformative ways. In this matter, to appear more scientific means giving less information. Researchers have to write as if they have something to hide.

Nominalization: processes and things

There is nothing intrinsically wrong with words such as 'nominalization', 'passivization' or 'de-agentialization'. It is not a crime against nature to construct these nouns or to utter them out aloud. By using terms such as globalization, privatization, nationalization, we can discuss broadly what might be happening in the world and what we think should happen.

We will find writers and speakers using these words in newspapers, magazines and television debates. I am not seeking to ban these words, as if I were the controller of Newspeak, attempting to reduce the vocabulary available to speakers. The problem is not the words themselves. The problems come with the ways that social scientists use them, treating them with exaggerated respect and acting as if they provide the means to technical precision, while persistently using such terminology in ways that leave a gap between the concept and the world.

I want to consider 'nominalization' as an example. There is no intrinsic reason why this word should have vague, jumbled meanings, for at face value it seems to be a necessary, technical term in the discipline of linguistics, which, in relation to other social sciences, is a comparatively technical discipline. But, as I hope to show in this section, linguists use the word in various different ways. The problem is not peculiar to 'nominalization' per se, for social scientists will use other technical concepts just as imprecisely. In Chapter 8, I will touch on the social psychological concept of 'categorization'. In many ways, 'categorization' is as baggy as 'nominalization'. The trouble is that the specialists do not handle their big nouns with care, but they rush to use them, knocking over verbs in their haste and barging other parts of speech out of the way. In their rush, they fail to tie the big words firmly to the grounds of human actions, leave them flapping loosely, but flamboyantly, in the wind.

As we saw in the previous chapter, before Peter Berger introduced the concept of 'reification', he did not catalogue different ways of reifying, or specify what people might do in order to be said to be reifying. Similarly, van Leeuwen does not tie concepts like 'existentialization', 'temporalization' and so on to the actions of those that might be considered to be existentializing or temporalizing. Again, the nouns come first. But isn't this similar to Newton and Priestley, formulating their special technical terms and saving their readers the trouble of reading and re-reading long-winded clause after long-winded clause?

There is a crucial difference. The human actions, which social scientists summarize with their technical terms, are unlike the movements of particles that Newton and Priestley were describing. Both natural and social scientists present their technical terminology as if it supersedes, and compensates for, the deficiencies of ordinary language. However, in the case of the social sciences, ordinary language is very much part of the world that is being described. In 'temporalizing' or 'reifying' or 'de-agentializing', people will typically be acting in ways that involve uttering far less exalted words. Social scientists generally fail to root their terminology within this world of actions and ordinary language. Normally physicists and chemists try to tie their words for physical processes closely to their own experimental procedures and to the movements of the physical entities that they study. The big problem is that the ordinary way of talking about human actions – with identifiable agents and verbs in the active voice – carries more information, both in actual social life and in the world of theory, than does the apparently scientific style.

Of course, social scientists, unlike ordinary speakers or writers, typically propose definitions for their key terminology, as if that prevents their official words from becoming wayward. Norman Fairclough is one of the leading critical discourse analysts, having written extensively and perceptively about how those in power use language ideologically. In his book *Discourse and Social Change* (1992) he discusses the issue of nominalization and specifically offers a definition of the concept: it is 'the conversion of a clause into a nominal or noun' (p. 27). We can note the phrasing: Fairclough does not reverse, or unpick, the process of nominalizing by defining the noun in terms of a clause, which might specify the action of nominalizing. Instead, he defines the noun in terms of a noun phrase, and, more specifically in terms of another abstract term 'conversion'. Thus, Fairclough's definition of 'nominalization' comprises agentless terms and does not specify what anyone might have to do, in order to nominalize or to convert clauses into nouns.

Most critical discourse analysts would broadly accept Fairclough's definition that 'nominalization' denotes a process by which a clause is converted into a noun. The question is how the process occurs – or rather, what people have to do in order to make the process occur. If one looks closely it becomes clear that linguists are not consistent in their use of 'nominalization' but use the word to cover very different sorts of process (for details, see Billig, 2008b and 2008c). It is as if one word fits all and it does not matter if there is terminological chaos behind the plausible definition.

Some linguists use the word 'nominalization' to refer to the etymological processes by which particular sorts of new nouns, especially those denoting processes, enter the language. First, someone has to formulate this new word, deriving it from an existing verb or from a clause; and then others have to take up the new word so that it becomes an accepted part of the language's vocabulary. In this sense, 'nominalization' would describe the sort of events which must have occurred, when towards the end of the nineteenth century the word 'nominalization' entered the English language and became established, not in everyday speech, but in the technical vocabulary of linguists. Accordingly, some linguists use 'nominalization' to refer to a historical process which results in words like 'nominalization'.

By contrast, other linguists – and sometimes the same linguists at other times – do not use 'nominalization' in this historical sense, but will use it to describe a process that occurs within a single text. They will describe how an author moves in the course of a single piece of writing from describing a process in terms of a clause to ascribing a single word to name that process. In this form of nominalization, the author does not have to be the person who invented the noun in the first place. When Halliday was referring to nominalization in the works of Priestley and Newton, he was principally using the term in this way. He was not necessarily implying that Newton was the etymological inventor of 'refraction' or that no one had used the word 'attraction' before Priestley. But he was suggesting that these writers were putting these words to new uses, as they moved from using clausal descriptions to using these nouns to denote what they had just described in those clauses. Here 'nominalization' does not refer to a historical process, but a process within a single text.

There are further senses of the term. Some academics have used the word to refer to the psychological process by which an individual person might cognitively transform a clause into a single noun. This could happen, for example, when someone is writing an official set of regulations. They will be thinking of the rules in terms of plain, clausal language, and then they will convert these thoughts into something more official-sounding, which they will then write down. Something similar might occur with 'passivization'. You might think a thought in the active voice and then turn it round into the passive. Linguists, who follow transformational grammars or who believe that we are liable to think first in 'congruent' ways, might well use 'nominalization' and 'passivization' to refer to the ways that people might grammatically transform their inner mental thoughts.

Then there are linguists, who use 'nominalization' to refer to some sort of ideal process, rather than one that occurs in time, whether that be historical, mental or even textual time. Fairclough (2008b) has claimed that many linguists principally use 'nominalization' in this ideal sense. Languages possess grammatical rules by which nouns can be formulated from verbs, or passive voices from active ones, etc. 'Nominalization' and 'passivization' can refer to these grammatical rules of transformation, rather than to processes by which people actually use the rules. It is, of course, a moot point how one could know that these rules exist, unless people perform the action of turning verbs into nouns etc. Anyway, this is another meaning of 'nominalization'. When linguists use the word in this sense, then they are referring to an ideal grammatical process – a conversion – that does not occur over time as actual processes do. For many non-linguists, who see things as either happening or not happening, this sort of a process can appear a bit baffling, or to use Fowler's term, somewhat mystificatory.

So, we can see that linguists do not agree among themselves that there is one particular sort of process which should properly be described as 'nominalization'. Instead they are liable to ascribe the word to very different kinds of processes, including a process which is not actually a process. That, however, is not the limit to the semantic anarchy. Despite the definitions describing 'nominalization' as a process, some linguists use the word to refer to a linguistic entity rather than a process. Corpus linguists, like Douglas Biber, will say that they are counting the number of nominalizations within a particular body of texts; they identify these nominalizations as nouns with endings such as '-tion', '-ness', '-ment' etc. When they do this, they are treating 'nominalizations' as the linguistic entities, and not as the processes by which these entities may have been produced either etymologically or textually.

As corpus linguists count the number of 'nominalizations' within collections of materials, so they treat 'nominalization' as a count noun – that is, a noun that takes a plural. Count nouns refer to entities that can be counted and corpus linguists, in defining 'nominalization' as a particular sort of noun, can count 'nominalizations'. However, those linguists, who consider 'nominalization' to be a process, treat it as a mass noun, in common with many other social scientific izations and ifications, which denote processes. For example, 'globalization', 'massification', 'mediatization' and 'reification' are all mass nouns: you cannot have four 'massifications' or eight 'mediatizations', just as you cannot count 'salt', 'electricity' or 'hopefulness'.

Regarding 'nominalization', here then is further messiness. 'Nominalization' can refer either to very different sorts of processes or to a sort of linguistic entity. It can be used as a mass noun or as a count noun. It seems that linguists are not disturbed by this outgrowth of uses and meanings. They still continue to use the word as if 'nominalization' really and clearly exists as something. The surprise is not that this has happened but that linguists do not seem bothered by it: there is no 'crisis' of nominalization. Linguists, including critical linguists, carry on using the term without apparently noticing that it comes with a profusion of meanings. If linguists, as specialists in language, do not seem to notice how a key technical word can pass from being a mass noun to a count noun and back again, then how are the rest of us expected to notice?

I have come across one researcher using 'nominalization' in a very different sense. This researcher was examining what difference it made if school teachers addressed their pupils by name (Hilsdon, 1997). The author must have felt that it was insufficient to write about teachers calling their pupils by name. This easily understood and easily described action had to be dressed in an impressive concept: 'nominalization'. It did not seem to bother the author – or the editors of the journal in which the article appeared – that other academics might be using this word in other ways. Such diversity of meaning is apparently no drawback when it comes to favouring long words over simple clauses. In fact, it might even be a bonus for the author can appear to be linking their specific piece work with other types of research.

Once again, we can see that putting the big izations into place does not achieve precision, but now we are in a better position to see why not. So long as you keep using words like 'nominalization', you do not have to specify exactly what they mean and to what sorts of processes they refer. Moreover, you can formulate theories linking one ization with another, as if you are solving problems by slotting your fictional things together. For example, you might assert that 'nominalization leads to de-agentialization'. But as you do so, you will be leaving a large gap between the world of theory and the world of actions – and no amount of further big nouns will fill that gap, for each will bring its own gap to the theory.

The basic problem is that our clauses contain more information about social actions than our formal nouns do. It is so much harder to unpick the big nouns and to imagine what actions comprise the 'thing' that they denote. However, if we use clauses to describe actions, then we will be more likely to think about what is going on. Suppose we want to formulate a general rule and instead of saying that 'nominalization leads to de-agentialization', we phrase this as a general clausal statement in the active voice: 'When someone nominalizes, they will be likely to de-agentialize.' If we put forward this statement, then it would be easy for someone to ask us (or for us to ask ourselves): 'How exactly do you nominalize or de-agentialize? What sort of actions do you have to take? Does it matter how you nominalize? Can you give me an example of someone nominalizing and de-agentializing?' If we then try to answer such questions, we will find ourselves going into the sorts of detail that we can avoid when we stick with the big nouns, treating them as things.

That should give us pause for thought. Perhaps the real function of these big nouns is not that by using them we can formulate better theories or that we can clarify what goes on in the world. It could be that we find them useful for another reason. When we use these nouns, we do not have to be clear – we do not have to think hard about what we really mean, especially when we are writing for others who regularly use these same words. In our own safe circles, where we all will be exchanging the same semantic tokens, we can leave the gap between the world and the words as wide as we want.

Promoting the nouns

There is a further rhetorical turn that those who write either ideologically or scientifically can find useful. Having emptied their prose of people, acting as agents, they can refill it with things that act like people. In this way, writers can depict fictional things, rather than people, as the agents of the world. Critical discourse analysts have described how ideological writers make this move. There have been a number of excellent analyses of economic language, suggesting that right-wing economists often reify the social world by treating economic concepts, such as 'market forces', as if they were objective entities (e.g., Fairclough, 2003, pp. 143ff.; Muntigl, 2002; Mautner, 2005). More than this, they ascribe motives to these so-called 'objective entities', making them act as if they were human. For example, we can read about market forces that dictate/demand/forbid, as if these forces spring to life to perform the human actions of dictating, demanding and forbidding. Moreover, these strange forces seem to crowd out actual people and their actions. The result is that the humans, who have power over others through their trading and owning, become invisible. In their place, abstract economic forces take on the role of quasi-humans, demanding obeisance from the real humans.

Right-wing supporters of current economic arrangements are not the only people who make these sorts of rhetorical moves. One study compared the frequency of inanimate entities that appeared as the subject of active verbs in scientific journals and in popular magazines (Master, 2006). This grammatical pattern occurred much more frequently in scientific journals where writers of research articles often made abstract concepts the subject of verbs such as 'make', 'use' and 'allow'. Jay Lemke (1995), in his book *Textual Politics*, discusses how this move can occur in scientific reports. The authors linguistically delete human agents as the authors use 'agentless passive clause structures' and nominalize the descriptions of processes. Then, according to Lemke, the authors present 'the nominalized processes ... as agents in the place of human agents' (p. 60).

In the previous chapter, we saw something similar occur with authors writing about the concept of 'reification'. They tended not to depict people going about reifying, but wrote about what 'reification' could do. It was the same with 'mediatization' and psychoanalysts can treat 'repression' in the same way. In this chapter, we have already seen how Fowler and his colleagues wrote about 'nominalization' doing things like depopulating, depersonalizing, facilitating etc. They claimed that nominalization 'permitted habits of concealment' (1979, p. 80). When analysing regulations for applying to university, they commented that 'the passive structure, allowing agent-deletion, permits a discreet silence about who if anyone might refuse to admit the applicant' (1979, p. 41).

'Allowing' and 'permitting' are activities, which we usually ascribe to human agents, particularly those with some sort of power. A police officer might permit a driver to continue along a road or a parent might allow a child to eat some chocolate. They have to utter words or make gestures in order to grant such permission. But how can a grammatical structure be said to permit actions to occur or not occur? The linguists mean: if we nominalize or use passive verbs, then we need not specify who is doing the actions. The linguists are expressing this idea, through their own nominal-izing (i.e., 'agent-deletion', 'the passive structure', 'nominalization' etc.) and by ascribing the power of permission to such entities. In their own statements, grammatical constructions, rather than human agents, have the power of permitting and forbidding.

Of course, one might counter by saying that this is a convenient, metaphorical way of writing that prevents endless repetition and awkward clause-making. And no harm is done by writing in this way: no one really imagines a nominalization actually standing there, like a policeman in uniform beckoning the traffic to advance. On the other hand, we could say that this rhetorical trope is particularly useful if you want to promote your approach or to emphasize the importance of the concepts that form the basis of your approach. By depicting the concepts as agents in the world, you will be accentuating their importance, or, to use current slang, bigging them up.

Social scientists often use this trope when describing their own theo-retically favourite concepts and things. In discussing the 'congruent mode of grammar', where a verb means a happening and a noun means an entity, Michael Halliday comments: 'But if grammar can construe expe-rience in this way, it can also reconstrue it in other terms' (2006, p. 14). Actually, it is humans, not grammar, that construe or reconstrue experi-ence although they might do so by means of grammar. This is not a passing figure of speech. On the next page Halliday claims that 'the grammar can always turn one class of word into another' (p. 15) and he offers an example where 'the grammar is reconstruing a happening as if it was a kind of thing' (p. 15). A few pages earlier, he had commented that 'grammar transforms experience into meaning' and 'that what grammar does is to construct a semiotic flow – a flow of meaning' (p. 11). Seemingly, it is grammar, not people, doing all these things.

Douglas Biber, another linguist whose work I have discussed, compares academic texts with other genres of writing. He is arguing that academic writing often is less explicit than other forms of writing, despite the fact that we assume it to be more precise. He puts his point in the following way: 'Academic texts have systematically chosen grammatical styles of expression that are less explicit than alternative (more explicit) grammatical styles' (Biber and Gray, 2010, p. 13). Of course, academic texts do not literally choose their own grammatical styles. Their authors make these choices, just as Biber and Gray have chosen to make 'academic texts' the subject of their sentence; their text has not done this for them. Similarly Halliday writes that 'the text itself creates its own grammar, instantially as it goes along' (2006, p. 143). Here one entity, the text, creates another entity, its grammar, without any people intervening. It is as if there is a world of things that do our writing and speaking on our behalf: and we, the experts, are revealing these important hidden actors. Our own destiny is bound up with the destiny of our creations, for the more important these thing-like actors are portrayed to be, the more important are our theories about them.

In earlier chapters, I have given some examples of academics promoting their own approaches, which they claim to be able to do things. We saw how supporters claimed that 'phenomenography' *favours* a dynamic approach and *provides* good opportunities, ascribing to their approach the powers of favouring and to providing good things. In the previous chapter, supporters of 'mediatization' talked of their approach in a similarly active way. If I am to follow the strategy of taking examples where I find them, I should provide some examples from the writings of critical discourse analysts. I do so at the risk of upsetting figures such as Norman Fairclough and Ruth Wodak, notable scholars whose work I admire. Because of this – rather than despite it – I am offering several examples from their writings about critical discourse analysis.

Lilie Chouliaraki and Norman Fairclough begin their book *Discourse in Late Modernity* with the statement 'Critical discourse analysis (henceforth CDA) has established itself internationally over the past twenty years' (Chouliaraki and Fairclough, 1999, p. 1). It is as if a thing 'CDA' is capable of establishing itself. Then this thing takes on the character of a human, capable of doing what humans do: the authors write that CDA 'can strengthen its analysis of language' (p. 2), that it 'can take further' lines of research (p. 2), and that it 'brings critical social sciences and linguistics together . . . setting up a dialogue between them' (p. 6) and so on. This thing also has opinions: CDA 'takes the view that a text can be understood in different ways' but 'CDA does not itself advocate a particular understanding of a text, though it may advocate a particular explanation' (p. 67).

Fairclough, Mulderig and Wodak (2011) also ascribe a number of psychological capabilities to critical discourse analysis. They outline how CDA 'sees discourse' (p. 357) and how it 'sees itself' and how it 'aims' to make opaque aspects of discourse visible (p. 358). Moreover, CDA is capable of making claims (p. 368), highlighting various things (p. 369), and achieving much success (p. 373). Wodak and Meyer (2010) discuss how it is 'interested in' analysing power and that it 'aims to investigate' social inequality (p. 10). And in all its various forms CDA 'understands itself' to be based in theory (p. 23).

Of course, one can see the advantage in writing this way. Writers do not have to keep referring to the analysts, who might include themselves. They can achieve a measure of distance (and modesty) by talking about the perspective and ascribing their own aims, intentions and successes to the perspective. There is no deceit involved. No one really believes that the approach actually functions like a person, or that it can exist and have these aims, intentions and successes without people having aims, intentions and successes. Talking about the approach doing all this gives the approach solidity. It exists as something in itself – something that has established itself. In this respect, the psychological verbs act like the acronym: they set the approach in place as an established part of the academic scene.

This sort of phrasing resembles a style of writing that is common in advertising. This is a style where the product is presented as if it operates itself. Marianne Hundt (2007 and 2009) has suggested that advertisers often use a voice, which is neither active nor passive, but somewhere in between. She has called this 'mediopassive', after the grammatical voice which linguists have identified in certain ancient Semitic languages. These new 'mediopassives' are slightly different. The verbs do not have specific grammatical forms, but their grammatical subjects are syntactically their customary objects. They occur in advertisers' statements when the products appear as the grammatical subject, although they are, in practice, the objects of the actions being described. 'The curtains are selling well': the curtains are not selling anything, but they are being sold. 'The car drives smoothly': someone has to drive the car to find out whether it is smooth or not. 'The door opens easily': the door does not open itself but it has to be opened. Hundt has traced how this form of expression has become increasingly common in English over the past hundred years.

Hundt suggests that 'mediopassives' might be used whenever someone wants to depict a process 'as independent of external influence', or whenever 'an agent is difficult to identify' (2007, p. 167). Advertisers, boasting about the qualities of their products, want to present their products as performing well, with the good performance not being dependent on the skills of those who must operate the product. Accordingly, the advertisers grammatically delete the agent, setting the product off on its own, running itself, selling itself, driving itself and establishing itself.

Hundt is at pains to stress that 'mediopassives' are not confined to advertising, but academics also use them. Like advertisers, academics often wish to describe processes as if occurring on their own. Hundt offers some examples from her own discipline of linguistics – such as 'morphemes that attach to roots' and 'vowels that raise' (p. 167). The morphemes do not actually do the attaching or the vowels the raising. The examples, that I have presented, suggest that academics, especially in the social sciences, may frequently use this way of writing when describing their key concepts or their own approach.

We should not automatically assume that advertising and academic writing are completely different sorts of genre and that it is just by chance that both advertisers and academics might use similar linguistic constructions for omitting agents. Academics also have products to promote and they will praise their own theories and approaches, recommending them to readers. They will want to say that the product operates well – has insights, produces findings, exposes what is hidden. Anyone using the product will have these benefits and understandings. It does not take an unusually skilled individual to reap the rewards, just as any driver would drive the car smoothly or open the doors with ease. The product seems to run itself, and readers, particularly student readers, are invited to try it out.

At this point the mythology of advertising meets the scientific claims of the social sciences. The result is rather like the mediopassive construction itself – neither one thing nor the other. This is neither literal nor metaphorical writing. Social scientists do not offer their constructs as if they were only metaphors. They offer their 'reifications', 'nominalizations' and 'mediatizations' as describing real, not metaphorical, processes. On the other hand, they do not root these constructs firmly in the world. Instead these words seem to swirl about, while the writers claim that the words are doing things that they cannot possibly do. It is the same with approaches and theories. The more convinced we are of their usefulness, the more we write about them in impossible ways. And the more we commit an error that seems easier to recognize in others than in ourselves – namely, the error of describing how things happen in the social world without mentioning how people might make them happen, or, indeed, who the people are who make them happen.

7   Some sociological things: governmentality, cosmopolitanization and conversation analysis

At this stage, I need some more examples. My general strategy, so far, has been to take examples where I find them, although on occasions I have departed from this strategy. As I have been writing about the ways that academics use language, inevitably many of my examples have come from academic experts in the study of language. Accordingly, there is a nagging doubt whether my choice of examples might reflect this particular field and that the writings of social scientists from other areas may be free from the faults which I have been criticizing. To quell this doubt, I must look at a wider set of cases.

I cannot cover all the social sciences, so in this chapter I will be concentrating on sociology, and I will be suggesting that sociologists, through their use of nouns, can rhetorically create sociological things, whose reality they uphold. I still have a problem with how to select my examples. It would be wrong to go searching for poor quality articles from obscure journals and then to declare self-righteously: 'Isn't it awful? I told you so!' I will need to ensure that I am taking good quality examples from significant bodies of work.

In selecting my first three sociological examples, I have used a strategy to ensure that I am looking at important pieces of work. I have taken examples from the special issue of the *British Journal of Sociology*, which appeared in 2010 to mark the journal's sixtieth birthday. The editors reprinted, with specially commissioned commentaries, what they held to be the two most significant articles from each of the journal's six decades. The articles, which I will be looking at, were selected to represent the best of the 1990s and 2000s: they include a piece by two Foucauldian scholars and articles from two eminent 'globalization' theorists – Ulrich Beck and John Urry. It is no coincidence that these are theoretical, or rather pro-grammatic, articles, because many sociologists, particularly those in Britain, currently hold theory in high regard.

It would have been unbalanced to have left the field to British and/or European theorists, for they do not represent sociology as a whole. Therefore, I have selected a fourth approach, which is in many respects the antithesis of the previous three. Conversation analysis concentrates on the small-scale details of human interaction, rather than the big sweep of history or the ambitions of grand theory. Its intellectual origins, together with much of its current work, come from the United States. Despite these differences, I will be suggesting that conversation analysts share with the other three a preference for nouns and for creating sociological things.

I will need to examine closely the ways that these sociological authors write. The first three examples are largely unpopulated pieces of work, dealing with sociological things rather than people. Of course, many others have previously criticized macro-sociologists for ignoring people; for example, Thomas Scheff has been doing so for a good number of years with great insight and humanity (Scheff, 1990, 1997 and 2006). Rather than tackling big questions of theory or methodology I will be focussing on some of the little details of language that these sociological writers use.

In the case of conversation analysis it is particularly fitting to look at the rhetorical details, for the adherents of this approach stress the virtues of examining the fine points of social life in preference to big theoretical formulations. I hope that I will not try the patience of readers by looking at the details. However the details are necessary, for otherwise I would risk giving the impression that I am complaining about serious social scientists on the basis of little more than personal prejudice and general grumpiness.

Establishing governmentality as a sociological thing

Let me begin with the Foucauldians and the way that they have created 'governmentality' as a sociological thing. Claire Moon was the *British Journal of Sociology*'s editor, who was responsible for choosing the two articles that made significant contributions to sociology in the 1990s. She chose 'Political Power Beyond the State: Problematics of Government', written by Nikolas Rose and David Miller and first published in 1992, and also an article by the British sociologist, John Goldthorpe. In her introduction, Moon made it clear that, in choosing the Goldthorpe piece, she was paying tribute to the latter's lengthy and distinguished career. If Goldthorpe represented a British sociological tradition that began well before the 1990s, then the Rose and Miller piece was, in Moon's opinion, offering sociologists something radically new (Moon, 2010).

According to Moon, the Rose and Miller piece had been important for sociology because it had played a central role in establishing 'a new mode of enquiry into the social: "governmentality"' (2010, p. 266). The concept of 'governmentality' comes from a lecture of the same name, which Michel Foucault delivered at the Collège de France as part of his course 'Security, Territory and Population' during the academic year of 1977–8.

His lecture on 'governmentality' was soon translated into English and published by the journal *Ideology and Consciousness* (1979). The French edition of the whole lecture course did not appear until 2004.

Moon may have described 'governmentality' as a new mode of enquiry into 'the social', but this new mode did not involve devising any new methodological techniques. Nor were Rose and Miller presenting a new set of empirical findings to illuminate a previously unexamined topic. In fact, they were proposing a new programme for sociologists, together with a new word for understanding the notion of government – 'governmentality'. As we shall see, whatever this new thing, governmentality, might be, it seems to be doubly real: the word indicates something that supposedly exists in the world and also something that exists as a sociological mode of inquiry.

The word 'governmentality' is crucial for appreciating the contribution that Rose and Miller's paper has made to sociology. I will briefly discuss how this noun came into sociology and how sociologists, such as Rose and Miller turned it into something that was more than just another conceptual noun. If I were a Foucauldian, I might claim to be offering a brief 'genealogy' of the concept of 'governmentality'. But in the present context the word 'genealogy' would add little of substance to what I am doing except that I would be explicitly linking my work to Foucault and his followers.

Taking inspiration from Foucault, Rose and Miller were arguing that sociologists have too narrow a concept of 'government'. Most sociologists, they argued, tend to link 'government' with the specific actions of the state, but in modern times the power of governing is not just to be found in the official institutions of the state. Indeed, the official institutions possess the means to reach into all aspects of social life. People govern themselves and others, and they do so according to patterns of knowledge that the state and other institutions produce. Foucault's message, in his course to the Collège, was that, in order to understand modern methods of governing, we have to look beyond the formal mechanisms of state government.

This was a bold idea, for it challenged assumptions about what constitutes 'government'. To express this wide role of government, Foucault proposed the word 'governmentality', which, according to Rose and Miller, provides a more realistic view of modern governance than does the standard notion of the state. At the start of their article, they quote Foucault suggesting that the modern state was a 'mythical abstraction' (Rose and Miller, 2010, p. 273; Foucault, 2000, p. 220). By contrast, the concept of 'governmentality' was describing something much more solid, more real and more deeply influential than the mythical state.

In his lecture Foucault claimed that 'governmentality' referred, amongst other things, to 'the ensemble formed by the institutions, procedures, analyses, and reflections, the calculations and tactics that allow the exercise of this very specific albeit complex form of power, which has as its target population, as its principal form of knowledge political economy, and as its essential technical means apparatuses of security' (2000, pp. 219–20). In passing, we can note how typically modern these translated words of Foucault appear: they contain fifteen nouns, two verbs and no people. Things like analyses, reflections and calculations are the actors who allow the exercise of power. We do not see anyone exercising power: there is instead a made up thing – 'the exercise of power'.

With characteristic scholarship, Foucault illustrated the origins of 'governmentality' by referring to some largely forgotten, old texts such as Guillaume de La Perrière's *Miroir Politique*. Foucault's point was that a wider meaning of 'to govern' was emerging in the sixteenth century. A writer like La Perrière was using the word in a variety of senses, writing about governing households, children, souls, families, convents etc. and not just governing the state. These older writers were showing that to govern meant more than controlling institutions or peoples; it meant governing things and acquiring knowledge. The captain of a ship, for instance, did not just govern his crew in a narrow sense but he had to control the ship and know about the seas, the weather, the winds, and so on.

In this way, Foucault was linking the new word 'governmentality' to an older history of the word 'to govern'. Foucault did not actually invent the word 'governmentality', which he conceded was an 'ugly' word (2009, p. 115). In taking up the word, Foucault was giving it new meaning, deliberately linking two words semantically: *gouverner* (to govern) and *la mentalité* (mentality) (see Lemke, 2002 and 2007). Foucault did this to construct a concept that would stress the impossibility of understanding modern government without understanding the making of modern individuals and their mentality. Foucault's semantic linking of the two words is interesting. One word is a verb and the other is a noun. When the two are combined, the verb disappears and a single noun emerges. It is as if there is a mathematical formula for creating modern academic concepts: Verb + Noun = Longer Noun.

We can see the triumph of the big noun over the verb in the part of Foucault's lecture from which Rose and Miller's early quotation comes. Foucault suggests that he is interested in the historical development of governmentality and how it came to be the guiding practice of the modern state. He writes of the way that the mediaeval state of justice became transformed during the fifteenth and sixteenth centuries into 'the administrative state', which itself 'becomes "governmentalized"'. He goes on to say that what is important for modernity is not 'the statization of society but the "governmentalization" of the state' (Foucault, 2000, p. 220).

In this passage, Foucault has gone from introducing the noun 'govern-mentality' to extending this noun grammatically. He uses the suffix 'iza-tion' to indicate the historical process of producing 'governmentality'. In between the introduction of these two nouns, a new verb briefly makes an appearance – 'governmentalize'. In the English translation this verb only appears in the passive voice, without any mention of the agent who might have been doing the governmentalizing.

The original French, however, is slightly different from the English translation because in the original Foucault used a reflexive verb with the past participle, rather than the passive voice of 'governmentalize'. Literally Foucault writes that the administrative state 'found itself bit by bit "governmentalized"' (Foucault, 2004, p. 112: 's'est trouvé petit à petit "gouvernementalisé"'). The reflexive voice emphasizes the extent to which this process of becoming governmentalized was enacted upon the state, with the state finding itself so 'governmentalized'. Significantly, Foucualt does not use 'gouvernementaliser' as a reflexive verb with the state simultaneously as the subject and the object: he does not say that the state governmentalized itself. Whoever or whatever might have been doing the governmentalizing is not identified. The reflexive voice, which does not exist in English as a specific grammatical construction, is similar to the mediopassive voice, which I mentioned in the previous chapter. Speakers and writers can use the reflexive voice to depict things happen-ing, or objects acting, as if on their own accord.

Whether or not the passive voice in the English translation fully repre-sents the reflexive verb in the original French does not matter here. The English translations have been important in making 'governmentality' into a sociological thing (whether the early 1979 translation or the later one which Rose and Miller use). What *is* important is another aspect of the passage which Rose and Miller cite. The verb (whether the English 'governmentalized' or the French 'gouvernementalisé') briefly appears, at least as a past participle, and then it disappears without the lecturer or his translators using it in the active voice. The verb has done its job of acting as an etymological staging post between 'governmentality' and 'governmentalization'.

When Rose and Miller came to select their quotations from this pas-sage, they overlooked the verb. They take up the big nouns – governmen-tality and governmentalization – but not the verb. 'Governmentalize' (or rather 'governmentalized') has played its short grammatical part.

Foucault has used it as a syntactic midwife for bringing 'governmentaliza-tion' into the world. This big noun is destined to become, as it were, a famous man of affairs. The midwife is forgotten.

Establishing governmentality

It is well known that towards the end of his life Marx became irritated by some of his followers, declaring, according to Engels, 'What is certain is that I am no Marxist' (quoted in McLellan, 1973, p. 443). Foucault, too, was no Foucauldian but not because he disowned his followers. He died several years before Rose and Miller paid tribute to his work in the *British Journal of Sociology*. I do not want to suggest that Rose and Miller mis-represented Foucault's work, but in a much simpler sense, Foucault was no Foucauldian: he was not following another thinker, adapting their ideas in order to create a new sociological mode of inquiry. The differ-ences are evident in the way that Foucault used the word 'governmental-ity' and in the ways that his followers came to use it.

There is something very old-fashioned about Foucault's lectures to the Collège de France. It is not just that he cites obscure writers from the early modern period and that he presents no 'literature reviews', in which he positions his own work in relation to the approaches of his contempora-ries. His lectures were lectures: he did not seem eager to rush them into print to boost his tally of publications. Nor did he place key lectures – such as that on 'governmentality' – in influential sociological journals. Instead, he addressed his audience directly. And most importantly, he addressed them as individuals, who might be interested in his ideas, rather than as potential academic producers whom he wishes to recruit to a new mode of enquiry. In this regard, Foucault was not a Foucauldian, spreading the Foucauldian message and seeking to promote a Foucauldian subdiscipline.

Rose and Miller, in publishing their article in a specialist journal of sociology, would have presumed that their readers were academic sociol-ogists, who would likely be producers of sociological research. Their readers would be just the sort of people who would be in a position to take up the project of establishing 'governmentality' as a new sociological approach. To see how this new mode of sociological enquiry may have been established, we should examine what sorts of arguments Rose and Miller were making about the new concept of 'governmentality'. Moreover, we should also look at the ways that other social scientists have taken up this concept. For reasons of space, I can only comment very briefly on both aspects.

First, there is the article. The authors were not providing an empirical investigation of 'governmentality', producing new facts that would disprove old theories of the state. Nor did they offer a case history of a specific event or an institution, and then claim that 'this is just the sort of thing that we mean by "governmentality"'. There is no tightly organized theoretical framework, precisely defining 'governmentality', 'governmentalization' and other concepts, and specifying exactly how they all might fit together. Rather, they offer 'governmentality' as a guiding principle for understanding the nature of power. Their article works as an argument against previous assumptions and in favour of new ones: government is not to be equated with the state; power does not just flow downwards from those occupying formal positions of power; power is contained in knowledge.

Although the authors offer no data or detailed examples, they write confidently as if they are giving the facts of the matter. In this respect, their article resembles Peter Berger's early work on the sociology of reification, which assumed that reification really existed. Rose and Miller take it for granted that 'governmentality', either as a thing or as a collection of things, exists and that 'governmentalization', as a process, has actually occurred. The authors assert towards the start:

Political power is exercised today through a profusion of shifting alliances between diverse authorities in projects to govern a multitude of facets of economic activity, social life and individual conduct. Power is not so much a matter of imposing constraints upon citizens as of 'making up' citizens capable of bearing a kind of regulated freedom (Rose and Miller, 2010, p. 272).

Note three features about this passage. The first is that the authors confidently assert how power is (and is not) exercised. The second is that their assertiveness is accompanied by a rather non-specific tone – 'profusion', 'diverse', 'multitude of facets'. It is as if the authors are saying that power is so diffuse, and has so many forms, that they need not locate it exactly. Third, there is an absence of people exercising power. The verb in the first sentence of the quote is in the passive voice – 'political power is exercised' without identifying the agents who might do the exercising of power. The second sentence mentions 'citizens' but these citizens are the objects, not the agents, of power: they are the beings whom power is 'making up'. In this sentence power (and not people exercising power) is grammatically the subject, that is 'making up' the citizens, who are the object. We have seen this grammatical pattern previously in relation to 'mediatization'.

Within the article generally, things and passives predominate. When people appear, they tend to be objects, not agents. Here the authors are discussing the state:

the state can be seen as a specific way in which the problem of government is discursively codified, a way of dividing a 'political sphere', with its particular characteristics of rule, from other 'non-political spheres' to which it must be related, and a way in which certain technologies of government are given a temporary institutional durability and brought into particular kinds of relations with one another (Rose and Miller, 2010, pp. 274–5).

This is one sentence containing five verbs, all in the passive voice and none with identifiable agents. There is the same general, non-specific tone: 'certain technologies' and 'particular' (but unspecified) kinds of relations and 'particular' (and equally unspecified) characteristics of rule. There is also the sort of formal tone that noun phrases can bring – 'temporary institutional durability', which is a thing that is given (by whom?) to other things, namely 'certain' technologies of government.

The article continues in much the same style. Nouns and noun phrases are in abundance when Rose and Miller describe what sociologists should be studying if they wish to study the mechanics of power:

We need to study the humble and mundane mechanisms by which authorities seek to instantiate government: techniques of notation, computation and calculation; procedures of examination and assessment; the invention of devices such as surveys and presentational forms such as tables; the standardisation of systems for training and the inculcation of habits; the inauguration of professional specialisms and vocabularies; building designs and architectural forms – the list is heterogeneous and in principle unlimited (Rose and Miller, 2010, p. 281).

The sentence starts with two verbs in the active voice. 'We' are the subject of the first and the 'authorities' (seeking to instantiate government) are the subject of the second. The authors do not specify who 'we' are, but presumably it is the sociological community to which the writers belong and whom they are seeking to recruit to their vision of sociology. It is not sufficient for their readers to agree with the authors but they need to be dispatched with projects for research. Hence, the authors list what 'we' need to be studying.

The list is interesting because it comprises nouns and noun phrases, which are, in the main, processes that are presented syntactically as if they are things. These are things such as techniques of calculation, procedures of examination, inculcation of habits, inauguration of vocabularies etc. In this way, the authors are depicting a world of interlocking things as the objects of sociological study. 'Governmentality', which itself appears as a thing, comprises all these other things and the list, we are told, is potentially infinite. Our work will never be complete for there will always be more things for us to investigate.

Rose and Miller were effectively saying to social scientists 'if you want to study power and government, you should be looking at these sorts of things, rather than the things that you have been looking at'. Their article has been an undoubted success and this tells us something about the meaning of academic success today. To be successful an article needs readers who are producers and who will use the article to produce more research. Moon alluded to citations, when she explained why she selected the piece (2010, p. 266). She pointed out that the Rose and Miller article was the most highly cited article published in the *British Journal of Sociology* during the 1990s. As I write these words (in July 2011), the article has been cited in nearly 1,500 publications (data from Google Scholar). Very, very few sociological articles score as highly as that.

In a rough sort of way, we can show the rise of 'governmentality' as a field of study. When the editors of the *British Journal of Sociology* accepted Rose and Miller's article in April 1991, there had only been two previous academic articles containing the word 'governmentality' in their title. The first had been *Ideology and Consciousness*'s publication of Foucault's lecture. Four years later, an article appeared in the journal *Screen*. After 1992, when Rose and Miller's article appeared, the number of articles with 'governmentality' in the title started to rise, gently at first but then accelerating. In the late 1990s, about five such articles were being published yearly. During the first half of the 2000s the average was around fifteen a year. By the end of the decade, the figure was averaging approximately forty a year and rising (data from Web of Science).

Researchers have been naming and studying different forms of governmentality. Many have taken 'neo-liberal governmentality' as their topic. There have been studies of global governmentality, civic governmentality, parental governmentality, dietary governmentality, colonial governmentality, post-colonial governmentality, white governmentality, green governmentality and so on. By now, there is a substantial and diverse body of work that has become known as 'governmentality studies'. Anyone, who is interested in finding out how the area has developed, should consult the interesting and committed account which Nikolas Rose and his colleagues have provided (Rose, O'Malley and Valverde, 2006).

With the development of 'governmentality studies' has come a new twist in the semantic story of 'governmentality'. Academics no longer solely use the word to indicate the sorts of phenomena that Foucault in his lecture was referring to or which Rose and Miller were urging sociologists to study: 'governmentality' now also refers to the sociological studies themselves. Mitchell Dean's book *Governmentality* first appeared in 1999. When the second edition was published in 2010, it contained a new introduction entitled 'Governmentality Today'. In writing of 'governmentality today', Dean was not updating readers on the developments of governmental practices in the years since the first edition. He was discussing the field of governmentality studies and its present standing in the academic world.

Rose, too, uses the word in this sense. When considering developments in governmentality studies, he and his colleagues mention several criticisms that others have made of their approach. Specifically, they seek to counter 'certain accusations that governmentality is guilty of homeostasis' (Rose, O'Malley and Valverde, 2006, p. 98). They are not defending the practices of governing bodies against the accusation of homeostasis – they are defending their approach against this charge. Similarly, they have a section 'The Legacy of Governmentality' in which they discuss the legacy of the academic approach, not the legacy of governments and their various apparatuses. Rose and his co-authors also use a turn of phrase that I discussed in the previous chapter whereby academics ascribe psychological agency to their approach. They write about 'governmentality' (or the 'governmentality approach' or 'governmentality studies') as insisting upon things, rejecting things, being not guilty of things, and so on.

In this way, supporters of governmentality studies, present 'governmentality' as possessing a double reality. Governmentality is assumed to exist as a feature of the modern world; and it also exists within the world of social sciences as an established approach. These realities are related, for the research programme, which Rose and Miller were proposing, was not to see if governmentality existed: there was no testing of a 'governmentality' hypothesis. In this regard, the introduction of 'governmentality' resembles Berger's introduction of 'reification' and also the introduction of 'mediatization': the proposers of these concepts were confident that their chosen words described things that actually existed.

Rose and Miller were hoping that sociologists, in following their line, would come up with examples of governmentality. Each example would reveal further real things such as neo-liberal governmentality, white governmentality, green governmentality etc., etc. The more that researchers produced these things, the more real governmentality would become in both senses of the term. Governmentality then ceases to be a programme for future research but it becomes an established entity – an established reality – within the sociological world.

How to write about 'governmentality' and other things

It is appropriate that the word should be used in these two senses, for Foucault and sociologists like Miller and Rose believe that the world of the social sciences is connected with the phenomena of governmentality. They argue with good reason that in the modern world the agents of government have done much to encourage the development of the social sciences. Opinion polling, the gathering and analysing of statistical information about populations and the use of psychological treatments have all become part of governing the modern state and its citizenry (e.g., Osborne and Rose, 1999; Rose, 1996). In their article, Rose and Miller wrote that 'as government depends upon these sciences for its languages and calculations, so the social sciences thrive on the problems of government' (2010, p. 280).

But there is a disturbing possibility. Could governmentality (the academic thing) be part of governmentality (the government thing)? It is not difficult to apply the arguments of Rose and Miller to the contemporary academic world. I have already mentioned citation scores as ways of measuring the extent to which individual academic articles are cited in other academic articles. Academics have developed a new science of 'bibliometrics', as an area of specialist research with its own technical journals. Academic managers and governing agencies use citation scores and other bibliometrics to help them assess whether academics, institutions and disciplines are being sufficiently productive, and also to inform their decisions for distributing funds within the academic world. And academics can use the scores to promote their discipline, subdiscipline and themselves.

Even radicals working in contemporary academia cannot escape from these bibliometric methods of assessing and accounting. This is the world in which the Rose and Miller article appeared. The publishers of the *British Journal of Sociology* present the journal's 'impact factor', or its average citation score, in their publicity. The editor, who selected Rose and Miller's article for the special issue, mentioned that high citations were a precondition for her choice. 'Citation statistics' have not come from outside the academic world as if an alien imposition, but we academics have created the means by which we govern ourselves. This is precisely what Rose and Miller were discussing in their article.

But how should academics study this sort of thing and, in particular, what sorts of words should we use to study the processes that seem to ensnare us? Many followers of Foucault trace the meanings of words, in order to examine the history of 'discursive formations', which are used in regulating modern citizens. Thus, Rose and Miller named 'the inauguration of professional specialisms and vocabularies' as one of the things that sociologists should be investigating (2010, p. 281). But what sort of words should analysts use when they wish to expose the governing power of academic vocabularies? Does it matter if they use the type of terminology which they are seeking to expose?

Often academics, who wish to reveal how governmental agencies exert power over academics, try to avoid using the self-same concepts which governing agencies use. In this way, analysts might hope to put a distance between themselves and the existing 'discursive formations' of power. This is one reason why Foucault adapted rare words or invented new ones. When he was giving his lectures at the Collège de France, governments were not talking about 'governmentality'. By adapting an obscure, even ugly, concept for his own purposes, he hoped to stand back from the unrecognized power of governing agencies and thereby to reveal that power.

However, words do not exist in isolation but, as Roger Fowler and his colleagues observed, there are formal and informal styles of writing. Bureaucrats and managers will use formal styles which enable them to absent themselves from their texts; by using long nouns and passive verbs, they can present their demands as established facts. We can note the prevalence of noun-only-phrases in this official style of writing: 'citation scores' and 'impact factors'. Such terms, which appear to denote objective facts in the academic world, fit neatly into the official writings of academic managers, the science of bibliometrics and more generally into the lives of academics. The phrase 'governmentality studies', too, has the same nouns-only form. This thing has itself become an object that managers can audit and assess, computing the citation figures for 'governmentality studies', and calculating the approach's capacities for attracting economic funding. Supporters of 'governmentality' can package and promote their work so that the word 'governmentality' no longer stands distinct from the processes that its users had hoped to describe critically.

Does this matter? The problem lies in assuming that we could investigate critically 'the inauguration of professional specialisms and vocabularies' by formulating our own specialist vocabularies for the purpose. It is naive to imagine that we can escape the world of 'governmentality' simply by using a word or several words that our governors do not use. The issue cannot just be about individual words, for exchanging one set of formal nouns for another set would still leave untouched the predominance of nouns and noun phrases. To use Michael Halliday's expression, much writing in the sciences and social sciences is an edifice of things. Adding another thing to the edifice will not necessarily enable us to see how academics continue to fill their edifices with things of their own creation.

The way of escape, even if only temporary, may lie in the little words, rather than in creating further large ones. The formal ways of writing, which managers and academic social scientists take for granted, is a style for those who take themselves seriously. It is hard to use this style to puncture authority, except as a direct parody (and academics do not tend to take kindly to direct parodies of themselves). However, sometimes if we describe what the managers and academics are presenting as technical things, in the plainer language of everyday actions, then the 'thingness' and its power, can appear to dribble away.

Take 'citation scores' and 'impact factors'. These are official terms for fictional things, whose reality seems simultaneously to obsess and to burden academics. I cannot exempt myself. This power is not diminished by dignifying these things with the name of 'academic governmentality', but their intrinsic absurdity might be better revealed if we use the small words of everyday actions. I am aware of the approximate citation scores for my own publications. Why have I bothered to find this out? Sometimes I have an excuse: I must use citation numbers when preparing for an official auditing exercise. But sometimes I have no excuse: I have simply looked at the citation figures for my own work, hoping to discover gratifyingly high scores. As Nikolas Rose would recognize, we willingly govern ourselves.

The term 'citation score' gives this activity some sort of power, even dignity, but when I turn the activity into small words, the official terms seem to lose their hold. Without the official words to hide behind, our vanity and insecurity can become embarrassingly plain. Why, I might ask, am I bothering to find out how many times other academics have mentioned my work? And why do I feel pleased if the number is high? What difference does it make? It doesn't seem to matter how the others are mentioning me, whether they do so in passing or at length, whether in complimentary or critical tones. All that matters is that I am mentioned, again and again. It gets worse. Sometimes, I have compared my scores with those of others. I am pleased if I am mentioned in more articles than they are, and my mood will be spoiled if their numbers surpass mine. It is as if I am pathetically pleading with the academic world: 'Please, please mention me; you only need mention me in passing; just drop my name; I don't care where or how; just mention me, please; oh, and don't bother mentioning Dr X or Professor Y.' Do I really think like this? Do I really care about the numbers? Yes, I must do. What a knob head.

As I have discussed previously, writers can use noun-only-phrases to convey a sense that the things, which they are naming, exist as objective things. This is especially true of academic terms such as 'citation scores', 'impact factors' and 'governmentality studies'. However, not all noun-only-phrases function like this. There is an older linguistic tradition in English of using two nouns to insult and deflate, rather than to boost and promote. Sometimes one of the two nouns will refer impolitely to a body part. In our current ways of writing the social sciences, the official sort of noun-only-phrase is almost compulsory. By using such noun phrases, we display the credentials of our earnestness, without realizing that, in this regard, our prose will resemble that produced by officials and management. By contrast, the older sorts of noun-only phrase, with their sharp short nouns, can be just right for deflating pretentiousness and undermining authority. Yet, serious academics consider it taboo to use these terms. We take ourselves far too seriously to demean ourselves by using unseemly, inferior language. Knob heads.

Changing words for changing times

The two articles, which the editors of the *British Journal of Sociology* selected to represent the first decade of the new millennium, are both interesting (Beck and Sznaider, 2010; Urry, 2010). I will discuss them at less length than I discussed the Rose and Miller article because their subject matter is not related to the topics which I am discussing in quite the way that Rose and Miller's piece was. Both the articles for the 2000s, nevertheless, are significant pieces of work and both claim to point the way towards a new sort of sociology that is fit for present times. The principal authors of the articles, Ulrich Beck and John Urry, are eminent sociologists with many achievements to their name. However original might be their vision for a new sort of sociology, neither of these authors was providing a sharp grammatical break with the past. Both were offering new sets of nouns, rather than breaking free from the supremacy of nouns.

Beck and Urry argue that the classic ideas of sociology are now outdated and that, if sociologists are to understand the changing world about them, they need new concepts. According to Beck, classic sociologists, such as Durkheim and Weber, conceived of sociology as the study of 'society'. Their image of a 'society' was strongly influenced by the nation state, for they imagined a 'society' as being located in a particular place and having an organized social structure etc., etc. In consequence, they unwittingly constructed the whole of sociology in the image of the nation state. Beck and Urry, along with many other theorists of 'globalization', claim the contemporary world is not principally comprised of nation states or separate 'societies'. Instead, we live in an interdependent world, where people, objects and images regularly traverse national and other boundaries.

To understand this fluid, restless world, we need new categories which will capture the social world of today and which will reject the idea of 'society' as the basic model for all social arrangements. Beck and Sznaider argue that sociologists need to adopt a cosmopolitan perspective and 'cosmopolitanization' is their key concept. Similarly, John Urry advocates that sociologists, instead of studying fixed social forms, should be studying 'mobilities'. 'Cosmopolitanization' and 'mobilities' are new sociological things for new times.

Like the Rose and Miller article, these two articles for the 2000s offer new programmes for doing sociology, with Beck specifically subtitling his article 'A Research Agenda'. All three articles are largely unpopulated: in their respective papers, Beck and Urry do not depict people living cosmopolitan lives, or journeying across the globe or even staying at home, while things and images travel distances into their sitting rooms. These articles are dominated by theoretical things, which the authors fit together. Their authors are basing their new modes of enquiry around new concepts – and this means new nouns, new jigsaw pieces.

It is clear that Beck, just like Rose and Miller, believes that his new concepts, and the new sociology built around these concepts, will be more realistic than the old sociology. Accordingly, Beck does not put forward cosmopolitanization as an interesting hypothesis that needs to be tested. Beck and Sznaider use the phrase 'really-existing cosmopolitanization' a number of times; for example, writing about the need 'to understand the really-existing process of cosmopolitanization of the world' (2010, p. 387). They contrast their realistic cosmopolitan sociology with the 'unreal science of the national' (p. 390), rather like Foucault contrasted the unreal image of the state with the reality of governmentality.

Beck and Sznaider are at home with technical concepts, particularly izations, ifications and isms, which they employ profusely. They write that one reason why a cosmopolitan outlook would be so beneficial for sociology is that without it 'one cannot even understand the re-nationalization or re-ethnification trend in Western or Eastern Europe' (Beck and Sznaider, 2010, p. 384). They suggest that 'realistic cosmopolitanism . . . should be conceived, elaborated and practiced not in an exclusive manner but in an *inclusive* relation to universalism, contextualism, nationalism, transnationalism, etc' (p. 399, emphasis in original).

Somewhat surprisingly, Beck and Sznaider claim that cosmopolitan sociology will have space for people – and to a far greater extent, so they claim, than other recent sociologies. They don't phrase it quite like that:

> The cosmopolitan horizon becomes institutionalized in our own subjective lives. A cosmopolitan sociology, therefore, brings the subject back into the social sciences after systems theory and poststructuralist theories have tried to construct a social science without subjects (Beck and Sznaider, 2010, p. 391).

This statement uses grammatical forms that, as we have seen, are familiar in this sort of writing. The first sentence, in which Beck and Sznaider describe how ordinary people might think in cosmopolitan ways, is written in the passive voice: the cosmopolitan horizon 'becomes institutionalized'. There is no description how this might happen or what 'we', or other people, might have to do to make it so. Quite the reverse, 'we' are the objects of unspecified processes. But actually 'we' do not appear: the institutionalizing takes place 'in our subjective lives'. Another thing – 'our subjective lives' – appears instead of the writers presenting 'us' thinking, feeling, doing, etc. In this way, people are doubly absent, for they are even absent when they are being written about.

The second sentence brings us actors, who operate in the active voice. These actors, however, are not persons but types of sociology. There is the good sociology which brings 'the subject' back, and the bad sociologies which have 'tried' to dispense with subjects. The subject, who is to be brought back by the good sociology, is grammatically an object, not a subject. We might note that Beck and Sznaider prefer to talk about 'the subject' rather than 'people'. It sounds much grander, more official, and less personal. The definite article – the 'the' – adds cachet. By using 'the subject', the authors turn 'people' into another theoretical thing.

John Urry, in his article, continues his project to develop a 'post-societal' sociology (e.g., Urry, 2000). At the start of his article, Urry claims that 'the social as society' has been transformed into 'the social as mobility'. He is proposing some categories that should be relevant for developing a new sociology of mobility. He does not, however, formulate fresh 'ifications' and 'izations' or generally use the sorts of big categories that Beck does. Urry's terms are shorter, snappier and less obviously technical. His key term is 'mobilities' and he claims that sociologists today should be concerned with 'the diverse mobilities of peoples, objects, images, information, and wastes' (2010, p. 348). If you think that 'people' are being sociologically noticed in the opening paragraph of this article, you should look again. The author is not writing of the diverse mobilities of 'people', but of 'peoples'. The singular of 'peoples' is not a person, but 'a people'. Urry is using an abstraction and people as persons are absent from this description of diverse mobilities.

It is still a parade of nouns, for Urry has not sought to express his fundamental idea in terms of a verb. Presumably, peoples, objects, images etc. cannot have 'mobilities' unless they move or are moved by forces, persons or things. But the verb disappears before the noun, as Urry grammatically translates the fluidity of moving into the solidity of a plural noun: 'mobilities'. This is something – another thing – that sociologists can study and can organize as a topic. The other categories, which Urry introduces, are also nouns or noun phrases, such as 'scapes', 'flows', 'networks', 'inhuman hybrids' etc. These are not big izations: Urry is not the sort of social scientist who assumes that insight is directly correlated with the length of a word. Certainly, his new sociology has some refreshing features.

I do not intend to discuss how Urry's concepts might contribute to sociology. My point is much more restricted, for it concerns the way that he removes people from his analyses. This does not just follow from his choice of nouns as key categories. Urry is not like Beck, who claims to put 'the subject' back into sociology just at the moment when he is flattening people under the heavy weight of his nouns. In fact, Urry provides some interesting reasons why people are of decreasing sociological importance in the contemporary world. For Urry, people are no longer just people, and things are not just things: we have human and inhuman hybrids, continually moving, flowing, combining and recombining.

This is one reason why Urry places such importance on the concept of 'network'. In some respects, it is networks (and 'flows' and 'scapes'), rather than people, that do things in the contemporary world. According to Urry, networks 'produce complex and enduring connections across space and through time between peoples and things' (p. 354). They also possess abilities: networks have different 'abilities to bring home distant events' and 'to overcome the friction of regional space' (p. 354). Importantly, Urry does not talk of 'really-existing global networks', in the way that Beck writes of really-existing cosmopolitanization. Urry recognizes that 'a network' is a metaphor, but it is 'the appropriate metaphor' to capture the present intersection of peoples and things (p. 354).

Urry is writing confidently about the ways that people live their lives and how their scope for action is limited. To know how people act or how they do not act – and particularly to know that their capacity for acting is limited by the things that surround them – one has to observe their lives closely. Any sociology of mobilities should be examining how people move, how things move towards them, how people and things have become interlocked etc., etc., rather than making confident assertions in the abstract. Caroline Knowles (2010) makes a similar point in her commentary on Urry's article for the anniversary edition.

But Urry could counter by claiming that sociologists need new ways of understanding how people live their lives. In Urry's vision, networks and mobilities are the actors that are doing things and transforming people. He takes a principled stand against a person-based social science, arguing that sociologists should not focus their attention on studying human actors. Flows, scapes and networks are comprised of hybrids, not humans, and, thus, it is inappropriate, according to Urry, to use 'conceptions of agency', when writing about people (p. 357). It is as if our creations have run out of control, and they are now controlling us, or rather we have become merged into them. The result is that there is no longer 'an autonomous realm of human agency' (p. 357).

Urry is commenting on the way that technologies 'carry' people, money, images etc. within and across national societies. He suggests that such technologies 'do not derive directly and uniquely from human intentions and actions' (p. 354). They are connected with other machines, technologies and objects. It may be true that no one has pre-planned all the technological connections and interconnections. No one had envisaged the completed pattern before it all started. But that is true of most social patterns: no one planned the mediaeval feudal system in advance and the Pilgrim Fathers did not sail across the Atlantic with a blueprint plan for the USA in their minds. Even if current technologies were not deliberately planned to exist as they do, their existence still depends directly on a whole complex range of human actions. If we all stopped acting – if no one was working in power stations, switching on machines, connecting cables, inserting parts on workbenches, testing programs, digging up raw materials, tapping on keyboards, looking at screens, cleaning offices, sending messages, receiving messages, paying money, receiving money, attending meetings, more meetings and yet more meetings – and if we stopped doing all this and much, much more besides, then the technologies would stop buzzing away. They cannot act without us.

Urry's point is that the flows and movements are so complex that they are unpredictable. Not even social scientists can predict what is going to happen next. An extra grain of sand here may (or may not) result in an avalanche somewhere else. We, as humans, act on a local level, taking our decisions for small, restricted reasons. Most people know 'almost nothing about the global connections or implications of what they are doing' (p. 360). This negative statement about most people is written in an active clause. What is active is unimportant: 'However, these local actions do not remain simply local since they are captured, represented, marketed, circulated and generalized elsewhere'; thus they are 'carried along the scapes and flows of the emerging global world' (p. 360). The voice has shifted from the active to the passive, from the negative to the positive, from the unimportant to the important. No agents are identified: no one is doing the capturing, representing, marketing, carrying along the scapes and the flows. They just happen. The world is out of human control.

Urry is presenting an interesting vision with humans in the thrall of hybrids and networks. He realizes that it is not an altogether literal vision, but it is exaggerated and metaphorical. The problem is not the vision itself, but that it is being proposed as the basis for a new sort of sociology. The more successful that the manifesto proves to be, the more literal will be the writing of its followers. The next generation of mobility sociologists will take the absence of humans for granted. They will 'know' the dangers of treating 'human agency' as an autonomous realm, for they will learn this as they acquire their 'mobilities perspective'. Mobilities will be their academic trade – the object of their production – as well as the mode of enquiry which they will promote. They will be seeking grants to study network A, or global scape B or transnational flow C, treating each as a really existing thing that *must* be investigated in funded programmes of research. They will be aware that those who control the awarding of grants will be unlikely to invest the money, for which they are publicly responsible, to investigate mere metaphors.

Academic success will bring literary solidity, for those, who establish the new disciplinary approaches, will have invested too much in their sociological things not to believe in their reality. They will treat their theoretical metaphors as literal and their fictions as real. As likely as not, the new words will gather extra meanings. Just as 'governmentality' now names a specialist academic area, so 'mobilities' and 'cosmopolitanization' will probably come to denote specialist areas of sociological study. There may be some semantic surprises awaiting us in the future, but we can predict that sociologists, whatever their theoretical stripe, will still strive to make their chosen nouns stand out from those of their competitors.

Conversation analysis and its conversational things

So far in this chapter, I have been looking at the type of sociologists, who deal with big historical processes, such as the changing nature of government in the modern era or the rise of global interconnections, and who have created new sociological things such as 'governmentality', 'cosmopolitanization' and 'scapes'. Like the experts in 'reification' and 'mediatization', these sociologists have not tied their constructs closely to what people do. In consequence, their big sociological things can float free of human actions. Nevertheless, not all sociologists write like this and I want to discuss a type of analysis which could hardly be more different.

At first glance, conversation analysis would seem to avoid the sorts of difficulties that I have been identifying. Conversation analysts examine in microscopic detail the procedures and organization of ordinary talk and, in doing this, they try to take a rigorously empirical stance, examining what people do when they interact together. Above all, they seek to base their analyses on the actions and assumptions of the participants, rather than on the presumptions and theories of the analysts.

In consequence, conversation analysts consciously avoid many of the features of big sociology. They do not speculate about historical processes or wide patterns of social change; their topics are not things like governmentalization, globalization or mediatization; and they do not want their theoretical concepts to float free of human actions. One might expect, therefore, that conversation analysts would put human actions above fictional things, and verbal clauses above nouns; but, as we shall see, matters are not quite so simple.

As a way of doing research, conversation analysis developed out of the pioneering work which Harvey Sacks did in California during the 1960s and early 1970s. He published little during his lifetime, but after his tragically early death in 1975 his lecture notes circulated among his students and admirers, before being published (Sacks, 1995). Sacks wanted to understand the ordinary rules and procedures of everyday life, believing that people regularly do intricate things which social scientists had previously overlooked. One matter, which caught his attention and which became fundamental to conversation analysis, was that conversation typically depended on participants swapping turns to speak in regular, orderly ways. For this to happen, participants must have ways of displaying when they are coming to the end of their speaking turn and potential speakers must know how to recognize these signs in order to take the floor at appropriate moments. No one had examined in detail what these signs might be and how speakers actually begin and end their own speaking turns to coordinate with others.

Sacks realized the importance of recording conversations and then listening to them over and over again, taking into account micro-pauses, intakes of breath, intonation, hesitations etc., etc., as well as the actual spoken phrases. Sacks did not do this to obtain profiles of individual speakers – whether, for instance, some speak or hesitate more than others – but to see whether the micro-features were part of a system by which participants organized their turns of talking. At the time, many orthodox sociologists considered that this was an extraordinary way of going about sociological research, abandoning the big issues to concentrate on tiny mumblings. Today Sacks's insights have grown into a major means for investigating social life.

I do not intend to comment on debates about the value of conversation analysis but my concern is with the way that conversation analysts write and how they rhetorically create their own conversation analytic things. Sacks, in the opening lecture of one of his courses, used to tell his students that the world in which they lived was 'much more finely organized' than they imagined (1984, p. 414). We might say something analogous about academic styles of writing. Academics might consider it obviously 'proper' to write in the way that they do, but, if we look closely, their small grammatical choices may be less obvious and more consequential than they might imagine.

Regarding the style in which conversation analysts write, we can say that it is distinctive in a number of ways. Although conversation analysts might be studying ordinary talk, and although they might base their analyses on the actions and speech of participants, they tend to write in highly technical ways. Regularly they reject ordinary ways of describing human actions. In fact, they ordinarily do not use the word 'ordinary' to describe what they are rejecting. Instead they will use 'vernacular', particularly when rejecting 'vernacular' terms in favour of specialist ones (see, for example, Schegloff, 2000, justifying why he was going to avoid using the word 'interruption').

For outsiders, the technical papers of conversation analysts can be hard going and their phrasing can appear a bit precious – but that is true of much academic writing in the social sciences. Part of the trouble (but by no means all of it) is that conversation analysts generally write for insiders and have devised a large number of new technical terms to describe the micro-features of conversational talk. Most of the new terms are noun phrases, and comparatively few are verbs. In the main, conversation analysts tend not to devise new words as such, but prefer to combine existing words in new combinations.

Some of their technical terms are triple noun phrases, often with regularly used abbreviations: 'membership categorization device' (MCD), 'transition relevance place' (TRP), 'turn construction unit' (TCU), 'overlap management device' etc. There are also double noun phrases, such as the important term 'adjacency pair'. This refers to a pair of conversational turns, which normally follow directly, one on another: if a participant says the first of the pair, technically named as the First Part Pair (FPP), then they will expect the recipient to follow with the Second Part Pair (SPP). These sorts of pairs occur in questions/answers, in greetings and in farewells. For example, when one speaker says 'goodbye' to another, they will act as if they expect the receiver to acknowledge this by also formulating a farewell; and if the receiver does not formulate a farewell, they will be expected to produce a reason why the leave-taking should be delayed. In this sense, the two tokens of farewell will constitute an adjacency pair, where the first will be followed by the second. Sacks discussed 'adjacency pairs' in his lectures and subsequent conversation analysts have taken the phenomenon to represent something very important about the sequential nature of conversation.

In the course of their research, analysts have taken it for granted that they are identifying new things in their conversational data and these newly discovered things must be named. This is reflected in the difference between their technical vocabulary and many of the sociological izations, which I have previously discussed. The latter tend to be mass nouns without plural forms, while conversation analysts tend to devise count nouns, which have plural forms and which can be counted as separate entities. Thus, one can have several 'adjacency pairs' or 'transition relevance places' in a given transcript. Rather ironically, conversational analysts do not generally count the things that their count nouns describe, although exceptionally they have been known to do so (e.g., Heritage and Greatbach, 1986). However, by using count nouns, conversation analysts are indicating that their discovered entities possess thing-like properties.

Sacks set the tone in his lectures. When lecturing on adjacency pairs, he commented: 'I would say that greetings are instances of a class of objects that I call *adjacency pairs*' (1995, p. 189, emphasis in original). He gave no indication here to suggest that adjacency pairs were only metaphorical objects. Generally, the writings of conversation analysts seem to fit Halliday's notion that scientists create an edifice of things by grammatically transforming processes, occurring over time, into things which seem to possess the solidity of objects. 'Adjacency pairs' are processes which occur sequentially over time, as first one speaker and then another speaks (or, in some cases, forgoes to speak). As such, adjacency pairs are not objects, but the word 'adjacency' suggests things concretely adjacent to one another, side by side in space, rather than processes unfolding in time one after another.

We can see metaphorical thingness in other terminology, which seems to translate time into space. For example, 'transition relevance place' is an important concept for understanding the orderly sequencing of conversation: participants must design their turns with transition relevance places, so that their recipients can pick up signs that the turn is coming to an end and they may have an opportunity to speak. The transition relevance place cannot literally be a place. It must be a moment, which occurs in time and which, if a hearer does not respond by starting to talk, may pass. In their classic paper on turn-taking, Sacks, Schegloff and Jefferson (1974) commented briefly in a footnote on their choice of the term 'transition relevance place', and especially on their choice of the word 'place', but without remarking on the fact that the 'place' is not literally a place (pp. 705–6).

Of course, conversation analysts are aware that these so-called objects exist in time rather than space: Schegloff, for example, refers to the 'nextness' of adjacency pairs, but he still considers this nextness to be a form of adjacency (2000, p. 19). As new generations of researchers are recruited to use the established terminology, so they will accept the terms as appropriate for naming conversational objects. In one textbook, aimed at students, a conversation analyst describes adjacency pairs. He describes them as 'a sequence of two utterances' which possesses four prime characteristics, the first of which simply is that they are 'adjacent' (Wooffitt, 2001, p. 53). It is not only textbook writers who are turning the time between utterances into space. In one study, researchers investigated how speakers use intonation to signify that they might be coming to the end of their speaking turn. The researchers defined 'transition relevance place' as 'the space between the TRP-projecting accent' of the current turn and the onset of the next turn (Wells and Macfarlane, 1998). Literally, there can be no space between two turns, which are separated in time.

Of course, no one will believe that the two parts of an 'adjacency pair', are actually physical things that are situated side by side, like two adjacent houses or two adjacent fields. But the term is not used as a metaphor. By treating a term, which contains spatial meaning as if it were a literal description of a process occurring over time, conversation analysts emphasize that they are discovering and discussing things. In this way, they are able to create objects out of actions that occur over time.

Creating the things of conversation

We need to ask whether it really matters if conversation analysts create and use a heavily noun-based vocabulary of technical terms. They have a strong tendency to seek to name actions, which can be described with active verbs, with nouns as if they were things. For example, they will write about 'self-repairs', rather than speakers repairing what they have just said; or about 'second assessments' rather than a speaker assessing after they or another has already assessed. When Schegloff (2000) analyses how a speaker might stretch a syllable in order to keep speaking and not concede the floor to another, he calls this 'a stretch', thereby going from verb to noun.

There is always the possibility that by emphasizing objects in their writings, established conversation analysts might be unwittingly encouraging their students to produce slack analyses. The students might start thinking that the way to analyse conversational material is to try to spot the things that it contains, as if it were sufficient merely to say 'there's an adjacency pair' and 'look at this transition relevance place' (Antaki et al., 2007). But, of course, birdwatching is not the same as zoological research. The originators of conversation analysis – and those who are developing it today – did much more than spot previously established objects; they had to create these objects, noticing what had not hitherto been noticed.

There is another danger – and it is one which I have discussed in relation to other tendencies to nominalize verbs in the social sciences. The analysts create things out of what people do; and then, when the analysts formulate statements of theory, they depict these things as actors, doing what people do. Although conversation analysts try to avoid doing this, at least in a simple way, they can write about what particular 'devices' might do, as if the devices, not the speakers, were the actors. I have mentioned the textbook chapter, in which a conversation analyst describes being 'adjacent' as the first characteristic of 'adjacency pairs'. The fourth characteristic is that 'a first part requires a second part' (Wooffitt, 2001, p. 53). The part itself does not literally require a second part, but the speaker of the first part is requiring a response by speaking in a particular way. We know what the writer is meaning and it can be simpler to use a verb that seems to attribute agency to the so-called conversational object rather than to the person using the object.

Anthony Liddicoat in his textbook *An Introduction to Conversation Analysis* writes similarly about adjacency pairs. He writes that 'the first turn of the pair initiates some action' and that 'the second turn responds to the prior turn and completes the action which was initiated in the first turn'. Surely it is the speakers themselves that are initiating, responding and completing the actions, rather than their utterances. The writer goes on to say that 'adjacency pairs set up expectations about how talk will proceed and if these are not met then the talk is seen as being problematic' (Liddicoat, 2007, pp. 106–7). This statement not merely personifies what adjacency pairs might do, but it eliminates all speakers. The writer switches from the active voice, when attributing agency to adjacency pairs, to the passive voice, when describing what happens if the expectations *are not met*: then the talk *is seen* as problematic. This is stated as a general rule and it is literally a rule about things, not about people, who are absent even as the agents who might see the talk as problematic.

From Sacks onwards, conversation analysts have sought to remain close to their data. They do not deploy technical concepts in the abstract but when, for instance, discussing 'adjacency pairs', they will do so in relation to examples. There is, accordingly, less chance of major gaps developing between what people do and the concepts that analysts are using to describe what people are doing. There is little danger of impersonal writing on the scale that can be found in some of the theories of 'mediatization', 'cosmopolitanization' and even 'reification'. Nevertheless, as conversation analysts use their technical concepts and relate these to the actions of people, gaps can appear.

Analysts report that there are a number of stages in conversation analytic research, going from recording the conversational material, transcribing it, selecting extracts to investigate in detail, proposing inter-pretations, formulating general rules of procedure, returning to the data to check etc. Back and forth the analysts go from data to interpretation and back again. Many research papers possess a rhetorical sequence. After discussing some general issues relating to the analysis of talk, the writers present the data in commendable detail and then produce interpretations of what the participants are doing. At this stage, they may give some background information and refer to parts of the conversation which have already occurred and which the analysts have not selected to examine in depth.

Experienced analysts can provide great insight into what the partici-pants are doing and how they are going about their conversational busi-ness. Typically at this early stage in the report, they use non-technical language to describe what the participants are doing. For example, Schegloff (2000), in analysing how participants resolve the problem of speakers talking at the same time, presents a conversation with a partic-ularly tricky moment: a wife seems to be accused by her husband of exaggerating and by her daughter of acting irresponsibly. Schegloff points to the moment when Dick, the husband, attempts to defuse the situation with a joke and he tries to make a pun that he has been trying to make previously. Here Schegloff does not use technical terminology but he describes what the participants are doing with ordinary verbs in the active voice: 'Dick is trying again to make a pun'; Dick makes a remark 'which Anne takes as a euphemism for being called *a liar*'; and when Dick finally gets to tell his joke, 'he pretends to address himself to his granddaughter'; and so on (Schegloff, 2000, p. 26).

At this stage, analysts like Schegloff are using the sorts of verbs (such as 'pretends' and 'tries') which they will not use during the more formal parts of their analysis. In fact, some analysts distinguish this preliminary stage from the real analysis. Paul ten Have (2009) describes how the analyst 'first tries to understand what the interactants are doing' (p. 261). He stresses, however, that understanding what the interactants are doing is not 'the purpose of the research' but is a 'necessary requirement for the next step, the analysis proper'. This next step is to formulate the proce-dures 'used to accomplish the actions-as-understood' (pp. 261–2). We can see, even in these brief comments, a move from an active statement about what people 'are doing', to an impersonal, passive voiced statement about procedures 'used to accomplish' actions.

When it comes to formulating general procedures on the basis of the so-called proper analyses, then passives often come into their own. Here is Schegloff (2000) describing 'the overlap resolution device', whose prin-ciples he has formulated on the basis of analysing several episodes such as that of Dick and his family. Schegloff writes that the device – and we might note the very 'thingness' of the notion of a 'device' – 'is locally organized', it 'is party-administered' and it 'is interactionally managed and recipient-designed' etc. (p. 45). All the verbs are in the passive voice. Schegloff here does not describe anyone as doing anything: he has put his device there in the centre of things.

It is the same when Sacks, Schegloff and Jefferson (1974) introduced the key notion of 'recipient design', explaining that the term referred to the ways 'in which the talk by a party in a conversation is constructed or designed in ways which display an orientation and sensitivity to the particular other(s) who are the co-participants' (p. 727). Again, the passive verb is to the fore: the talk 'is designed' and 'is constructed'. But the noun phrase 'recipient design' is being introduced to replace these verbs, even in their passive voices. In this way, analysts can talk about 'design' without talking about a designer or anyone doing the designing. In their explanation of 'recipient design', they use the active voice of 'display' when they use the words 'display an orientation and sensitivity' to others. However, the subject of this active verb is not a person – namely the talker or the designer of the talk – but it is the talk itself, or, to be more precise, it is the way the talk is constructed that displays the orientation and the sensitivity. People are dropping out to be replaced by things, including the thing 'orientation'.

Orienting to semi-technical terms

As well as creating and using formal technical terms, such as 'overlap resolution device' or 'adjacency pairs', conversation analysts also use a range of other terms which, for the sake of simplicity, might be called 'semi-technical'. Conversation analysts go to painstaking lengths to create, explain and deploy their formal terminology, which, at all stages, they seek to tie to examples. However, not all the distinctive terminology that conversation analysts use is the product of such careful analyses. At first glance, the word 'interactant', which I have quoted ten Have as using, seems to be a technical term. The word is not in the *Oxford English Dictionary* and ordinary speakers are highly unlikely to use it. There is, however, a big difference between 'interactant' and terms like 'adjacency pair'. When ten Have talks about 'interactants', he does not preface his use with definitions, examples and analyses. He simply uses the word as if he expects his readers to understand the word. The term, therefore, is neither properly technical nor properly ordinary: it is semi-technical.

Conversation analysts have a batch of semi-technical terms and phrases, and unlike their formal terminology, which is heavily biased towards nouns and noun phrases, this semi-technical vocabulary includes adjectives, such as 'candidate' and 'hearable', and verbs like 'to orient' or 'to orientate'. The noun 'orientation' is also a semi-technical term. One does not normally have to read far into a textbook on conversation analysis before coming across 'orient' or 'orientate'. On the fourth page of *Conversation Analysis*, Hutchby and Wooffitt refer to the structure of 'situated social interaction' as being something that 'participants actively orient to as relevant to the ways that they design their actions' (2008, p. 4). Liddicoat, on the fifth page of his textbook, claims that 'participants themselves orient to the order being produced' (2007, p. 5). Neither book explains what 'orient' means.

Personally, I do not really know what it means to orient to an order or to a structure, whether actively or otherwise. You don't hear people – at least those without training in conversation analysis – saying 'Oh, I was just orienting to the order of our chat.' In ordinary terms, people have to be doing something else before the analyst will say that they are orienting to structures, orders, devices or whatever. But, as ten Have says, conversation analysts are not particularly interested as such in the things that people are doing. Given that conversation analysts do not formally define 'orient', we have to understand the word's meaning by seeing how they use it.

Let me attempt this by looking at a section from Hutchby and Wooffitt's textbook, as the authors discuss how participants might come to speak at the same time. They present an extract from a conversation between Nancy and Edna. At one point, Edna says 'Oh my gosh' (for convenience, I have omitted the standard transcription symbols that Hutchby and Wooffitt use). Nancy comes in with a high-pitched exclamation, while Edna continues talking, so that at this moment the two speakers are overlapping. Hutchby and Wooffitt explain Nancy's high-pitched exclamation: 'it is quite possible that Nancy at this point treats Edna as responding to her joke' (a joke which Nancy has previously made). But Edna continues talking and demonstrates that her 'Oh my gosh' is not a response to the joke but the start of a comment that she proceeds to make. The authors comment that 'the overlap caused by Nancy can be seen as the product of her orientating to the first possible completion point in that turn'. From this, they go on to formulate a general principle: 'even apparently "disorderly" talk can be seen as the product of participants' orientations to the rule-set' (Hutchby and Wooffitt, 2008, p. 56).

The sentences, which I have quoted from, correspond to the stages of analysis that ten Have describes. The first sentence corresponds to the stage before the analysis proper, with the authors interpreting what the participants are doing. They use ordinary language with an active clause to say that Nancy is 'treating' Edna as 'responding' to her joke. The authors present the second sentence as if they are reformulating the ordinary language of the first into analytic language. Nancy is now seen to be 'orientating', rather than 'treating'. The third sentence drains out all the particularities of Nancy, Edna and what they happened to be doing. The authors are proposing a general statement about 'disorderly' talk and participants' observations. The verb 'orientate' has become a noun – 'orientations'. The authors present the three sentences as if they lead one to another without substantial change. But we can look for possible changes, especially to see what using 'orientate' might add or subtract, and whether there are gaps between using ordinary language and technical language.

The verb. First, there is the change of verb from 'treat' to 'orientate'. The phrase – 'treating Edna as responding to a joke' – tells us more about what Nancy was doing than does 'orientating to the first possible completion point'. It tells us about the joke, and that Nancy thinks that Edna is now responding to that joke. This information is omitted from the second sentence. As we move from an ordinary verb, which the analysts use to describe what the participants are doing, to 'orient', or 'orientate', we generally lose information, for 'orient', or 'orientate' are much less informative than ordinary verbs. That is, of course, the point of using them. The analyst can redescribe an infinite amount of acts that participants might be performing as 'orienting' or 'orientating', without having to specify precisely what they mean by these verbs. What analysts are doing – when moving from verbs such as 'treating', 'expecting', 'paying attention to', 'responding to', 'trying to' etc. – is rather like moving from the active to the passive voice. Active sentences can be translated into passives but typically not vice versa. From the statement that 'Nancy is treating Edna as responding to her joke', we can formulate a sentence using 'orientate'. However, if we hear that 'Nancy is orientating to a possible completion point', we cannot formulate the sentence that Nancy must have been treating Edna as responding to a previous joke. She might have been doing a million other things.

One might argue that there is nothing problematic in this for, in using the verb 'orientate', conversation analysts are deliberately using a term that is wider than all those ordinary verbs that people use to distinguish between different actions. As such, the analysts want to treat an infinite number of different actions as being functionally equivalent. In this respect, we might formulate an informal explanation of 'orientate', as used in the example from Hutchby and Wooffitt: 'If someone shows that they are expecting another to finish speaking, then they can be said to be orientating to a possible completion point'. There are all manner of different ways of showing that you are expecting another to finish speaking, but, because ordinary language does not provide a ready verb, which stuffs all these different actions into the same category, analysts have had to adapt one for this purpose. One might say that is precisely the point of using 'orient' or 'orientate'. But why don't the analysts then define this verb or, at least, explain what they are doing with it? Why do they just use it? Is it because they are using the word to cover gaps?

The object. As the writers move from using 'treating' to 'orientating' so they change the grammatical object of the actions that they are describing. When using 'treat', the grammatical object is Edna and her responding to Nancy. With the verb 'orientate to', Nancy is no longer treating Edna but orientating to the sort of conversational object that the analysts have noted. In this regard, we are moving from a sentence that uses the sort of words that the participants might have used about themselves to one that uses the analysts' terminology. The grammatical object no longer is a piece of action unfolding over time, but it has become an object itself, namely a completion point. We might note also a move from being tentative to being sure. The first sentence states that 'it is quite possible that Nancy at this point treats Edna as responding ...' The second sentence omits 'it is quite possible' and now it is claimed the overlap 'can be seen as the product of her orientating to the first possible completion point'. The phrase 'can be seen' is ambiguous. On the one hand it seems to assert, with 'can' implying that one can justifiably see X. On the other hand, it also qualifies, or hedges, in a standard academic way by not being an outright assertion that X *is* the case. Whatever the meaning of 'can be seen', the phrase is more assertive than 'it is quite possible that'.

There is something else that adds to the feeling of definiteness in the second sentence. Nancy is not just orientating, but she is orientating to a first possible completion point, whose reality the authors seem to be asserting rather than suggesting. More than this, the authors are moving from describing to explaining. Rather than describing what the participants might have been doing, they are suggesting that the overlap may have been the 'product' of Nancy's orientating to the first possible completion point. In this way, the second sentence does more than reformulate the descriptions contained in the first sentence. In fact, the sentence loses much of the specificity of the first sentence. Instead, the authors are moving their theoretical things – the orientating and the completion point – into positions of explanatory importance.

However, the argument that these things have produced the effect, which is to be explained, contains a slightly circular element. We can only know that there is a possible completion point because Nancy has intervened and thereby overlapped. Had she said nothing in reaction to

Edna's 'Oh my gosh', we would have had no reason for supposing there was a first possible completion point. So, the overlap is being accounted for in terms of an entity (the first possible completion point) whose existence we only know about because there has been that overlap.

The noun. Between the second and the third sentence there is a further move towards making the analytic things seem more concrete. In this third sentence, the analysts widen their focus to writing about phenomena in general, not about particular forms of those phenomena. Thus, the authors move from completion points to 'rule-sets', and from overlaps to 'disorderly' talk in general. In this sentence, participants are no longer said to orientate, but they have things called 'orientations' and 'disorderly' talk is held to be the product of these orientations. It is as if the orientations, rather than the participants, are the actors that produce the 'disorderly' talk. Of course, no one would explicitly assert this as a literal fact, but the analysts are using a form of expression that is common in social scientific writing and that social scientists use when they are emphasising the importance of their theoretical things.

There is also a loss in this third sentence. The analysis of Nancy's interjection was based on the idea that she had misunderstood the signals from Edna. She believed that Edna was laughing at her joke, when she was not. The general statement in the third sentence refers to apparently 'disorderly' talk being the product of 'rule-sets'; it does not say that 'disorderly' talk might be the product of speakers making mistakes when applying 'rule-sets'. The sentence does not contain the idea of misinterpretation, but it asserts that 'participants' orientations to the rule-sets' produce 'disorderly' talk, not their 'mis-orientations'. By this omission, the authors strengthen the idea that conversations are highly structured. However, they are omitting from the general statement, which they formulate on the basis of the episode, a crucial element of that episode – indeed, the element that makes it meaningful in ordinary terms.

By replacing ordinary verbs with a semi-technical verb like 'orient', conversation analysts can change the way that they describe conversationalists: no longer are the conversationalists acting in ordinary ways but they are acting in accordance with the things that are central to the analysts' concerns. To do this successfully, analysts need a verb which is far less specific than the verbs of ordinary language whose meanings have been refined by constant use in everyday life. Analysts would not want to define 'orient' too rigorously or discuss its usage too closely for that would turn it into a technical term and restrict how they use it. Instead, conversation analysts need their semi-technical terms to be semi-technical, rather than self-consciously formal, so that they can use them to cover gaps between the ordinary verbs and their technical terminology.

Of course, these gaps might be small – certainly much smaller than the gaps in much sociological theory. Nevertheless, as we have seen, when conversation analysts move from ordinary language to general formulations, they can still leave little gaps behind them. Leaving gaps might be inevitable, as analysts move rhetorically from describing what specific people are doing, to formulating general statements about theoretical objects, whose reality as objects the analysts take for granted but which can only exist because people are acting messily and uniquely. And into these gaps, analysts can then smuggle small packets of extra meaning, as if these were aid parcels for their own theoretical assumptions.

Doing being a social scientist

Harvey Sacks may have sought to discover conversational objects, to which he could affix somewhat awkward, noun-filled names, but he also used another rhetorical turn of phrase, which was much more original in its grammatical form and which stacked up verbs rather than nouns. In his opening lectures, Sacks used to tell his students that ordinariness was not ordinary but there were complicated ways of 'doing "being ordinary"' (Sacks, 1984). He meant that you had to show your ordinariness by performing it. Sacks would put into inverted commas the 'being ordinary' part of his double verb serving. Here, I intend to remove those marks, for they might suggest that the phrase 'being ordinary' functions grammatically as a noun, which has been formed out of a verbal participle. I prefer to emphasize that it is academically possible, if unusual, to double one's verbs.

Conversation analysts have not generally taken up this rhetorical trope from Sacks; they do not write about 'doing being a syllable-stretcher' or 'doing being a completion point ignorer'. That would be too great a rub against conceptual and rhetorical grains. Besides Sacks was not using his double verbs as a prelude to inserting a technical, rather than ordinary, term. However, Sacks's trope is useful for understanding why conversation analysts employ their semi-technical and technical terminology to the extent that they do.

In Chapter 3, I discussed how postgraduates become fully-fledged academics, by doing a number of academic things, and especially by using the appropriate technical language of their subdisciplinary speciality. What are the sorts of things that you have to do in order to do being a conversation analyst? At data sessions or in group seminars, you have to say things like: 'I hear interactant X orienting to the First Part Pair' or 'Y's orientation to the Second Part Pair is hearable at this point'. You won't be accepted as fully belonging – as fully doing being a conversation analyst – unless you can mobilize such phrases, and many more besides, at the appropriate Technical Phrase Display Point.

The new recruits will not use the semi-technical terms because they have judged from personal experience that these turns of phrase are superior to their equivalents in ordinary language. Nor will they have obtained the semi-technical terms from an official glossary for they will not find them there. It is much more likely that they have heard the elders of the parish speaking like this and they are adopting this style in order to do being a proper conversation analyst. It is the same across the social sciences. There are other ways of talking which are required if the recruit wishes to do being a Foucauldian, a Lacanian, or a mediatization theorist.

Just as there are the turns of phrase that you should use if you wish to display your linguistic credentials, so there are some that you should not use. This is particularly noticeable in the conversation analytic parish. Your reputation will not be enhanced by quoting Deleuze, Derrida or Ulrich Beck, as you analyse your First Part Pairs. Conversation analysts tend not to look to outsiders for extra ingredients to add to their analytic recipes. The line is that doing conversation analysis is difficult enough without having to import ideas from elsewhere, especially if those ideas are ungrounded in conversational data. The recruit will soon learn that there is little to be gained professionally from ploughing through the writings of Deleuze or Beck. It is better that they study the work of the major figures in conversation analysis, such as Emanuel Schegloff, Gail Jefferson and Anita Pomerantz, whose styles they should follow.

Outside of conversation analysis, things tend to be a bit more relaxed. If you want to do being a social analyst, it is good to throw in a quote or two from a classic writer. A touch of Aristotle or Weber, Plato or Nietzsche will show that you are not just a specialist in neo-liberal governmentality or educational policy cosmopolitanization; but you are also a bit classy. There are, of course, changing fashions in the amount of points you can gain from citing individual classic figures. Marx has gone down in value of late; Engels has plummeted; and Lenin is untradeable. Heidegger has been up for a while, having recovered from his nasty Nazi blip. It takes the sort of scholarship, which Foucault regularly demonstrated, to cite historic writers that virtually no one else has heard of.

Things, such as Beck's 'cosmopolitanization' and Schegloff's 'pre-resolution stretch', would seem to come from sociological environments that could not be farther apart. But it is not just a matter of theoretical things. There are also broader rhetorical styles, and semi-technical turns of phrase. The first three approaches, which I have discussed in this chapter, seem to have more in common rhetorically with each other, than any of them does with conversation analysis. However, there is something that the adherents of all four are likely to share, although this might not be immediately apparent. None will probably gain much credit from their peers if they were seriously to cite the approach which I will be discussing in the next chapter. All would distance themselves from the language and outlook of experimental social psychologists.

8 Experimental social psychology: concealing and exaggerating

In this chapter, I will be turning from sociology to social psychology, in order to examine some of the literary practices that experimental social psychologists customarily use. In a way, this is a move from the centre of the social sciences to its boundary with the natural sciences. The majority of social psychologists like to think of themselves as scientists, conducting proper experiments. Many would be surprised to hear that they have a literary style, because they would claim just to stick to 'the facts' and to write with the sort of clarity that befits any natural scientist. But, as I want to argue in this chapter, it is not quite so simple and experimental social psychologists have some rhetorical habits which are well worth critically examining.

Some very vocal critics have contrasted the waffle of the social sciences with the precision of the natural sciences. If one paid attention to scientists such as Richard Dawkins and Alan Sokal, one might gain the impression that the root of all problems in the social sciences lies in the pretentiousness of continental literary theory. In the words of Sokal, much big theory today is 'fashionable nonsense', designed to impress those who lack the intellectual resources and scientific education to see through its pretences (Sokal and Bricmont, 1999). Dawkins asks his readers to imagine being 'an intellectual impostor with nothing to say, but with strong ambitions to succeed in academic life'. What sort of literary style would you adopt? He answers: 'Not a lucid one, surely, for clarity would expose your lack of content' (Dawkins, 2003, p. 47).

These critics seem to suggest that the antidote to the intellectual fraudsters lies in being more scientific. Impostors, possessing impressive verbiage and no substance, would soon be found out in the world of science. If social scientists could be a bit more like natural scientists, then the problem of unnecessary obscurity and empty words would be resolved. However, transporting the literary practices of the natural sciences into the social sciences brings its own difficulties. The topics of the social sciences concern people, not things or physical processes, and, as I have suggested previously, there are problems when social scientists rhetorically treat people as things.

Experimental social psychologists, as I hope to show, are particularly liable to turn human actions into objects and to end up writing about the social world as if they were writing about things. This would not be so bad, if their writing at least had the benefit of being precise, but technical concepts, which might appear precise in theory, can be highly imprecise in practice. As we shall see, experimental social psychologists can use impressive-sounding terms very loosely, so that the same word comes to stand for very different sorts of psychological processes and entities.

In order to demonstrate what is going wrong with the rhetorical practices that social psychologists use, I will need to look at some experimental procedures in detail. This may be a bit tedious, but it is worth taking the trouble to compare what social psychologists are doing experimentally with the way that they write about what they are doing. If you take the trouble, you can notice something unexpected. These advocates of the scientific approach routinely conceal important aspects of their experimental findings and just as routinely they exaggerate their results. They exaggerate and they conceal so regularly that they cannot be aware of what exactly they are actually doing, as they follow supposedly scientific procedures.

Social psychology as an experimental science

First, I must declare an interest. My academic background was in experimental social psychology. I obtained my doctorate in the subject and my first papers were experimental reports. I was fortunate that my doctoral supervisor was Henri Tajfel, who, unlike many other social psychologists, was no narrow experimentalist. Tajfel was a genuine intellectual with interests across the arts and the social sciences. Although I turned away from doing laboratory experiments soon after my doctorate, my admiration for Tajfel persisted. If anything, it has deepened over the years, as I come to appreciate the profundity of his insights, as well as the debt which I owe him. As I have explained elsewhere, I believe that Tajfel's paper 'Cognitive Aspects of Prejudice' (1969) is one of the most intellectually important and creative articles in the history of modern social psychology (Billig, 2002).

I say this because I want to make clear that I am not excluding either myself or my teacher from the criticisms that I will be making. Later in this chapter, I will be using a couple of examples from Henri Tajfel as illustrations. I am not doing this to devalue his legacy or as a belated, pathetic act of rebellion. Quite the contrary, it is my way of stressing that some of the very best experimental social psychologists write in ways that I will be criticizing. I do not have to scrabble around the second division for examples. I am talking about deeply ingrained, disciplinary practices, not individual faults. Nor do I exempt myself. I learnt the standard procedures for analysing, presenting and discussing data. Just in case anyone is thinking of trawling through my early writings, in order to see whether I was guilty of the very faults that I am now accusing others of committing, let me spare them the bother. I was. In those days I was a good boy, still trying to do what I had been taught to do.

The majority of experimental social psychologists suffer from a double insecurity. They tend to work in psychology departments, alongside other academic psychologists, such as cognitive psychologists, perception psychologists, physiological psychologists and so on. As such, they share a general disciplinary insecurity. In most universities and colleges, psychology departments are part of the sciences, rather than the arts or social sciences. This is not an administrative accident, but it reflects the history of psychology as an academic discipline. Academic psychologists, ever since Wundt founded his laboratory at Leipzig in the late nineteenth century, have generally prided themselves on being both experimental and scientific. Kurt Danziger, an experimentalist turned historian of psychology, has written of the discipline's 'wishful identification with the natural sciences' (1997, p. 9). The result is that most psychologists crave to be recognized as proper scientists. As a corollary of this, they wish to distance themselves from the arts and the social sciences, which they see as soft, easy and unscientific. And they have a continual insecurity: proper scientists – the biochemists, physiologists and chemists – will not recognize them as real scientists but will look down on psychology as a soft subject. And the more they fear the disdain of proper scientists, the more they will disdain those that they hold to be beneath them in the hierarchy of 'real' science.

Social psychologists find themselves in a doubly insecure position, for they are marginal figures in a marginal discipline. Within psychology, the highest status is given to those who appear the most scientific, so that psychologists at the biological or physiological end of the discipline carry greater weight than social psychologists, whose topics often overlap with those of sociologists and other social scientific softies. Unlike the biological psychologists, social psychologists do not require laboratories filled with expensive equipment or attract funds from the big grant-awarding bodies of the natural and medical sciences. As a result, many experimental social psychologists overcome their insecurities by repeatedly stressing their scientific credentials. They will distance themselves from their sociological neighbours, who are on the wrong side of the imaginary boundary, which separates the natural sciences from the social sciences.

The result is that the members of no other discipline in the social sciences, with the possible exception of economists, pride themselves on being scientific as much as do experimental social psychologists. They tend to be unimpressed by current literary or social theorizing, but they will look towards the cognitive and natural sciences for their ideas and methodological practices. In their articles, they are unlikely to cite the sorts of sociologists, whom I discussed in the previous chapter, but they will prefer to fill the bibliographies at the end of their papers with references to other experimental studies. They cling fast to the belief that the route to knowledge is through the accumulation of experimental findings, and not through flashy philosophical, literary or sociological speculation. They tend not to look kindly on social psychologists, who might once have been reasonable experimentalists, but who have chosen to go off and do non-experimental things. No one, least of all those unsure about their position in the world, likes a traitor.

Sometimes introductory textbooks provide a good indication of the way that academics want to project publicly the image of their discipline. The big introductory textbooks for social psychology, aimed at first year university students, can make interesting reading. In the opening pages, the desire to be seen as scientific is often evident, as their authors link being scientific with doing experiments. Crisp and Turner (2010) declare at the start of *Essential Social Psychology* that 'social psychology is the scientific study of social behaviour' (p. xxviii). On the following page they assert that 'experiments are the best way to confirm or refute theories of social behaviour' (p. xxix). Another textbook asserts: 'Social psychology is a *science* because it uses the scientific method' (Hogg and Vaughan, 2011, p. 5, emphasis in original). We should note the wording. Social psychology is not *a* science because it uses *a* scientific method: it is a science because it uses *the* scientific method, as if there is a single method, which all scientists use, whatever their discipline. The authors then link the scientific method with doing experiments. They claim: 'Systematic experimentation is the most important research method in science' and that is why 'social psychology is largely experimental' (p. 9).

Such comments offer a clue about disciplinary anxieties. We would not expect a textbook of chemistry or physics to begin by emphasizing the scientific nature of their discipline. It would not occur to readers that chemistry or physics might be anything other than scientific. For instance, the word 'scientific' does not appear at all in the text of *Introductory Biomechanics* (Ethier and Simmons, 2007). The authors of *Solid State Chemistry* make no mention that the discipline, which they are introducing, is scientific or experimental. On the first page they declare that solid state chemistry is based on the need to understand the structure of crystals and that this is accomplished through X-ray crystallography (Smart and Moore, 2005, p. 1). They do not then add words to the effect 'and this makes our subject very scientific indeed'.

There are other differences between introductory textbooks in psychology and the natural sciences (Smyth, 2001). Biology textbooks tend to present the 'facts' of the discipline without saying who had discovered those facts and how they had discovered them. Psychology textbooks, by contrast, describe experiments and justify any generalizations in terms of the experimental evidence, as if psychologists are less confident of their facts than are natural scientists. Psychologists have no periodic table of unquestioned 'facts' to support their science, nor discoveries to match those of the circulation of the blood or the structures of crystals. Worse still, many of the firm 'facts' that psychologists in the past have announced to the world, such as those based on IQ tests or personality inventories, have a habit of collapsing into controversy. For example, analysts have been recently questioning whether the measures of 'self-esteem', which social psychologists have used in literally thousands of studies, actually predict any important behavioural responses (Scheff and Fearon, 2004).

Again, social psychologists are doubly exposed. The topics of social psychology are, by and large, topics about which ordinary people can be expected to have opinions – for example, whether everyone has prejudices, whether opposites attract, whether we can trust our first impressions of other people etc., etc. Non-specialists tend not to have firm opinions about the structure of crystals or the biomechanical properties of the elbow. Accordingly, social psychologists often claim that their scientific experiments have provided them with a knowledge which surpasses the opinions of non-experts. In *Social Psychology*, Kenneth Bordens and Irwin Horowitz claim that without scientific social psychology we might as well just ask our grandmothers about how people behave. However, modern social psychology, by being scientific, provides an advance on 'bubba psychology' (2001, p. 256).

Smith and Mackie (2000) explain at the start of their textbook that we cannot rely on our ordinary common sense, for it often provides contrary nuggets of wisdom: such as birds of a feather flock together and opposites attract. Both maxims might sound reasonable but which is correct? They cannot both be. Hence, we need scientific evidence to sort out which one is correct. This sounds promising. It might reassure first year students that they are embarking on studying something worthwhile. By the time they get to the end of their textbook, they might notice that the promises have not really been delivered. After nearly 600 pages of scientific evidence,

Smith and Mackie summarize some of the main discoveries of social psychology. The authors list 'the principle of superficial versus extensive processing' as one of the key findings. This principle says that we make snap judgements when the stakes are low but 'give considerable thought to matters of importance' (2000, pp. 586–7).

The principle of superficial versus extensive processing: it sounds impressive, just like a proper scientific principle. The word 'processing' has a technical quality. In effect, the principle states that sometimes we think deeply and sometimes we react unthinkingly – and we tend to think deeply when the stakes are high and react unthinkingly when the stakes are low. Now, there's something that would never have occurred to an untrained grandmother. Almost certainly she would not have thought of transforming the verb 'to think' into the noun 'processing'.

Gerd Gigerenzer is a psychologist, who is deeply critical of the ways that many psychologists conduct their so-called scientific enquiries. He has complained that social psychologists have a habit of proposing explanations which are not proper explanations. They are merely pseudo-explanations, re-describing in technical language the very thing, which is to be explained. Gigerenzer (2010) recalls Molière's parody of Aristotle offering a pseudo-explanation for the effects of opium. Why does opium make us sleepy? Because it possesses dormative properties. Why do we give considerable thought to important matters? Because the principle of extensive processing is operating.

Concepts as nouns

Not only do experimental social psychologists want to improve on ordinary, unscientific common sense, but they also want to go beyond the chaotic, unscientific language that ordinary, non-specialists use. They want technical terms to describe the sorts of things and processes that they claim to discover in their laboratories. In Chapter 4, I quoted the social psychologist, Daryl Bem, arguing that ordinary words were too imprecise and too burdened with extra meanings for the purposes of scientifically minded social scientists. Hence, social psychologists formulate their own concepts, over which they can exert precise control. At least, that is the official justification for the use of technical terminology. As we shall see, the practice is rather different.

When social psychologists feel the need for new technical terminology, they, like other social scientists, tend to devise nouns and noun phrases: they use terms such as 'deindividuation', 'superordinate identity', 'ideocentrism', 'meta-contrast ratio', 'social schemata' etc. It is easy to see why writers would find technical terms convenient. One long noun can do the job of several smaller words. It is simpler to use the word 'deindividuation', rather than repeatedly employ a clause such as 'being in a state of mind of not feeling oneself to be an individual whom others might recognize'. Therefore, Philip Zimbardo (1969), who has enjoyed a long and distinguished career in experimental social psychology, adopted this word when he studied the behaviour of crowds; and this is one reason why many subsequent researchers have continued to use this handy, technical term.

Nouns and noun phrases dominate social psychology, as they do in other branches of the social sciences. Social psychologists investigate topics such as 'identification' rather than people identifying; 'attitudes' rather than people attitudinizing; 'social representations', rather than people socially representing (for a lack of studies of 'socially representing', see Billig, 2008a). In each case, the topic is described by a noun rather than a clause or a verb. Later in this chapter, I will look at a phenomenon which social psychologists have recently spent much experimental effort in examining: people reacting automatically to signs or words. Social psychologists prefer to go beyond the clausal description of 'people reacting automatically to signs' and they identify the general phenomenon by a single, specially constructed noun – 'automaticity'.

I have already mentioned Henri Tajfel's important article, 'Cognitive Aspects of Prejudice' (1969). Tajfel argued that prejudice rests upon ordinary, rather than upon extraordinary, mental factors. He pointed to the importance of three processes by which we give meaning to the social world. He used a noun or noun phrase to describe each of these processes: categorization, assimilation and the search for coherence. Instead of using verbal participles, categorizing, assimilating and searching for coherence, Tajfel described the processes syntactically as if they were entities, rather than actions being performed by people.

The question is not whether it is correct for experimental social psychologists to invent technical terms. Given the nature of academic inquiry today, it is inevitable that they do, although there is no intrinsic reason why their invented terminology should be weighted in favour of nouns rather than verbs – and, as I have argued, there are good reasons to reverse this imbalance. The real question, however, is whether social psychologists are living up to the standards by which they justify using technical terminology. Are they actually improving on the alleged imperfections of ordinary language? The evidence, as we shall see, does not clearly favour the experimentalists over the grandmothers.

I want to consider the concept of 'social categorization', which has been widely used by social psychologists. This concept lies at the heart of Henri Tajfel's work, especially his 'Social Identity Theory', which has become one of the main developments in social psychology over the past thirty years. The concept also provides the mainstay of 'Self-Categorization Theory' which John Turner originally developed as a branch of Social Identity Theory and which has been influential in its own right (e.g., Turner, 1987). 'Social categorization' is a central component of other outgrowths such as Leadership Categorization Theory (Hogg, 2010) and the Elaborated Social Identity Model (Drury and Reicher, 2000). I should also add that the concept formed the topic of my own doctoral research many years ago.

First, we can note that the concept of 'social categorization' is not self-evidently clear. The term bears out what Douglas Biber says about the noun phrases that academics formulate: the relation between the individual words is frequently ambiguous and so you cannot tell what the phrases mean without belonging to the circles, in which the phrase is being used (Biber and Gray, 2010). The word 'social' in 'social categorization' could refer either to the subject or the object of the categorizing. It could be describing instances where the act of categorizing is being performed socially rather than being performed by a lone individual. On the other hand, 'social' could be referring to the object of categorization – where, for instance, a social group, not a physical object, is being categorized, whether or not by a lone individual or a group of people. In fact, social psychologists tend to use 'social categorization' in the second sense. Leadership Categorization Theory is a theory about the ways that people categorize leaders, not how leaders categorize, and certainly not how leaders categorize theories. You have to be on the inside to know these things: you cannot infer them simply from looking at the meanings of the words.

Like linguists using their word 'nominalization', experimental social psychologists use 'categorization' and 'social categorization' quite loosely, to indicate both processes and entities and as both a count noun and a mass noun. Like 'nominalization', experts mostly define 'categorization' as a process. The entry on 'social categorization' in *The Blackwell Encyclopedia of Social Psychology* opens with the statement that 'this process cuts to the very heart of social psychology' (Spears, 1995, p. 530). In 'Cognitive Aspects of Prejudice', Tajfel described 'categorization' as a process, without specifying what type of process it might be. He was principally discussing how people use categories of language in acts of stereotyping, such as describing Scandinavians as 'tall' or Italians as 'short': to do this people need to use language categories both for the groups, which they are stereotyping, and for the traits which are being ascribed to those groups. People, however, can use these group categories to perform very different acts of categorizing. For instance, speakers can categorize by acts of deciding, of asserting, of sorting, or merely by using a particular word when making claims about what is happening in the world (Edwards, 1991). There is, in short, no single act of categorizing.

In 'Cognitive Aspects', Tajfel quoted from Gordon Allport, to the effect that categorization introduces order and simplicity into the psychological world. Allport was not just referring to the use of language, but also more generally to cognitive, or mental, processes. Cognitive scientists tend to use 'categorization' in this sense, referring to mental (and therefore unobservable) processes by which the mind (or brain) groups stimuli according to their properties. Thus, animals, which have no language, will be said to engage in this sort of categorization in order to make their sensory world meaningful, for example implicitly categorizing stimuli as 'food' and 'non-food', 'predator' or 'non-predator'. Other social psychologists also treat the concept of 'social categorization' in this cognitive way. For example, Rupert Brown, who studied under Tajfel and who has contributed much to the study of prejudice, describes categorization as 'a fundamental process' which is 'an inescapable feature of human existence'. Like Tajfel, Brown mentions Allport and the use of language categories, and he specifically states that 'categorization is a cognitive process' (Brown, 1995, p. 41).

So, social psychologists use the term 'categorization' to describe very different sorts of processes. Categorization is something that an individual perceiver might accomplish mentally. In this case, the perceiver might be categorizing automatically and without conscious awareness, as stimuli are grouped together in the act of perception. There again, categorization could be an outward, social act, involving the explicit use of language, as the person declares that someone is a member of a particular group. A speaker can perform many different sorts of overt act which can count as 'categorization'. Thus, social psychologists use the concept of 'categorization' to refer to an individual or a social process, a mental or a linguistic process, a conscious or an unconscious process. All can be lumped together under the heading 'social categorization'.

It is like linguists describing very different sorts of processes as 'nominalization'. Actually, the parallel goes further. Just as linguists sometimes use 'nominalization' to describe entities as well as processes, so social psychologists use 'social categorization' to describe entities. John Turner (1987), in outlining his self-categorization theory, wrote: 'A social categorization may be defined as a cognitive representation of a social division into groups' (p. 27). Turner is not defining 'social categorization' as the process by which a social division into groups is made; nor as the process by which a representation of such a division is formed. No, it is the representation itself that he is defining as 'a social categorization'. By referring to 'a social categorization', he is using 'categorization' as a count noun; by contrast, those who use the term to describe a process usually use it as a mass noun, without singular or plural. Turner makes plain that by 'social categorization', he is referring to a cognitive, not a linguistic, representation. As a cognitive entity, a 'social categorization' cannot be observed directly and its existence can only be inferred. Turner does not specify the things, or processes, from which we might infer the existence of 'a social categorization'. In this account 'a social categorization' may be a thing, but it is a highly nebulous sort of thing.

Social psychologists do not seem unduly bothered by the profusion of meanings which have gathered around the concept of 'social categorization'. The major journals of experimental social psychology tend not to publish articles that analyse the meanings of major concepts. They prefer new experimental studies. The general lack of concern with the precise use of words is illustrated by a small, intrinsically unimportant rhetorical habit that many followers of social identity theory show: the habit of writing about 'social categorization processes'. Greenland and Brown (2000), for example, begin a chapter, examining the relations between categorization, intergroup anxiety and intergroup contact, with the statement: 'One of the main contributions of social identity theory to the contact hypothesis has been to emphasize categorization processes' (p. 167). A recent experimental study claims to be addressing the problem how 'social categorization processes' might affect empathy (Tarrant, Dazely and Cottom, 2009, p. 443).

Of course, neither statement is likely to mislead or worry its readers, the majority of whom will be fellow experimental social psychologists. Nevertheless, both statements are curious. As we have seen, Brown, like many other social psychologists working in this area, defines 'categorization' as a process. If categorization is a process, then what are 'categorization processes' or 'social categorization processes'? Are they processes of processes, or, to be a bit mathematical, the sum of processes squared? The crucial question is not 'What is a social categorization process?' but 'Why are social psychologists not bothered by the idea?' How is it that they can read (and write) about 'social categorization processes' without noticing anything semantically strange about the phrase? They might take it for granted that ordinary language is nowhere near as precise as their own terminology; but by their own actions, they show that precision is not the point of their own exercises.

A world of variables, not a world of people

So far, I have concentrated on the way that social psychologists define concepts such as 'social categorization'. If that looked messy, with social psychologists offering different sorts of definitions for the same terms, then things are about to get even messier. The definitions do not tell us how experimental social psychologists actually use their concepts in practice. Here, we will see something curious. Theoretically, social psychologists try to create a pure world of variables, describing what happens when one variable meets another variable. But, in practice, there is virtual anarchy in the way that social psychologists turn their pure variables into experimental manipulations.

For experimentalists, 'social categorization' can never be just an interesting idea, but it has to be something that can be transformed into an experimental variable, to be investigated experimentally along with other variables. In the previous section, I mentioned studies that looked at the effect of categorization on empathy (Tarrant, Dazely and Cottom, 2009), or examined how categorization related to intergroup anxiety (Greenland and Brown, 2000). On the basis of their experimental results, experimentalists will seek to construct theories that formulate general statements about the relations between variables. In their theories, social psychologists will be depicting a world of interacting variables, rather than a world of interacting people. They will not stop there. The theoretical work is a step towards conducting further experiments to support the theoretical ideas. These experiments will give rise to further statements about the relations between variables, and these statements will, in their turn, necessitate more experiments. The business, happily, is without a foreseeable finish, but this world of variables tends to become increasingly self-enclosed and detached from the world of actual people.

Social psychologists routinely 'operationalize' their concepts. That means that they transform a concept, which they wish to examine, into an experimental procedure. For example, Henri Tajfel conducted a classic series of experiments which have become known as the 'minimal group experiments'. Using the language of variables, one might say that Tajfel wanted to see whether a meaningless social categorization could be sufficient to produce some sort of group identification (Tajfel et al., 1971). In the classic minimal group experiment, the procedure involved the experimenters telling the participants, who were young boys, that they were members of 'Group Y' rather than 'Group X'. The act of social categorization seems clear: the experimenters were doing the categorizing. Social categorization here is not presumed to be an internal cognitive process, but it is an overt social act which the experimentalists perform through language by telling others something. In this experiment, there seems to be a straightforward tie-up between the concept of 'social categorization' and the experimental procedure.

Gerd Gigerenzer, whose criticisms of experimental social psychology I briefly mentioned earlier, has complained that there is often a huge gap between the concepts that social psychologists use theoretically and the way that they operationalize these concepts in their experiments (Gigerenzer and Brighton, 2009; see also Katzko, 2006). Certainly this is true of 'social categorization'. Experimentalists have operationalized this variable in a multitude of different ways. Some of these bear little relation to the way that Tajfel examined 'social categorization' in the original minimal group experiments. It would take an enormous, and not particularly profitable, labour to document the different experimental actions (and entities) that social psychologists have called 'social categorization'. I will, instead, give a couple of examples from studies that I have already mentioned.

Tarrant, Dazely and Cottom (2009), in their study on categorization and empathy, examine how university students rate another student, who is described as being in a distressing situation. The experimenters wanted to see how much empathy the real students would show for this hypothetical student. In one condition, the hypothetical student is identified as attending the same university as the real students. In another condition, the hypothetical student attends a neighbouring university. The experimenters operationalize 'social categorization' in terms of the way that they describe a hypothetical student. The experimenters are not actually engaged in categorizing the participants in the experiment, as they were in Tajfel's experiment; nor, as far as the participants are concerned, are the experimentalists engaged in an actual act of categorizing. The mere act of using the name of a university here counts as 'social categorization'. It is as if any statement, which mentions where someone else lives, works or studies, is an act of 'social categorization'.

Greenland and Brown (2000) describe how they studied 'group categorization' and its effect on 'intergroup anxiety' in a sample of Japanese students, studying in the United Kingdom. They operationalize the variable of 'group categorization' somewhat differently. Greenland and Brown describe 'intergroup categorization' in terms of being 'aware of nationalities and culture' (p. 175). In this case, just being aware of other nationalities counts as 'categorization', even if there is no overt act (whether on the part of the participants or the experimenters) of categorizing. Here we find the concept of 'categorization', which in any case started off in a rather baggy condition, becoming even baggier.

The aim of the experiments is not to find out what the people actually do in the experiments, but it is to see the effects of key experimental variables on other variables. The people, taking part in the experiments, are ciphers for testing what the variables apparently do to each other. The experimenters, in formulating their theoretical statements, depict the variables as actors in this world of interlocking variables. It is variables, rather than people, who do things in this strange world of variables.

The article about categorization and empathy contains a number of statements that describe variables interacting with other variables. Generally these are unpopulated statements: 'Self-categorization theory argues that once a social identity is made salient there is a depersonalization of the self – an enhanced perception of the self and other members of one's group as interchangeable – which in turn facilitates group behaviour' (Tarrant, Dazely and Cottom, 2009, p. 428). Social identity is made salient: the authors do not say who does this and how they do it. And depersonalization facilitates group behaviour. All this seems to occur without human intervention, as one depersonalized variable nudges another into action. It is like observing a spectacle of automata, as each figure artfully releases a spring to set the next one into motion.

The authors write of their own research results: 'Empirically articulating the link between self-categorization, empathic experience and helping intentions helps explain previous research which has shown an effect of social categorization on helping behaviour' (p. 439). Again: look, no people. But, look again. The authors are assuming that previous research has studied 'social categorization', just as they have done. It is as if there is a thing called 'social categorization', not a range of very different activities, which social psychologists are stuffing into the ever expanding portmanteau of 'social categorization'.

There is irony in the way that social psychologists can categorize many different things and processes as 'social categorization'. Their own use of the category of 'categorization' is providing evidence for Tajfel's ideas. When we group things together under the same category, Tajfel claimed that we are liable to treat these things as if they were more similar to each other than they actually are (Tajfel, 1981). Social psychologists are calling a range of different actions and entities 'social categorization'. The danger is that they exaggerate the similarities between all these different things, processes and actions. We see this in the way that social psychologists try to formulate general theories of 'social categorization' – as if this were a definite entity that might affect other entities and processes in a regular manner. One might think it strange that social psychologists can write in general terms about the possible distortions of 'categorization' without pausing to consider whether this affects their own 'categorizations' – including their categorization of 'categorization'.

The language of variables offers a cumbersome, noun-filled way of talking about what people do. Typically it is less subtle and less precise than the normal clausal way of talking about actions. In Chapter 6,

I discussed how researchers often use the passive voice when describing their procedures. I gave an example from an experiment, which was examining whether white Australians, who had aboriginal friends, were more willing to meet aboriginal Australians than those who did not have aboriginal friends. The authors present the thinking behind their study. They use two sentences, of which the first is impersonal and describes a pure world of interlocking variables. The second describes people:

> Whereas intergroup anxiety is by now an established mediator of intergroup contact and cross-group friendship, the present study also sought to explore cognitions of rejection as a cognitive mediator predicted by cross-group friendship, and predictive of intergroup anxiety, as well as a range of attitudes towards the outgroup. Specifically, we propose that people with cross-group friends cease to expect outgroup members to reject their attempts at contact and friendship (Barlow, Louis and Hewstone, 2009, p. 391).

These two adjacent sentences are very different in style. The first sentence is heavy with noun phrases such as 'cognitive mediator', 'intergroup anxiety', 'cognitions of rejection'. It is entirely unpopulated. The second sentence seems to rephrase the first sentence, translating it from the world of variables to a world populated with 'people', 'friends' and 'outgroup members'.

We can see how the noun phrases of the first sentence appear as clauses in the second: 'cognitions of rejection' becomes a clause about expecting 'outgroup members to reject their attempts at contact and friendship'. A thing – 'intergroup friendship' – is changed into people: 'cross-group friends'. In describing the rationale for the study the authors move from unpopulated to populated phrasing. In the first sentence, we learn that 'the present study also sought to explore . . .', as if the study possessed the motives for exploration. The second sentence is more direct and personal: 'we propose . . .'

If the two sentences seem to be saying something similar, but in different ways, then why do the authors need both? Surely the first one – the one using the scientific phrasing – should suffice. It depicts the world of variables, with things such as 'intergroup anxiety' and 'cognitions of rejection' affecting one another, or acting as 'mediators'. How exactly the variables do this, the authors leave unclear. It is the second sentence that is more specific. The authors state that people with intergroup friends 'cease to expect' outgroup members to reject them. The nature and the direction of the mediation, as well as its unfolding over time, are specified: people, who once expected aboriginal Australians to reject them, stop expecting this when they acquire aboriginal Australians as friends. In short the second sentence contains more information and clarity than the first.

This is not just my interpretation. The authors indicate this, by their use of the first word of the second sentence: 'Specifically'. It is a revealing word. The authors could have reversed the order of the two sentences, and started the technical statement with 'specifically'. That would have implied that the 'ordinary' statement was too vague. But they do not do this. Instead, they indicate that the theoretically worded statement needs to be supported by an ordinary statement that specifies what is going on, in terms of people, their actions and their feelings. This is an interesting admission. It appears to confirm that the pure world of variables poorly describes the world of people.

What's going on? How many?

For years, experimental social psychology has been marked by baggy concepts, operationalized baggily. It is small wonder that, despite all the experimental testing, questions never seem to be properly resolved. How could they be, when the technical concepts have so many different meanings, whether in theory or in experimental practice? Years ago, Paul Meehl, the great expert in the methodology of psychology, noted that in social psychology, theories are rarely refuted or decisively corroborated. According to Meehl, it is a sad fact that in social psychology 'theories rise and decline, come and go, more as a function of baffled boredom than anything else' (1978, p. 49). If anything, the situation has become even worse since Meehl was writing. The number of theories has increased, and not just because social psychology, like other academic disciplines, has expanded. Gigerenzer (2010) has said that psychologists treat theories like toothbrushes: no one would wish to use someone else's. Today, social psychologists are eager to present small changes of emphasis, regarding which variable should count as the key one, as a separate theory, equipped with its official label and acronym. Supporters of these mini-theories then do battle on the pages of the journals. After each experimental skirmish, no one surrenders, but back come the protagonists for more of the same. This carries on until a new troop is spotted advancing over the horizon, carrying in their bags fresh supplies of data and big words.

For experimental social psychologists doing experiments is the great glory of their discipline. And the greatest glory of all is to produce statistically significant results. The top journals rarely publish experimental reports that fail to report significant differences. Over the years, social psychologists have developed conventional ways of doing research which aspiring doctoral students must acquire. Successful careers will be the reward for following these procedures assiduously and for obeying the productive logic of the world of variables. But there is one thing that success will not bring: that you will actually know what is going on in the experiments that you read about or, indeed, in the experiments that you conduct. In fact, your expertise will teach you how not to know what is going on.

That sounds an extraordinary claim. To understand why I am making it, it is necessary to look at the way social psychologists design their experiments, analyse their results and write about their findings. Suppose that you wanted to conduct an experiment, in order to test whether 'social categorization' affects the degree of empathy, you might do something very similar to what Tarrant, Dazely and Cottom (2009) did. You randomly divide your participants into two groups. The participants in both groups are faced by almost identical experimental tasks. The only difference is that half the participants are asked to rate a hypothetical member of their own university, and that the other half rate a hypothetical member of a neighbouring university. You then calculate the 'empathy' scores for the two groups and apply some statistical analyses ('t' tests and/or analyses of variance) to discover whether there are statistically significant differences between scores of the groups of participants. If there are, you then have the makings of a publication. If not, then you must try again, modifying your procedure. When you come to writing your article, you will present the mean scores of the two groups, together with the results of the statistical tests showing significant differences. Having presented your evidence, then you can conclude that social categorization affects empathy.

This is a standard design for social psychological experiments, to be found again and again in the journals. Students will be taught how to design such experiments, how to feed their data into a computer and how to select appropriate statistical tests. They will learn that they should draw conclusions about the effects of 'categorization' (or about the effects of whatever variable they are experimentally investigating) only if the computer printout for the program of statistical tests shows 'significant' differences. A 'significant' difference is one where the value of 'p' (or the probability value of obtaining those particular differences by chance) is 0.05 or less.

In essence, Tarrant et al. followed these sorts of procedures. In Experiment 1, they found that participants rating a member of their own university had a mean empathy score of 7.40, whereas participants rating a member of a neighbouring university had a mean empathy score of 6.13. Applying analyses of variance and 't' tests, the authors reported that these differences were statistically significant. They also did more complicated analyses, involving several other variables, with the aim of assessing the relative strengths of their various variables. There was also something they did not do: they did not present the scores of any individual respondent.

Why should this matter? According to Gigerenzer it matters greatly. He accuses most psychologists of mindlessly using statistics, without under-standing the assumptions of the tests that they use (Gigerenzer, 2004 and 2006). Gigerenzer stresses that mean scores are unreal. No one would actually score 7.40 or 6.13 on the empathy test that Tarrant et al. used – just as no couple actually has 2.46 children although that may be the mean score for a particular population. Tarrant's test of empathy, like virtually every other test used by social psychologists, yielded a range of scores. The authors, following common practice, present the 'standard deviation' (or a measure of the spread of scores), along with the means.

Gigerenzer argues powerfully that you cannot really understand what people are doing in the experimental situation if you only know the mean scores and the standard deviations. To understand your experiment, you have to look at individual scores. Gigerenzer suggests that analysing individual scores gives real benefits: it allows 'researchers to minimize the real error, to recognize systematic individual differences, and – last but not least – to know one's data' (Gigerenzer, 2006, p. 248). He might have added that dealing with individual scores also allows the researcher to escape from the unreal world of variables.

In his own research, Gigerenzer is interested in the way that people make decisions. He uses simple language when describing the heuristics, or principles, that his participants use to make decisions. He writes about participants using guidelines such as 'if there is a default, do nothing' or 'consider the majority of people in your peer group and imitate their behaviour'. These descriptions – which are clausal and non-technical – better describe how participants are thinking than do the technical terms, like superficial and extensive processing, that most social psychologists use to describe decision-making (Gigerenzer and Brighton, 2009, p. 109). Gigerenzer also formulates a guiding principle that social psychologists should use when analysing their data: 'Do not test what the average individual does, because systematic individual differences may make the average meaningless' (p. 132).

There is one crucial piece of evidence lacking in most experimental social psychology reports today: frequency scores. Although writing about the significant effects of particular variables, the authors typically do not say exactly how many of the participants might have been affected by the variable in question. As we shall see, when statistically significant differences are found, the reports usually imply that all participants were affected. That implication has to be a fiction.

It is easy to say why the mean scores might be less informative than frequency scores. What does it tell us that 'empathy is experienced more strongly for ingroup members than it is for outgroup members'? (Tarrant, Dazely, Cottom, 2009, p. 433). Of course, it tells us that the overall mean scores are 'significantly' different: 7.40 as compared with 6.13. But that is telling us something about fictional groups, not about actual individuals. The mean scores are not greatly different. If the individual scores for both samples were plotted, there would be considerable overlap between the two groups.

What does such a finding mean in psychological terms? There are different possibilities. It could be that everyone is just a little bit more empathetic towards ingroup members than towards outgroup members. Or it could be that some people are much more empathetic to ingroup members, but others show no difference between ingroup and outgroup members. You could get the same mean differences either way. If it is not everybody who is affected then how many are? Statistically, it does not have to be a majority. We could get statistically significant differences between the two groups of participants, even if the crucial variables were only affecting a minority of the participants. That is the problem. Although the authors write about empathy being experienced more strongly for ingroup members than outgroup members as if it were a general finding, we simply do not know for how many of the participants it is true. From the data presented, there is no way of finding out.

This is part of a wider problem in experimental social psychology and, more generally in the social sciences – a problem which the economists Stephen Ziliak and Deirdre McCloskey have called the 'cult of statistical significance' (Ziliak and McCloskey, 2008). Empirical researchers are using statistics to demonstrate the existence of a so-called 'significant difference' between two populations, rather than enquiring about the size and nature of any differences. It is as if the search for significant differences has become an end in itself. Having found the precious statistically significant difference, researchers then treat populations as if they were entirely different. According to Ziliak and McCloskey, this has led researchers in the social sciences to misuse statistics and to misunderstand the assumptions of the statistical tests that they use (see also Lambdin, 2012).

Of course, not all writers of reports in experimental social psychology have followed the cult of the significant difference and have avoided presenting frequency data. One of the most famous of all experiments – Milgram's studies of obedience – did not contain complex statistics.

Milgram (1974) did not need to use statistical tests in order to demonstrate how striking his results were. He presented the frequencies of those giving supposedly dangerous electric shocks when told to: in his basic conditions roughly seventy per cent of his subjects obeyed to the full extent. That is meaningful data, not least because it tells you how many did not obey.

In terms of today's experimental practices, Milgram's way of presenting his results looks decidedly old-fashioned. In fact, one notable social psychologist has speculated that the editors of leading social psychological journals are now so fixated with sophisticated statistics, and with valuing the appearance of being scientific over genuine innovation, that Milgram would have trouble publishing his work today (Reicher, 2011). The journal editors would probably tell him to go back and analyse his result properly – and, as we shall see, that would mean making it more difficult for readers to see what happened in his experiments.

Trying to discover what is going on

Milgram's dramatic findings appeared to show that many ordinary people were prepared to obey an immoral order that was potentially harmful to an innocent victim, although whether that is quite what they showed is open to debate (e.g., Gibson, in press). Actually, Milgram's experiment would not be permitted today, because there are now ethical codes to prevent experimenters from systematically deceiving their participants and submitting them to the stress that Milgram did. Notwithstanding these restrictions, it is still possible for experimenters to design experiments that appear to produce unexpected, impressive findings. We can appreciate the dramatic nature of Milgram's findings, for we know how many of his participants were prepared to deliver the highest level of electric shock. However, as I want to suggest, it can be difficult to find out the equivalent information for today's seemingly dramatic experiments. In suggesting this, I should stress that I am not arguing against doing experiments, but I am criticizing the practices that experimenters currently use to analyse and present their results.

Experimentalists have produced some striking results in the area of 'automaticity' or 'priming'. They show participants being unconsciously influenced by an unimportant or passing stimulus: sometimes the stimulus is shown too quickly for the participants to be aware that they have seen it and sometimes it is so trivial that it would not have specifically caught their attention. When the participants are in a different situation, experimentalists note how their behaviour or thinking has actually been influenced by these prior stimuli. It all seems to happen without conscious awareness. John Bargh, a social psychologist at Yale University, is one of the leading exponents of this type of research. He writes that 'the past twenty-five years have seen amazing empirical advances in our knowledge of the kinds of psychological concepts and processes that can be primed or put into motion nonconsciously' (2006, p. 147). We might note in passing that 'prime' is one of the comparatively few technical concepts in social psychology that is a verb. Experimentalists write about priming their participants, by presenting them briefly with a particular stimulus whose effects they will assess in a later, different context. We can also note that, when it comes to making formal theoretical statements, Bargh and his colleagues tend to prefer the noun 'automaticity' to describe the phenomenon that they are studying.

John Bargh is the first author of a classic experimental study of 'automaticity' (Bargh, Chen and Burrows, 1996). In this paper, Bargh and his colleagues reported a series of experiments that demonstrated that stimuli, conveying a stereotype, could in a different context elicit participants to behave unconsciously in ways that conformed to the stereotype. The experimental results appear remarkable. Participants were asked to complete a word test; they had to form four-word sentences from five words which were presented to them. In one of the experiments, half the participants were presented with words that tended to be associated with rudeness and the other half with words associated with politeness. Then the respondents found themselves in a different situation where they were being kept waiting by an experimenter, who was talking with another person. Bargh wanted to see whether the participants would interrupt that conversation. He found that the participants, who had earlier received the words associated with rudeness, would interrupt sooner than those who had been given words associated with politeness. In another study, the participants were either given words associated with old age (e.g., 'old', 'grey', 'lonely' etc.) or neutral words. After completing this task, Bargh and his colleagues timed how long it took the participants to walk down a corridor. Again, there was a surprising effect. Those who had been exposed to the 'elderly' words (which did not include any terms specifically referring to slowness) walked more slowly than those who had not been exposed to such words. Interviews afterwards showed the participants were unaware that they had been influenced. Other participants, who were white, were subliminally shown the face of either a black male or white male. Those who had been shown the black male subsequently displayed more anger, when the experimenter had annoyed them by apparently losing their test results.

These are extraordinary findings. They demonstrate how participants can be influenced by apparently inconsequential stimuli. When such stimuli are associated with a stereotype, then participants automatically

seem to imitate some of the stereotyped behaviour. The young participants seemed to dawdle along the corridor like old folk; and they did this
just because they had been exposed to words like 'grey' and 'old'. Words
such as 'blunt', 'aggressive', 'bold' triggered participants to behave more
rudely than more neutral or polite words. Perhaps most worryingly of all, a
black face, which was presented too quickly for conscious perception,
made white participants respond more aggressively. Just like the old
Milgram experiment, very few people would have predicted these findings
in advance.

However, there is a big difference between Milgram's studies and those
of Bargh and his colleagues. Milgram provided his readers with frequency
scores – namely, how many of his participants obeyed or disobeyed the
experimenter. Bargh and his colleagues do not tell us how many of their
participants were, or were not, influenced by the priming stimuli. Instead,
the authors provide mean scores for their measures of displaying anger
and speed of walking. As we shall see, the measure for interrupting the
conversation provides a special case and the authors almost reveal the
crucial frequency scores. They manage, in the end, to hold back this
information. However, they let slip that the frequency of priming may
not be quite as widespread as it might at first sight appear.

Basically Bargh and his co-workers analysed the data in each of their
three experimental situations by comparing the scores of those who were
exposed to experimental stimuli with those exposed to control stimuli.
Thus, the ratings for displaying anger were obtained for all participants.
The scores of those participants, who had been subliminally exposed to
black faces, were compared with those who had not been subliminally
exposed to black faces. The mean difference for the two groups was not
great but it was found to be statistically significant. The statistics used do
not permit us to estimate what percentage of participants, who were
shown the black face, might have been influenced to display greater
anger than if they had seen a white face. We only know that as a group
they showed more anger. It is the same with the data about the speed of
walking. We do not know how many of those who had been exposed to the
'elderly' words slowed down their speed of walking. That is, we do not
know how many of the sample might have been affected by the priming
variable. This is important, because statistical tests are designed to pick up
small variations in the data from different samples. And if they do, then
researchers can label small variations as 'significant' variations, even
though the variable may be affecting only a minority of participants.

Bargh and his co-workers' first experiment (examining whether rudely
primed participants would interrupt a conversation more often and faster
than would participants who had been politely or neutrally primed)

encountered a statistical problem. Its data could not be analysed in the standard way, because too many participants overall did not interrupt at all. In consequence, the data, concerning the length of time it took to interrupt, was not 'normally' distributed: too many scores were bunched at the maximum end. The authors had to use a different sort of statistical test. The authors looked at the percentage of respondents who interrupted the conversation, in order to see whether the rude priming condition had a higher percentage of interrupters. This is the sort of data that tells us how many respondents might have been affected by the key variable. By knowing this, we should be able to estimate how many respondents were affected by the primes. In short, we should be able to get the frequency scores from the percentages.

Revealingly, the key information was not readily forthcoming in the paper. The authors do not present the frequencies – namely, how many participants in each condition interrupted the conversation. It would have been easy to present such data. Nor do they give the actual percentages, but they present the percentages visually in a histogram without specifying the numbers (Bargh, Chen and Burrows, 1996, p. 235, Figure 1). The histogram suggests that fewest respondents in the polite condition interrupted and slightly more than sixty per cent did in the rude condition. The authors tell us that, using non-parametric statistics, the differences were significant. But this still does not tell us how many participants in each condition interrupted or did not interrupt.

It should be easy to calculate these frequencies from the visual display of the percentages. To do that, all one has to know is how many participants there were in each condition. Amazingly, this figure is not provided. We know that there were thirty-four participants overall, but not how many were in each of the three conditions. Even if we cannot find out the information with any certainty, we can make a rough estimate, assuming that there would be approximately similar numbers in each condition. It is possible (but not absolutely certain) that in the rude condition, eight participants interrupted and five did not. Does this mean that the majority of participants had been affected by the rude words? Not necessarily. We would have to know how many of those in the neutral condition interrupted. We then would assume that in the rude condition the same proportion of participants would interrupt anyway and that their interrupting could not be attributed to the influence of the rude stimuli.

We can only estimate the actual frequencies of those who interrupted in the neutral condition. On the basis of the percentages that are visually represented in the histogram, two possibilities seem likely. Either four out of eleven of those exposed to the neutral words interrupted, or five out of thirteen did. If we assume that there were equal numbers of participants in the rude and neutral conditions, then comparisons between the two conditions are much easier. So, let us for the sake of convenience, assume that five out of thirteen interrupted in the neutral condition. That would be three participants fewer than the number in the experimental condition. From these numbers, we would be justified in saying that in the rude condition, the priming stimuli might have influenced three of the participants to interrupt, for the other five who interrupted might have done so anyway even if they had not been exposed to the rude words. In consequence, this evidence suggests that no more than three out of thirteen participants – or twenty-three per cent – were influenced by the rude variable.

Once the results are expressed in terms of people, rather than mean group differences, they look considerably less dramatic. Of course, skilled social psychologists know how to apply statistical tests to maximize the possibility of obtaining significant results, especially when the differences between samples are comparatively small. Certainly, in the other experiments, which Bargh et al. present, the differences between the groups are small and there is no reason to suppose that, because statistical differences have been found, the key variable must be affecting the majority of participants in the experimental groups. In fact, with small differences, it is more reasonable to assume the opposite.

We should note that it is only because something went wrong in one of the experiments that we are able to come close to getting a glimpse of the frequencies. Had all occurred according to plan, we would have only seen the group means and significant differences. We would not have been in a position to estimate that only a minority of participants in the crucial condition might have been affected by the priming variable.

This is nothing to do with the abilities of the experimenters. On the contrary, it indicates their professionalism and without doubt Bargh is a highly proficient experimentalist. The study was accepted to be published in the highest rated journal in social psychology. Neither the editor nor the reviewers would have found anything untoward in the authors' methods of analysis or in their ways of presenting data. That is exactly the point. The accepted procedures, when followed with due propriety, do not enable us to find out what was going on in the experiments. They seem, in fact, designed to prevent us from finding out basic information. Even when something goes wrong and the authors come close to using the frequency data, they do not make it easy for readers to ascertain what might have happened at the level of individual participants. One can presume that authors, editors and reviewers do not consider it important to find out how many of the participants (or, rather, how few of them) might have been affected by the variable whose effects were being investigated and whose significance was being proclaimed.

Writing about what happened

If experimental social psychologists often do not know how many of their participants were affected by the key experimental variable, then how do they write about their results? How is it possible that they can describe what the variable supposedly does without knowing much about the individual participants? The answer is that experimental social psychologists have developed conventional ways for describing their results which not only are vague, but which also manage rhetorically to produce the effect of exaggerating their findings. So, in a manner of speaking, exaggeration follows concealment.

The rhetoric is interesting. Let us return to the experiment about categorization and empathy. Small differences in the scores for participants rating the ingroup figure as compared with participants rating for the outgroup figure led the authors to conclude that 'empathy is experienced more strongly for ingroup members than it is for outgroup members' (Tarrant, Dazely and Cottom, 2009, p. 433). The clause is phrased in the passive voice. Using the passive voice obviates the authors from describing who is experiencing the empathy and how many participants might have been doing so. Do all, most, some, or just a minority of participants feel more empathy for ingroup members? If you use the passive voice, you don't have to specify.

There is also a way of using the active voice that enables you to avoid specifying the proportion of participants involved. Tarrant et al. use this form when describing the results of their third experiment: 'Participants exposed to an ingroup empathy norm reported more positive attitudes towards the outgroup than did those exposed to an ingroup objective norm' (p. 439). Note the wording: 'participants'. It is not 'some participants', 'most participants' or 'the majority of participants'. It is simply the undifferentiated category 'participants'. This phrasing comes with an advantage. It implies 'all' without actually specifying it. 'Most', 'some' or 'the majority of' all imply exceptions. If some participants are said to do one thing, then this would imply that others did not do it. Were the authors to state that 'most participants reported more positive attitudes towards the ingroup', then they would be implying two things. First they would have implied that they knew how many participants had shown more positive attitudes – and, given the statistical analyses that they conducted, it is unlikely that they knew this. Second, they would be implying that there were some participants who did not show more positive attitudes.

On the other hand, if writers just refer to 'participants' acting in a particular way, they do not imply that there might have been exceptions. They treat the participants as if they were an undifferentiated category. This is, of course, a fiction. One thing we know for certain is that in nearly all social psychological experiments participants are differentiated both mathematically and psychologically. The participants, as they did in the Tarrant experiment, produce a range of scores; they do not act as if with a single, united voice. Typically the effects in social psychological experiments are small and the variations between participants are large. That is why statistical analysis is necessary.

Bargh and his colleagues use tropes that are common amongst experimental social psychologists. When they discuss the results of their experiments, they tend to do so in two ways. They either use the language of variables, describing, for example, stimuli activating cognitive stereotypes; or they describe what 'participants' did (e.g., Bargh, Chen and Burrows, 1996, p. 239). They do this even when discussing their first experiment, when too many participants in the rudeness group failed to interrupt. The authors still write about 'participants' in an undifferentiated way. Referring specifically to the interrupting of conversations, they write that 'participants primed with rudeness-related stimuli' interrupted a conversation faster 'and, as a group, more frequently than other participants' (p. 235).

This is an odd way of putting it. The participants in the rude condition did not act 'as a group'. They acted as individuals. Nevertheless, the social psychologists are treating them as a group – a fictional group. Rhetorically, this enables the writers to treat the members of the 'group' in an undifferentiated manner. The writers can say that these participants 'as a group' interrupted more frequently than those in the other groups. This again is odd, since no participants could actually interrupt frequently. Each participant either interrupted once or not at all. Talking about the participants as a group interrupting more frequently has further advantages. You do not have to imply that a sizeable number did not interrupt; additionally you do not have to specify how many did interrupt.

It is as if the experimenters are not really interested in what actually happens in the laboratory. If they were, they would be seeking to discover what distinguishes those participants who seem to be influenced by the key variable from those who are not. They would, for instance, be asking why some participants, who had encountered 'elderly' words walked slowly down that particular corridor, whereas others did not. Were the latter participants thinking of different matters? Had they used the 'elderly' words differently in the first part of the experiment? Instead of comparing individuals who were affected with those who were not, the experimenters treat all the participants as indistinguishable members of their experimental group. Thus, they concentrate on comparing those who encountered the elderly words with those who encountered other sorts of words, treating both as if they were undifferentiated groups. The experimenters are not interested in those who encountered elderly words and continued to walk briskly. They write as if such people did not exist.

The exaggerations do not stop there. When experimentalists quote previous experimental studies they often simplify the results. Michael Katzko (2006) has given a number of examples of the way that later authors have quoted the study by Bargh et al., sometimes presenting explanations of findings as if they were the findings themselves. I would like to give a recent example of the way that Bargh has described his own work. He and a colleague were writing about priming and how it leads 'participants' to pursue goals. They wrote that 'relevant stimuli (primes) automatically activate a goal representation' and 'the goal will then be pursued even though there is no conscious awareness of the primes, the active intention towards the goal or the active guidance of goal-directed thought or behaviour' (Shalit and Bargh, 2011, p. 490). This description is free of people: the authors use the passive voice (the goal is pursued, rather than specifying a person pursuing a goal); they write of conscious awareness and active intention, not people being aware or intending. Above all, there is a sense of interlocking mechanisms: the stimulus sets in motion the representation which, in its turn, sets in motion the behaviour.

The phrasing here – and elsewhere – suggests that the process runs like clockwork. First, we have the stimuli and these 'automatically' activate the representations (whether of goals, stereotypes or whatever). And 'then' the goal is pursued (or the behaviour imitated). The word 'automatically' is both crucial and ambiguous. It is theoretically important because the psychologists are studying reactions which people make without being aware that they are making them. Hence researchers have called their general topic 'automaticity'. So, the reactions are described as 'automatically' occurring in this sense.

At the same time, the word 'automatically' also has its non-technical, ordinary meaning. The writers are depicting a sequence of events in which things are said to happen *automatically*: you only have to show the primes, and the process is automatically set in motion. The word 'automatically' here implies that the sequence of events is inevitable. The lack of general specificity in the phrase 'the goal will then be pursued', together with the temporal specificity of 'then', underlines this sense of inevitability, as one thing inevitably follows another. The sequence starts to unfold automatically when the primes are displayed, no matter to whom. That, we know, is an exaggeration. What makes this particular exaggeration possible is that the word 'automatically' retains both its technical sense of unconsciousness and its ordinary sense of sequence. We do not see here social psychologists trying to free their technical terminology from ordinary meanings, as Bem implies. On the contrary, both meanings are necessary for making exaggerated claims. The psychologists can justify, if challenged, their use of the word by citing its technical meaning. But, in using the word, they can imply more than can be technically justified.

This is not an isolated lapse, but we can see something similar occurring when social psychologists use other technical words that retain a general, non-technical sense. The word 'significant' is an example. Here are the authors of a textbook writing about the results of one of the Bargh experiments: 'Participants who were primed with the elderly stereotype took significantly longer to reach the lift than did participants who had been primed with neutral words' (Stroebe, Hewstone and Jonas, 2008, p. 5). We can note the familiar undifferentiated use of the term 'participants', suggesting, but not stating, that all of these participants took longer. They did not merely take longer, but they took 'significantly longer'. Social psychologists, if pushed, might technically justify the use of the adverb, because the group differences were shown to be statistically significant.

Even in its statistical sense, the word 'significant' can be misleading. Most social psychologists assume that results, which are statistically significant (i.e., where the statistical probability yielded by the test is 0.05 or less), are firm and replicable. Social psychologists hardly ever conduct replications, not least because journal editors prefer 'original research', with statistically significant results, to replications of previous work. This preference wrongly assumes that the replication of an experiment is likely to yield similar 'p' values (and therefore similar levels of significance) to the original study. Actually that assumption is misguided: the 'p' score produced in a particular study tells us little about what 'p' score would emerge had other participants from the same population been tested in exactly the same way (Cumming, 2008).

However, the word 'significance' also has the wider, non-technical sense of importance, and social psychologists can use the word ambiguously, with both meanings possible, as if what is 'statistically significant' must be actually 'significant'. The textbook authors, who were describing Bargh's study, did not qualify their use of 'significantly' to say that they were only using the word in the statistical sense. Indeed the sentence comes in the introduction to their textbook, before they had even mentioned statistics and while they were giving readers a foretaste of interesting studies to come. In reality, the group differences in Bargh's experiments were small and unlikely to be noticed by those without stopwatches and statistical packages. If the authors of the textbook had wished to use 'significantly' in the general sense, it would have been more accurate had they claimed: 'A number of participants, who were primed with the elderly stereotype, took insignificantly longer to reach the lift than did a number of participants who had been primed with neutral words.'

We can see why experimentalists might not be keen to remove ordinary meanings from their technical terminology. These double-meaning words can be handy for making claims about experimental results. Experts can slide between technical and non-technical meanings, exaggerating without noticing that they are exaggerating, boosting the importance of chosen variables, theories and approaches. Even those who are trained in experimental methods can act, like some of the participants in the automaticity experiments, without being aware of just what they are doing.

Rhetoric and repression

When he was studying how people make decisions, Gerd Gigerenzer formulated the sort of principles that decision-makers must have followed in order to come to the decisions that they did. We could formulate principles for the rhetorical decisions that experimental social psychologists might make. These might include principles such as: 'Treat individuals as groups both rhetorically and statistically'; 'Write in a way that conveys that small effects are big ones and use the word "significant" to accomplish this'; 'Do not specify how many experimental participants were affected by the key variable, but write non-specifically as if they all were'; 'Don't exactly lie, but don't let your readers know how few participants may have been affected by the key variable.' Of course, none of the writers, whom I have been discussing, actually thinks like this. They would not follow such principles as a deliberate strategy. Yet, all of them act as if these were their principles, as I also did many years ago, when I was conducting experiments on social categorization and ingroup favouritism. I never consciously avoided calculating exactly how many participants had favoured members of their own group. I just automatically calculated group means and went on from there.

As a result, I know from personal experience that social psychologists write like this without consciously deciding to conceal and exaggerate, for they are following the institutionalized practices of their discipline. Experimental social psychologists learn established ways of proceeding and they take these procedures to be the proper, scientific ways of doing research. They do not notice the side effects of their procedures – namely that they end up concealing and exaggerating. Instead, they take their routine exaggerations as accurate representations of what happened experimentally. Indeed, experimental social psychologists would be affronted to be told that they regularly conceal and exaggerate. How could they be exaggerating when they are only being scientific? How indeed?

All this rests upon social psychologists treating their world of variables as more important – even more real – than the participants in their laboratory experiments. The actions of the participants are merely a means for understanding the effect of variable upon variable. The world of variables is much cleaner than the world of people. In practice, the participants tend to disappoint. Their actions are messier and less uniform than they should be. Luckily social psychologists have powerful statistical tests for extracting the important effects from the rest of the random, human dross. In this regard, they resemble old-time gold panners, sifting the precious metal from the accompanying grit and gravel. But gold panners are not environmental scientists, who want to understand how the geological elements fit together. The gold panner is only looking for the single, pure substance on which their fortune depends. All else can be thrown away. Social psychologists, having obtained their significant effects, can return safely to the pure world of variables, putting aside the participants, who have failed to show the golden effect.

Here lies the experimentalist's equivalent of repression. Repressing, in this sense, is not a hidden mental process, taking place in the depths of the psyche, but it is accomplished by uncritically following institutionally backed procedures. Experimentalists, just like participants who dawdle in corridors or who interrupt conversations, can react thoughtlessly and automatically. The more experienced they are, the more they will follow practices that have become second nature – and, in this respect, the more thoughtless they will be. Respected experimentalists do not have to think twice, when sitting at their computers, whether to type the word 'participants' with or without a qualification of quantity. Unaware of what they are doing, their fingers automatically key in, without qualification, 'participants'.

There is no conscious plan of concealment, no intention to deceive, but the experimentalist's practices – both statistical and literary – ensure that the participants, who fail to match up to the ideal world of variables, are collectively repressed from consciousness. They do not appear in the final report. No one seems to ask after them. Everyone talks about those who made the variable, and therefore the experiment, such a success. No one mentions those whose actions might have imperilled the successful outcome. They become non-persons. They disappear. Who would have guessed that a science would rely on repression?

As we have seen, adherents of this science will sometimes justify its superiority over common sense by pointing to the contradictions of common sense. The ordinary person will hold views that are odds with each other: birds of a feather flock together; opposites attract. Social psychologists, by collecting scientific evidence, will sort out these contradictions. But what sort of explanations do experimental social psychologists produce? Often their theories appear tautological. Priming stimuli, we are told, 'automatically activate a goal representation' which in turn leads to the goal being pursued (Shalit and Bargh, 2011, p. 490). How do we know that the 'goal representation' has been activated? Because the goal has been pursued. Why has the goal been pursued? Because the goal representation has been activated. Once again, it's the dormative properties of opium.

Then, there are the descriptions of what happened in the experiments: 'participants' did this; 'participants' did that. In virtually every instance in which 'participants' are described as doing something, there will be some participants who did not do this. Sometimes the latter may be as frequent, if not more frequent, than the former – mostly there is no way of telling, given the sort of information that authors provide for their readers. What this means is that both positive and negative statements may be equally true. Participants walked slower if exposed to 'old' words. That may be true of some participants, but not others. Therefore, it is equally true to say 'participants did not walk slower'.

Experimental social psychologists might criticize common sense for containing diametrically opposite statements. As far as their own experiments are concerned, they appear to solve this problem. Their solution, however, is rhetorical, rather than empirical. They write as if all participants behave in a standard way and they ignore those who do not. The negations of their positive statements remain unwritten, even unthought. Yet these negations remain as empirically viable as the positive statements. This is an odd sort of empirical science.

9   Conclusion and recommendations

In many academic books, the conclusion provides the place for authors to be optimistic. After chapters of hard travelling, buffeted between theory and doubt, an author can now settle back and tell readers why the journey has been so worthwhile. The author can say that their work promises to improve things, whether it is correcting theoretical misconceptions, striking out on new academic paths or offering to help with the problems of the wider world. I should now be slipping into this sunny upland mood. Yes, I have outlined problems with the ways that academics in the social sciences write. Yes, I have identified some of the linguistic features that lie at the root of these problems. And, yes, here in my conclusion, I will do what is expected: make some recommendations so that we can all move forward to a better future. Yet, I fear that I can recommend until I am fit to burst, but nothing much will change. My recommendations, whatever they are, will just be whispers in the wind.

There may, however, be some readers who are surprised that I could be arriving at the conclusion quite so early. I have claimed to be discussing how social scientists write, but I have only considered a tiny fraction of the social sciences – some linguistics, some sociology, some social psychology, a few theories about globalization and the media and a bit of conversation analysis. Where is the social anthropology? Political science? Social geography? Large-scale empirical sociology? Had I looked at management studies, I would surely have found some choice examples to boost my arguments. Worst of all, I have been focussing on social sciences that are published in English, or have been translated into English. Out there, there is literally a world of social sciences that I have ignored. In my mind, I can also hear some American social scientists complaining that there have been too few Americans here (although they will not put it like that).

Even when I seem to cover an area, I am only scratching about, touching on a particular approach or an individual study, while ignoring thousands of others. Readers, who have got this far, might be suggesting that things are much better in their disciplines, subdisciplines or own work.

Why haven't I discussed theory X or the important work that the followers of Professor Y have been doing? I have been arguing that today it is impossible to keep up with reading across any individual discipline, let alone across the social sciences as a whole. We have to pick and choose what we read, even in our own supposed areas of expertise; if we are not rigorously selective, we will be submerged by the continuing outpouring of new publications. In consequence, we struggle to know what is going on in our own backyard – let alone what our neighbours are doing in theirs.

If readers complain that I have insufficiently covered the social sciences, then I can only say in my defence that, in this sort of work, one should start with areas with which one is familiar. It is no good blundering into strange fields, criticizing how the writers there use concepts, whose intellectual history one cannot appreciate. If someone else would be willing to study how social anthropologists or management scientists are using long nouns, then they should do so. I have been presuming that what is happening in the areas, which I know about, will not be so different from what is going on elsewhere in the social sciences. After all, the underlying pressures of work are likely to be similar across the social sciences, with our shared managers using similar types of managerial rhetoric for which we academics in the social sciences should take some responsibility.

Of course, I may have been exaggerating, or at least overlooking the possibility of exceptions, for there may well be some approaches and subdisciplines where technical nouns do not have the status that they have in the areas that I have been discussing. Certainly, many historians are committed to telling historical stories in their full human complexity without recourse to specialist terminology. Their writings often differ from those of sociologists who give the past a sociological treatment. In Chapter 7, I discussed Foucault's notion that the nature of governing has changed in the modern era. This is essentially a historical idea which a number of sociologists are currently developing with the aid of the big noun – 'governmentality'. In this regard, sociologists, writing about the past, tend to resemble linguistically those sociologists who write about the present. Their writing typically has a different character from that of historians, who seek to tell stories about past human dramas without the aid of sociological concepts. Such historians, however, are likely to see themselves as belonging to the humanities rather than to the social sciences.

Some readers may be disappointed that I have not provided examples of good writing in the social sciences. The problem is that the good writing invariably comes with extra baggage: it is always more than a literary style, for the good writer is also doing the social sciences in their own particular way. If, for example, I devoted a section to praising the writing of the sociologist Richard Sennett – a humane and insightful author – then readers might say to themselves 'Oh, he wants us all to do the sort of sociology that Sennett does; but my work is different, so his message does not apply to me'. I do not want my message to be restricted to one form of social science, nor do I want to appear to be endorsing a particular approach.

If any readers are disappointed that my examples seem to epitomize what should be avoided, rather than what could be followed, then I would say that this book is itself a piece of social scientific writing. I have tried to write simply, and to avoid automatically using the big concepts that are relevant to my themes: concepts such as 'massification', 'nominalization', 'reification', 'de-agentialization' and many more. By my own writing, I wanted to show that it is possible to write social scientifically without being in the thrall of such words. Whether I have succeeded is not for me to say. However, I can say that it takes much longer to try to write in this way. I would have completed my book much sooner, and with far less strain, had I believed that there can be no substitute for the big words.

I may have overlooked some notable havens in the social sciences where clear language and a suspicion of technical nouns are thriving. Perhaps some of these havens contain social scientists, who write in languages other than English. I can only apologize for failing to notice good guys, who deserve support, not neglect. If there are sanctuaries of clear writing, about which I am ignorant, then their existence does not necessarily disprove my arguments. The current ways of doing and writing social science do not need to enjoy total dominance in order for them to be the prevailing ways. A few obstructive academics, especially in outposts of independence, will not offset the majority. There may still be some social scientists practising what look like old-fashioned craft skills, but their existence scarcely impinges on the major academic conglomerates that continue to develop their business models, trading globally in some hefty linguistic units.

This is why I feel that any recommendations about how we should be writing can only be whispers in the wind. Perhaps a better analogy would be that I am stuck by the side of a large highway, as the trucks go pounding past, hour after hour and day after day. In a voice that can only be heard by someone standing very close to me, I speak against the roar: 'Wouldn't it be better if there were fewer trucks on this road, if their loads were lighter and their engines were quieter?' My words will have no effect; the trucks will keep thundering past whatever I think or say. It is the same with my criticisms of academic writing in the social sciences. I can say what I want in a book which most social scientists would not have time to read, even if they wished to. Things will carry on much as they are; too much has been invested for sudden changes. Academic social scientists are building successful careers and attracting significant research funds, while their managerial evaluators look on, demanding more and more. I just stand by the side of the road, muttering at the traffic.

Of course, nothing stays exactly as it is and social life is constantly changing, with its patterns often becoming clear only when it is too late to change course. Things are by no means constant in the academic world. Perhaps for some institutions and for some academics the research bonanza is starting to shrink, even coming to an end. Educating students will become the prime source of income for more academics, with the writing of research papers becoming a bonus that must not be allowed to interfere with the customer satisfaction that fee-paying students demand. If this occurs on a grand scale, then there might well be fewer academic papers being published in the future. But the result could be papers that are more, not less, hastily written. Everyone will still feel the need to write, but there will be even less time to do so adequately. With the availability of the internet, it will be easy to publish instant papers, so that there will be even more to read and academic language may become even clumpier and unpolished. In the richer institutions, it is hard to see that the status of research, and the financial rewards for doing research, will evaporate. With funds spread even more unfairly, the competition for rewards could become even fiercer. Then we might expect that academics will become even more sophisticated at promoting their personal and sectional interests, as well as their favoured academic concepts.

There is no doubt that the internet is having major effects on the world of academic publishing with the long-term outcomes being difficult to predict. Again, there is no reason for supposing that the conditions for favouring verbs over nouns, and non-technical writing over technical writing, are fortuitously falling into place. In the sciences, there are moves to change the way that top journals are funded. Instead of university libraries funding journals by paying the expensive subscription fees demanded by publishers, there are plans to make top journals free to access on the internet, while the authors – or rather their institutions and their funding bodies – bear the publishing costs. It is possible that some of the major journals in the social sciences may follow this model, becoming free to access but costly to publish within. This is likely to maintain, if not increase, the power of journal editors. Independent authors, or those who lack substantial institutional support, may find it even harder to publish in the major journals. The source of funding for the journals might change, but there is no reason to think that this might bring about radical changes in their content or in the linguistic preferences of their editors and reviewers.

If there were to be a major movement to simplify and slow down our ways of writing, there would already be some sign of its emergence. I have given seminars at a number of universities, discussing the themes of this book. After my talks, some academics, particularly younger ones, have come up to me and said that they agree with me. What they do not say is more significant. Not one has said: 'Haven't you heard? We all here belong to the worldwide movement for clearer writing. There's a growing, groundswell of support for our view. I'm really surprised you didn't know about it.' Instead, the young academics are more likely to say: 'Yes, I agree with you, but what can I do? It's worse than you say. I have to publish my thesis and get a research contract; I can't do anything now; perhaps, when I feel secure, I'll be able to speak out.' But when will they feel secure?

I should not exaggerate the importance of a few young academics who have attended my talks and who afterwards have spoken to me about their fears. They do not represent all social scientists of their generation. Those ambitious young social scientists, who are already forging ahead with their careers, will be far too busy to attend such a talk. They have so many conferences to prepare for, committees to attend, journals to co-edit, networks to nourish and, always, papers to finish. I fear that their hyperactive lives, rather than my complaints, contain the outlines of the academic future.

But perhaps my fears are stronger than my imagination. Social institutions, which one generation assumes to be permanent features of life, can crumble before the eyes of the next. The present patterns of academic life – the priorities of funding bodies, university managers, journal editors, academic publishers and academic leaders – may well pass within a generation and with them today's styles of conducting academic business will disappear. It is probable that future social scientists, working in conditions that I am unable to envision, will consider the present styles of writing to be pompous, wearisome and, above all, hopelessly old-fashioned. Maybe, the trend will be to write in simpler, more direct ways.

Although today I feel that my words will have little effect on the current 'realities' of academic life, I can dream unrealistically. When today's young social scientists have grown old, a few might recall reading a writer who believed he was just whispering in the wind, but whose own words reached out towards a future that he was incapable of imagining. This hope may be irrational, but, when we think of future generations, it is surely just as irrational not to hope.

Whispering in the wind

I can delay it no longer: I must offer my recommendations, more in a spirit of hope than in an upsurge of optimism. The present practices for writing the social sciences are too firmly rooted in a range of economically profitable activities for anyone to be seriously disturbed by an academic shouting 'Look out! I have some recommendations at the end of my book!' Maybe a whisper now will be joined by some youthful whispers later, and these whispers might one day become an audible hum.

George Orwell's 'Politics and the English Language' is the model and his short essay should be required reading for all social scientists and their students. In his essay, Orwell writes about the virtues of clear writing and the dangers of sloppy prose: bad writing and bad thinking were, in Orwell's view, inextricably linked and both were politically dangerous. He was distressed by the growth of meaningless, pompous words that politicians, bureaucrats and academics were regularly employing to make themselves appear important. At the end of his essay, Orwell included six rules, which, he said, sounded quite simple but which 'demand a deep change of attitude in anyone who has grown used to writing in the style now fashionable' (1946/1975, p. 156).

Orwell, of course, did not succeed in producing the deep change of attitude that he hoped for, and the trends, which he warned against, have grown worse since his times. He would have been appalled by the managerial language of today, which seems to fit his category of 'pretentious writing' that results in 'an increase in slovenliness and vagueness' (pp. 149–50). It is not hard to guess what would have been Orwell's views on social scientists who, linguistically speaking, are seeking to out-bureaucrat the bureaucrats or out-manage the managers. Not for a moment can I imagine that Orwell would have been impressed by some of the linguistic excesses that I have been discussing. He would have found much to mock: 'the ideational metafunction', which academics used as a synonym for 'content'; or the fuss about whether to use 'mediatization' as opposed to 'mediation' or 'mediazation'; and all the formal phrases, where big nouns are bolted together, one after another without any intervening prepositions. His general point continues to be apposite: 'One ought to recognize that the present political chaos is connected with the decay of language' (p. 157).

My point, however, is not to recruit Orwell as an ally to my cause, for I am a long-standing, unashamed recruit to his cause. But I have a somewhat different point to make. Orwell with his six brief rules was not able to stop the general pomposity and lack of clarity in managerial, bureaucratic and academic writings. As I have suggested, some of the trends, such as the spread of noun-only-phrases, have been growing apace in the last hundred years. If someone like Orwell could not devise rules that would successfully reverse these patterns of language, then why, on earth, should I believe that my recommendations could have any effect? All I can do is to follow Orwell's lead and to follow in his belief that we should all make an effort to try to write in simpler, clearer ways.

Accordingly, I make six recommendations that are guides for those who might already be persuaded that there is something going wrong with the way that social scientists are writing. On their own, these recommendations will not change anything, except that, if we bear them in mind as we write, then we might produce a few more adequate sentences than we might have done otherwise. I am not proposing that there are some fundamental laws of language, whose rightness needs to be asserted unequivocally, and which must never be broken. It is the balance that is wrong in much academic writing in the social sciences. There are too many long words, passive voiced verbs and clumpy sentences. In moderation, there is nothing wrong with occasional passives or well-constructed neologisms. But do we need to be constantly assailed by new words, whose supporters launch them onto the academic market like products to be promoted? I am not formulating rules to forbid particular syntactical constructions or to assert old-fashioned standards of 'correct' grammar. But I want to put forward six recommendations for re-setting our linguistic and conceptual balances.

1. We should try to use simple language and avoid technical terms as much as possible. We should not assume that technical terms are clearer and more precise than the ordinary ones, for, as I have been suggesting, they are often used less precisely and that is why social scientists often find them useful. It is actually harder to write the social sciences using simple words than it is by mobilizing the big noun phrases and izations. If we use ordinary words, then typically we must clarify what we mean, without hiding behind stacks of syllables.

   So as a rule, try to convert jargon-filled statements into simpler ones. Get into the habit of doing this when you read, otherwise you may find that your thinking is being taken over by the big words of others and that you fail to get beyond these big words. Certainly, attempt to translate every jargon-filled sentence that you are about to write. It could be that your ideas fail to survive the processes of translation and, when phrased in humble words, your thoughts seem to lose their shine or even disappear altogether. If this happens, then you should take this as a sign that your ideas were not particularly special in the first place – not that your translation must have been poor or inappropriate. Orwell wrote that if you simplify your language, then 'when you make a stupid remark, its stupidity will be obvious, even to yourself' (p. 157).

As a corollary to this recommendation, remember that it is easy to sound impressive in the social sciences when one uses big words. If a relative or friend of the family – especially someone who has not received university education – asks you about your research interests, try to answer as simply and directly as possible. If you find that you cannot answer them without using big words, which they do not understand, then you should treat this as your failing not theirs.

2. Try to reduce the number of passive sentences in your writing. Orwell included this recommendation, as well as the previous one, in his list of six rules. This is not an absolute rule. There can be aesthetic reasons for mixing active and passive sentences and sometimes you might want to use a passive verb to achieve a specific emphasis. So, passives can be used. However, we should try to make the active sentence our default sentence. That means that if you write a passive sentence, then you should try to turn it into an active one, only keeping it as passive if you have good grounds for doing so.

   In recommending the active voice as the default voice, we should remember that active sentences generally contain more information than passive ones. As I have argued in earlier chapters, sometimes social scientists, as well as bureaucrats and politicians, will use the passive voice because they do not have to specify how actions took place and who undertook those actions. Using the passive voice, then, becomes a means for the social scientist to avoid giving information. That is a bad habit to get into. And that is why we all should try to make the active voice our preferred voice, especially when we are writing about humans and their actions.

3. We should try to write clausally rather than nominally: and forgive me, if in saying this, I have just infringed my first recommendation, but I want to emphasize that I am not advocating a ban on technical terms, although I would like to see a greater proportion of them as other parts of speech besides nouns. What I mean is that we should try to undo the power that nouns seem to have over managers, bureaucrats and, of course, social scientists. Rather than rely on a noun or noun phrase – especially one that is a technical noun or noun phrase – we should try to express ourselves in clauses with active verbs. Otherwise we might find ourselves using language that habitually turns people into things and that, instead of understanding what people are doing, we habitually reify them with our terminology. This is likely to occur when we turn our verbs into abstract nouns and then favour those nouns over the verbs. Our izations and ifications bear something in common with sentences phrased in the passive voice: they often contain less

information than sentences phrased in the active voice with human individuals or groups as the grammatical subject of the action.

In championing the active verb over the formal noun, I am not allying myself with Gregory Bateson's friend, who, according to the social anthropologist, used to display a car sticker, declaring 'Stamp out nouns' (Bateson, 2000, p. 334). Of course, the slogan itself is self-contradictory. 'Nouns' is a noun and Bateson's friend would have been showing humorous self-awareness, unlike some linguists who warn about the dangers of 'nominalization' and 'passivization' but fail to see how they are using just the sort of language that they seem to be warning against.

I should stress that there is nothing intrinsically wrong with nouns or even with nouns formed from verbs (or nominalizations). Again it is a matter of balance and being precise. The balance has tilted too far in the favour of the big nouns and social scientists use these big words as if they are writing more precisely than those using shorter words, whilst actually they are often writing more vaguely. This means we should try to avoid using the nominally dense style that today comes almost as second nature to many social scientists. It also means we should try to be sceptical about the fictional things that we create with our big nouns and noun phrases. Above all, we should avoid writing in ways that lump together fictional thing after fictional thing, as if our words are too good for this world.

4. Treat all these recommendations as either guidelines or aspirations, but not as rigid rules. This is in the spirit of Orwell's sixth rule: that one should break any of his previous five rules, rather than write something barbarous. I am sure that readers would be able to find many instances, in this chapter and throughout the book, where I have failed to follow my own recommendations. I will have used verbs in the passive voice, as well as technical concepts. Sometimes, I will have done so, fully aware what I am doing. At other times, the sentences will have slipped out and then I will regret that I failed to check them more carefully.

Even Orwell admitted that he was unlikely to have maintained his own high standards in his essay and that his readers might spot turns of phrase which he could have improved upon. If a great writer like Orwell can make such an admission, then there is less reason for the rest of us to fret that we inevitably fall below the standards that we aspire to. If one fails to live up to one's standards then that is no reason to jettison those standards. It is a reason to try harder. We do not think of discarding the laws against burglary or against speeding, just because incidents of burglary and speeding continue to occur regularly.

Similarly, I see no reason to abandon my recommendations, because I might fail to follow them.

5. As social scientists, we should aim to populate our texts – to write about people rather than things. We should describe (and thereby imagine through our writing) what people do, feel and think. We should be suspicious of unpopulated writings which seem to depict social worlds full of things and empty of people. Moreover, as I have suggested, when as social scientists we move from describing people to describing theoretical things, we do not necessarily make the gain of being more precise. In fact, the reverse is often the case, as we fail to ensure that our concepts have a grip on the world.

   If we do feel the need to write theoretically – about things such as 'reification' or 'mediatization' or 'nominalization' – then we should bear in mind the virtues of using extended examples. We should always try to make our theoretical concepts serve the world, rather than use the world to serve our concepts. And if we want to explain what a big word means, then we should not seek to perfect an abstract definition or invent another big word to explain the troublesome big word, for that is the way to an infinite regress away from the world. Instead, we should try to use an extended example saying, in effect, to the reader: 'This is what I mean by x-ification; look closely at what the people are doing and I hope that you'll see what I mean.'

6. Lastly we should avoid becoming personally attached to our technical terms. We certainly should not use them as comfort blankets, reassuring ourselves that we know more than laypersons do. Moreover, we should avoid writing as if we are their sales representatives, promoting the unique virtues of our semantic products. In fact, we should try to resist writing as if we are advertising our favoured approach, theory or big word. Generally, we should aim to keep separate the activities of advertising and analysing.

   Throughout this book, I have cautioned against the belief that we need technical concepts in the social sciences because ordinary language is so deficient and that those who frame their thoughts in ordinary words will be necessarily limited in their thinking. It is easy for social scientists, who accept the superiority of their own technical terminology, to slip into a stance of professional arrogance.

   Sometimes common sense contains more insight than the newest complicated theories. Our heavy theoretical concepts can get in the way of understanding the social world. So, I will end by adapting an old proverb. Don't fall in love with your technical terms, because, as we know, love can make you blind.

References

Abbott, A. (2001). *The Chaos of Disciplines*. University of Chicago Press.

Adler, R., Ewing, J. and Taylor, P. (2008). 'Joint Committee on Quantitative Assessment of Research: Citation Statistics'. *The Australian Mathematical Society Gazette*, 35: 168–88.

Allan, K. (2001). *Natural Language Semantics*. Oxford: Blackwell.

Allan, K. and Burridge, K. (2006). *Forbidden Words: Taboo and the Censoring of Language*. Cambridge University Press.

Altbach, P. G. (1997). 'Problems and Possibilities: The US Academic Profession'. In M. J. Finkelstein and P. G. Altbach (eds.), *The Academic Profession*. New York: Routledge.

   (2005). 'Patterns in Higher Education Development'. In P. G. Altbach, R. O. Berdahl and P. J. Gumport (eds.), *American Higher Education in the Twenty-First Century*. Baltimore, MD: Johns Hopkins University Press.

Altbach, P. G., Reisberg, L. and Rumbley, L. E. (2009). *Trends in Global Higher Education: Tracking an Academic Revolution*. Paris: UNESCO.

Andreski, S. (1971). *Social Sciences as Sorcery*. Harmondsworth: Penguin.

Anonymous. (1854). 'The Principle of the Grecian Mythology: Or How the Greeks Made Their Gods'. *Fraser's Magazine*, 49, 69–79.

Antaki, C., Billig, M., Edwards, D. and Potter, J. (2007). 'Discourse Analysis Means Doing Analysis: A Critique of Six Analytic Shortcomings'. In J. Potter (ed.), *Discourse and Psychology*, Vol. 1. London: Sage.

Arendt, H. (1963). *Eichmann in Jerusalem: A Report into the Banality of Evil*. New York: Viking Press.

Banks, D. (2003). 'The Evolution of Grammatical Metaphor in Scientific Writing'. In A. M. Simon-Vandenbergen, M. Tzaverniers and L. Ravelli (eds.), *Grammatical Metaphor*. Amsterdam/Philadelphia: John Benjamins.

Bargh, J. A. (2006). 'What Have We Been Priming All These Years? On the Development, Mechanisms, and Ecology of Nonconscious Social Behaviour'. *European Journal of Social Psychology*, 36: 147–68.

Bargh, J. A., Chen, M. and Burrows, L. (1996). 'Automaticity of Social Behaviour: Direct Effects of Trait Construct and Stereotype Activation on Action'. *Journal of Personality and Social Psychology*, 71: 230–44.

Barlow, F. K., Louis, W. R. and Hewstone, M. (2009). 'Rejected! Cognitions of Rejection and Intergroup Anxiety as Mediators of the Impact of Cross-group Friendships on Prejudice'. *British Journal of Social Psychology*, 48: 389–405.

Barthes, R. (1995). *Roland Barthes*. London: Papermac.

Bateson, G. (2000). *Steps to an Ecology of Mind*. University of Chicago Press.

Bazerman, C. (2006). 'Distanced and Refined Selves: Educational Tensions in Writing with the Power of Knowledge'. In M. Hewings (ed.), *Academic Writing in Context*. London: Continuum.

Becher, T. and Trowler, P. (2001). *Academic Tribes and Territories*. Milton Keynes: Open University Press.

Beck, U. and Sznaider, N. (2010). 'Unpacking Cosmopolitanism for the Social Sciences: A Research Agenda'. *British Journal of Sociology*, 61: 381–403.

Becker, S. L. (1999). 'Looking Forwards, Looking Backwards: A Personal Perspective'. *Communication Studies*, 50: 22–7.

Belcher, W. (2009). *Writing Your Journal Article in Twelve Weeks: A Guide to Academic Publishing*. Thousand Oaks, CA: Sage.

Bellquist, J. E. (1993). *A Guide to Grammar and Usage for Psychology and Related Fields*. Hillsdale, NJ: Lawrence Erlbaum.

Bem, D. J. (1987). 'Writing the Empirical Journal Article'. In M. P. Zanna and J. M. Darley (eds.), *The Compleat Academic: A Practical Guide for the Beginning Social Scientist*. Mahwah, NJ: Lawrence Erlbaum.

Berger, P. L. and Luckmann, T. (1967). *The Social Construction of Reality*. London: Allen Lane.

Berger, P. L. and Pullman, S. (1965). 'Reification and the Sociological Critique of Consciousness'. *History and Theory*, 4: 196–211.

Bewes, T. (2002). *Reification of the Anxiety of Late Capitalism*. London: Verso.

Bhatia, V. K. (1993). *Analysing Genre*. London: Longman.

Biber, D. (1988). *Variation Across Speech and Writing*. Cambridge University Press.

  (2003). 'Compressed Noun-phrase Structures in Newspaper Discourse: The Competing Demands of Popularization vs Economy'. In J. Aitchison and D. M. Lewis (eds.), *New Media Language*. London: Routledge.

  (2007). 'Corpus-based Analyses of Discourse: Dimensions of Variation in Conversation'. In V. K. Bhatia, J. Flowerdew and R. H. Jones (eds.), *Advances in Discourse Studies*. Oxford: Routledge.

Biber, D. and Conrad, S. (2009). *Register, Genre and Style*. Cambridge University Press.

Biber, D. and Gray, B. (2010). 'Challenging Stereotypes About Academic Writing: Complexity, Elaboration, Explicitness'. *Journal of English for Academic Purposes*, 9: 2–20.

Biber, D., Conrad, S. and Cortes, V. (2004). '*If you look at . . .* : Lexical Bundles in University Teaching and Textbooks'. *Applied Linguistics*, 25: 371–405.

Biber, D., Conrad, S. and Reppen, R. (1998). *Corpus Linguistics*. Cambridge University Press.

Billig, M. (1991). *Ideology and Opinions*. London: Sage Publications.

  (1994). 'Repopulating the Depopulated Pages of Social Psychology'. *Theory and Psychology*, 4: 307–35.

  (1996). *Arguing and Thinking: A Rhetorical Approach to Social Psychology*. Cambridge University Press.

  (1999). *Freudian Repression*. Cambridge University Press.

  (2002). 'Henri Tajfel's "Cognitive Aspects of Prejudice" and the Psychology of Bigotry'. *British Journal of Social Psychology*, 41: 171–88.

(2006). 'Lacan's Misuse of Psychology: Evidence, Rhetoric and the Mirror Stage'. *Theory, Culture and Society*, 23(4): 1–26.

(2008a). 'Social Representations and Repression: Examining the First Formulations of Freud and Moscovici'. *Journal for the Theory of Social Behaviour*, 38: 355–68.

(2008b). 'The Language of Critical Discourse Analysis: The Case of Nominalization'. *Discourse & Society*, 19: 783–800.

(2008c). 'Nominalizing and De-nominalizing: A Reply'. *Discourse & Society*, 19: 829–41.

(2011). 'Writing Social Psychology: Fictional Things and Unpopulated Texts'. *British Journal of Social Psychology*, 50: 4–20.

(2012). 'Undisciplined Beginnings, Academic Success and Discursive Psychology'. *British Journal of Social Psychology*.

Blanshard, B. (1954). *On Philosophical Style*. Bloomington, IN: Indiana University Press.

Blyth, A., Bamberg, J. and Toumbourou, J. (2000). *BEST. Behaviour Exchange Systems Training: A Programme for Parents Stressed by Adolescent Substance Abuse*. Camberwell, Victoria: ACER Press.

Bondy, A. S. and Frost, L. (2001). 'The Picture Exchange Communication System'. *Behavior Modification*, 25: 725–44.

Bordens, K. S. and Horowitz, I. A. (2001). *Social Psychology*, 2nd edn. Mahwah, NJ: Psychology Press.

Bourdieu, P. (1993). *Sociology in Question*. London: Sage.

(2000). *Pascalian Meditations*. Oxford: Polity Press.

(2003). *Méditations pascaliennes*. Paris: Éditions du Seuil.

Bourdieu, P., Passeron, J.-C. and de Saint Martin, M. (1996). *Academic Discourse*. Cambridge: Polity Press.

Brennan, J., Locke, W. and Naidoo, R. (2007). 'United Kingdom: An Increasingly Differentiated Profession'. In W. Locke and U. Teichler (eds.), *The Changing Conditions for Academic Work and Careers in Selected Countries*. Kassel, Germany: International Centre for Higher Education Research.

Brown, R. (1995). *Prejudice*. Oxford: Blackwell.

Burawoy, M. (2005). 'Provincializing the Social Sciences'. In G. Steinmetz (ed.), *The Politics of Method in the Human Sciences*. Durham: Duke University Press.

(2009). 'The Public Sociology Wars'. In V. Jeffries (ed.), *Handbook of Public Sociology*. Lanham: Rowman and Littlefield.

Campbell, R. and Meadows, A. (2011). 'Scholarly Journal Publishing: Where Do We Go from Here?' *Learned Publishing*, 24: 171–81.

Chouliaraki, L. and Fairclough, N. (1999). *Discourse in Late Modernity*. Edinburgh University Press.

Coleman, J. (2009). 'Slang and Cant Dictionaries'. In A. P. Cowie (ed.), *The Oxford History of English Lexicography*, Vol. 1. Oxford University Press.

Couldry, N. (2008). 'Mediatization or Mediation? Alternative Understandings of the Emergent Space of Digital Storytelling'. *New Media Society*, 10: 373–91.

Crane, D. and Small, H. (1992). 'American Sociology Since the Seventies: The Emerging Identity Crisis in the Discipline'. In T. C. Halliday and M. Janowitz (eds.), *Sociology and its Publics*. University of Chicago Press.

Crisp, R. J. and Turner, R. N. (2010). *Essential Social Psychology*. London: Sage.

Culler, J. and Lamb, K. (2003a). 'Introduction: Dressing Up, Dressing Down'. In J. Culler and K. Lamb (eds.), *Just Being Difficult?* Stanford University Press.

(eds.) (2003b). *Just Being Difficult?* Stanford University Press.

Cumming, G. (2008). 'Replication and *p* Intervals: *p* Values Predict the Future Only Vaguely, but Confidence Intervals Do Much Better'. *Perspectives on Psychological Science*, 3: 286–300.

Dahl, T. (2008). 'Contributing to the Academic Conversation: A Study of New Knowledge Claims in Economics and Linguistics'. *Journal of Pragmatics*, 40: 1184–201.

Danziger, K. (1997). *Naming the Mind*. London: Sage.

Dawkins, R. (2003). *A Devil's Chaplain*. London: Orion Books.

Deacon, D. (2012). 'Mediatization and History'. Plenary talk delivered at Discourse, Communication, Conversation Conference, March 2012, Loughborough University.

Dean, M. (2010). *Governmentality: Power and Rule in Modern Society*, 2nd edn. London: Sage.

De Quincey, T. (1863). *Dr Samuel Parr or Whiggism and its Relation to Literature*. Edinburgh: Adam and Charles Black.

Donald, J. G. (2009). 'The Commons: Disciplinary and Interdisciplinary Encounters'. In C. Kreber (ed.), *The University and its Disciplines*. New York: Routledge.

Drury, J. and Reicher, S. (2000). 'Collective Action and Social Change: The Emergence of New Social Identities'. *British Journal of Social Psychology*, 39: 579–604.

East, J. (2010). 'Judging Plagiarism: A Problem of Morality and Convention'. *Higher Education*, 59: 69–83.

Economic and Social Research Council. (2009). *Postgraduate Training and Development: Guidelines*. Swindon: ESRC.

Editors (2003). 'Editorial, May 2003'. *Papers on Social Representations*, 12: 3.1–3.2.

Edwards, D. (1991). 'Categories Are for Talking'. *Theory and Psychology*, 1: 515–42.

(2012). 'Discursive and Scientific Psychology'. *British Journal of Social Psychology*, 51: 425–35.

Edwards, D. and Potter, J. (1993). *Discursive Psychology*. London: Sage.

English, F. (2002). *Student Essays: An Academic Literacies Perspective*. Subject Centre for Languages, Linguistics and Area Studies Good Practice Guide. Retrieved 28 May 2012, www.llas.ac.uk/resources/gpg/62.

Ethier, C. R. and Simmons, C. A. (2007). *Introductory Biomechanics*. Cambridge University Press.

Fairclough, N. (1992). *Discourse and Social Change*. Cambridge: Polity Press.

(2003). *Analyzing Discourse*. London: Routledge.

(2008a). 'Critical Discourse Analysis and Nominalization: Reply to Michael Billig'. *Discourse & Society*, 19: 811–20.

(2008b). 'A Brief Response to Billig'. *Discourse & Society*, 19, 843–4.

Fairclough, N., Mulderig, J. and Wodak, R. (2011). 'Critical Discourse Analysis'. In T. A. van Dijk (ed.), *Discourse Studies*, 2nd edn. London: Sage.

Fisher, J. C. (1991). 'A Short Glossary of Laser Terminology for Physicians and Surgeons'. *Journal of Clinical Laser Medicine and Surgery*, 9: 345–8.

Flowerdew, L. (2007). 'Corpora and Context in Professional Writing'. In V. K. Bhatia, J. Flowerdew and R. H. Jones (eds.), *Advances in Discourse Studies*. London: Routledge.

Foucault, M. (1979). 'On Governmentality'. *Ideology & Consciousness*, 6: 5–21.

(2000). 'Governmentality'. In M. Foucault, *Power: Essential Works of Foucault 1954–1984*, Vol. 3. Harmondsworth: Penguin.

(2004). *Sécurité, Territoire, Population: Cours au Collège de France (1977–1978)*. Paris: Gallimard.

(2009). *Security, Territory, Population: Lectures at the Collège de France, 1977–1978*. Basingstoke: Palgrave Macmillan.

Fowler, R. (1991). *Language in the News*. London: Routledge.

Fowler, R., Hodge, B., Kress, G. and Trew, T. (1979). *Language and Control*. London: Routledge.

Freud, S. (1914/1993). 'On the History of the Psychoanalytic Movement'. In S. Freud, *Historical and Expository Works on Psychoanalysis*. Harmondsworth: Penguin.

Freud, S. and Breuer, J. (1895/1952). 'Stüdien über Hysterie'. In S. Freud, *Gesammelte Werke*, Vol. 1. Frankfurt am Main: S. Fischer.

(1895/1991). *Studies on Hysteria*. Harmondsworth: Penguin.

Frey, B. S. (2003). 'Publishing as Prostitution? Choosing Between One's Own Ideas and Academic Success'. *Public Choice*, 116: 205–23.

Garbutt, R. (2009). 'Is There a Place Within Academic Journals for Articles Presented in an Accessible Format?' *Disability & Society*, 24: 357–71.

Gascoigne, T. and Metcalfe, J. (2005). 'Commercialisation of Research Activities in the Humanities, Arts and Social Sciences in Australia'. Occasional paper of Council for Humanities, Arts and Social Sciences, Department of Education, Science and Training, Australia.

Gemme, B. and Gingras, Y. (2009). 'The New Production of Researchers'. In A. S. Chan and D. Fisher (eds.), *The Exchange University: Corporatization of Academic Culture*. Vancouver, BC: University of British Columbia Press.

Gibson, S. (in press). 'Milgram's Obedience Experiments: A Rhetorical Analysis'. *British Journal of Social Psychology*.

Gigerenzer, G. (2004). 'Mindless Statistics'. *The Journal of Socio-Economics*, 33: 587–606.

(2006). 'What's in a Sample? A Manual for Building Cognitive Theories'. In K. Fiedler and P. Juslin (eds.), *Information Sampling and Adaptive Cognition*. New York: Cambridge University Press.

(2010). 'Personal Reflections on "Theory and Psychology"'. *Theory & Psychology*, 20: 733–43.

Gigerenzer, G. and Brighton, H. (2009). 'Homo Heuristicus: Why Biased Minds Make Better Inferences'. *Topics in Cognitive Science*, 1: 107–43.

Grafton, A. (2010). 'Britain: The Disgrace of the Universities'. *The New York Review of Books*, 8 April.

Gramsci, A. (1971). *Selections from Prison Notebooks*. London: Lawrence and Wishart.

Greenland, K. and Brown, R. (2000). 'Categorization and Intergroup Anxiety in Intergroup Conflict'. In D. Capozza and R. Brown (eds.), *Social Identity Processes*. London: Sage.

Grose, F. (1785/1963). *A Classical Dictionary of the Vulgar Tongue*, edited by E. Partridge. New York: Barnes and Noble.

Grubrich-Simitis, I. (1997). *Early Freud and Late Freud*. London: Routledge.

Grünbaum, A. (1998). 'A Century of Psychoanalysis: Critical Retrospect and Prospect'. In M. S. Roth (ed.), *Freud: Conflict and Culture*. New York: Alfred Knopf.

Gumport, P. J., Iannozz, M., Shaman, S. and Zemsky, R. (1997). *Trends in United States Education from Massification to Post Massification*. Stanford, CA: National Center for Postsecondary Improvement.

Halliday, M. A. K. (2003). *On Language and Linguistics*. London: Continuum.
   (2006). *The Language of Science*. London: Continuum.

Halliday, M. A. K. and Martin, J. R. (1993). *Writing Science*. London: Falmer Press.

Hearn, J. C. (2007). 'Sociological Studies of Academic Departments'. In P. J. Gumport (ed.), *Sociology of Higher Education*. Baltimore, MD: Johns Hopkins University Press.

Heritage, J. and Greatbach, D. (1986). 'Generating Applause: A Study of Rhetoric and Response at Party Political Conferences'. *American Journal of Sociology*, 92: 110–57.

Hewings, A. and Hewings, M. (2006). 'Anticipatory "It" in Academic Writing: An Indicator of Disciplinary Difference and Developing Disciplinary Knowledge'. In M. Hewings (ed.), *Academic Writing in Context*. London: Continuum.

Heywood, A. (2006). *Key Concepts in Politics*. New York: St Martin's Press.

Hilsdon, J. (1997). 'Nominalisation in the Classroom: Issues of Power and Identity'. *International Journal of Educational Development*, 17: 417–25.

Hitchings, H. (2005). *Defining the World: The Extraordinary Story of Dr Johnson's Dictionary*. New York: Farrar, Strauss and Giroux.

Hogg, M. A. (2010). 'Influence and Leadership'. In S. T. Fiske, D. T. Gilbert and G. Lindzey (eds.), *Handbook of Social Psychology*, 5th edn. New York: Wiley.

Hogg, M. A. and Vaughan, G. M. (2011). *Social Psychology*, 6th edn. Harlow: Prentice Hall.

Holmes, R. (1997). 'Genre Analysis and the Social Sciences: An Investigation of the Structure of Research Article Discussion Sections in Three Disciplines'. *English for Specific Purposes*, 16: 321–7.

Honneth, A. (1995). *The Struggle for Recognition*. Cambridge: Polity Press.
   (2008). *Reification: A New Look at an Old Idea*. Oxford University Press.

Hood, S. and Forey, G. (2005). 'Introducing a Conference Paper: Getting Interpersonal With Your Audience'. *Journal of English for Academic Purposes*, 4: 291–306.

Huang, M. and Chang, Y. (2008). 'Characteristics of Research Output in Social Sciences and Humanities: From a Research Evaluation Perspective'. *Journal of the American Society for Information Science and Technology*, 59: 1819–28.

Hudson, G. (1999). *Essential Introductory Linguistics*. Oxford: Blackwell.

Hundt, M. (2007). *English Mediopassive Constructions*. Amsterdam/New York: Rodopi.

(2009). '"Curtains Like These are Selling Right in the City of Chicago for $1.50" – The Mediopassive in American 20th-century Advertising Language'. *Language and Computers*, 69: 163–83.

Hutchby, I. and Wooffitt, R. (2008). *Conversation Analysis*. Cambridge: Polity Press.

Hyland, K. (2001). 'Humble Servants of the Discipline? Self-mention in Research Articles'. *English for Specific Purposes*, 20: 207–26.

(2005). 'Stance and Engagement: A Model of Interaction in Academic Discourse'. *Discourse Studies*, 7: 173–92.

(2009). *Academic Discourse*. London: Continuum.

Hyland, K. and Tse, P. (2007). 'Is There an "Academic Vocabulary"?' *TESOL Quarterly*, 41: 235–53.

James, C. L. R. (1963). *Beyond a Boundary*. London: Stanley Paul.

James, W. (1890). *Principles of Psychology*. London: Macmillan.

(1899). *Talks to Teachers*. London: Longmans, Green and Co.

(1911). *Memories and Studies*. London: Longmans, Green and Co.

(1920). *The Letters of William James*, edited by H. James. Boston, MA: Little, Brown and Company.

Jary, D. (1997). 'A Brief Guide to "Difficult" Sociological Jargon'. In C. Ballard, J. Gubbay and C. Middleton (eds.), *The Student's Companion to Sociology*. Oxford: Blackwell.

Jinha, A. E. (2010). 'Article 50 Million: An Estimate on the Number of Scholarly Articles in Existence'. *Learned Publishing*, 23: 258–63.

Johns, T. (2006). 'From Evidence to Conclusion: The Case of "Indicate That"'. In M. Hewings (ed.), *Academic Writing in Context*. London: Continuum.

Katzko, M. W. (2006). 'A Study of the Logic of Empirical Arguments in Psychological Research: "The Automacity of Social Behaviour" as a Case Study'. *Review of General Psychology*, 10: 210–28.

Kitchin, R. and Fuller, D. (2005). *The Academic's Guide to Publishing*. London: Sage.

Kivinen, O., Hedman, J. and Kaipainen, P. (2007). 'From Elite University to Mass Higher Education: Educational Expansion, Equality of Opportunity and Returns to University Education'. *Acta Sociologica*, 50: 231–47.

Klinenberg, E. (2005). 'Convergence: News Production in a Digital Age'. *The Annals of the American Academy of Political and Social Science*, 597: 48–64.

Knoch, U. (2007). '"Little Coherence, Considerable Strain for Reader": A Comparison of Two Rating Scales for the Assessment of Coherence'. *Assessing Writing*, 12: 108–28.

Knowles, C. (2010). 'Mobile Sociology'. *British Journal of Sociology*, 61: 373–9.

Kousha, K. and Thelwell, M. (2009). 'Google Book Search: Citation Analysis for Social Science and the Humanities'. *Journal of the American Society for Information Science and Technology*, 60: 1537–49.

Kreber, C. (ed.) (2009). *The University and its Disciplines*. New York: Routledge.

Kyvik, S. (2003). 'Changing Trends in Publishing Behaviour Among University Faculty, 1980–2000'. *Scientometrics*, 58: 35–48.

Kyvik, S. and Skodkin, O.-J. (2003). 'Research in the Non-university Higher Education Sector: Tensions and Dilemmas'. *Higher Education*, 45: 203–22.

Lambdin, C. (2012). 'Significance Tests as Sorcery: Science is Empirical – Statistical Tests are Not'. *Theory & Psychology*, 22: 67–90.

Laplanche, J. and Pontalis, J.-B. (1983). *The Language of Psycho-Analysis*. London: Hogarth Press.

Lea, M. R. and Street, B. V. (1998). 'Student Writing in Higher Education: An Academic Literacies Approach'. *Studies in Higher Education*, 23: 157–72.

Lee, J. J., Cheslock, J., Maldonado-Maldonado, A. and Rhoades, G. (2005). 'Professors as Knowledge Workers in the New Global Economy'. In J. C. Smart (ed.), *Higher Education: Handbook of Theory and Research*, Vol. XX. Dordrecht: Springer.

Lee, S. H. (2010). 'Command Strategies for Balancing Respect and Authority in Undergraduate Expository Essays'. *Journal of English for Academic Purposes*, 9: 61–75.

Leech, G. (2006). *A Glossary of English Grammar*. Edinburgh University Press.

Leech, G., Hundt, M., Mair, C. and Smith, N. (2009). *Change in Contemporary English*. Cambridge University Press.

Lemke, J. L. (1995). *Textual Politics: Discourse and Social Dynamics*. London: Taylor and Francis.

Lemke, T. (2002). 'Foucault, Governmentality and Critique'. *Rethinking Marxism*, 14(3): 49–64.

(2007). 'An Indigestible Meal? Foucault, Governmentality and State Theory'. *Distinktion: Scandinavian Journal of Social Theory*, 15: 43–66.

Liddicoat, A. J. (2007). *An Introduction to Conversation Analysis*. London: Continuum.

Lillis, T. and Scott, M. (2007). 'Defining Academic Literacies Research: Issues of Epistemology, Ideology and Strategy'. *Journal of Applied Linguistics*, 4: 5–32.

Locke, W. (2008). 'The Academic Profession in England: Still Stratified After All These Years?' In Research Institute for Higher Education, *The Changing Academic Profession*. Hiroshima University.

Lomas, L. (2001). 'Does the Development of Mass Education Necessarily Mean the End of Quality?' Paper given at Sixth QHE seminar, Birmingham, May 2001.

Lukács, G. (1923/1971). *History and Class Consciousness*. London: Merlin Press.

Lundby, K. (2009). 'Introduction: "Mediatization" as Key'. In K. Lundby (ed.), *Mediatization*. New York: Peter Lang.

Marková, I. (2003). *Dialogicality and Social Representations*. Cambridge University Press.

(2008). 'The Epistemological Significance of the Theory of Social Representations'. *Journal for the Theory of Social Behaviour*, 38: 461–87.

Martin, J. R. (2008). 'Incongruent and Proud: De-vilifying "Nominalization"'. *Discourse & Society*, 19: 801–10.

Martinez, I. A., Beck, S. C. and Panza, C. B. (2009). 'Academic Vocabulary in Agriculture Research Articles: A Corpus-based Study'. *English for Specific Purposes*, 28: 183–98.

Marton, F. (1986). 'Phenomenography: A Research Approach Investigating Different Understandings of Reality'. *Journal of Thought*, 21: 28–49.

(1994). 'Phenomenography'. In T. Husén and T. N. Postlethwaite (eds.), *The International Encyclopedia of Education*, Vol. 8. Oxford: Pergamon.

Marx, K. (1894/1959). *Capital*, Vol. III. New York: International Publishers.

Marx, K. and Engels, F. (1846/1970). *The German Ideology*. London: Lawrence and Wishart.

Master, P. (2006). 'Active Verbs With Inanimate Subjects in Scientific Research Articles'. In M. Hewings (ed.), *Academic Writing in Context*. London: Continuum.

Mautner, G. (2005). 'For-profit Discourse in the Nonprofit and Public Sectors'. In G. Erreygers and G. Jacobs (eds.), *Language, Communication and the Economy*. Amsterdam/Philadelphia: John Benjamins.

McLellan, D. (1973). *Karl Marx: His Life and Thought*. London: Macmillan.

McLennan, G. (2003). 'Sociological Complexity'. *Sociology*, 37: 547–64.

McMillan, K. and Weyers, J. (2010). *How to Write Essays and Assignments*. Harlow: Prentice Hall.

Meehl, P. E. (1978). 'Theoretical Risks and Tabular Asterisks: Sir Karl, Sir Ronald, and the Slow Progress of Soft Psychology'. *Journal of Consulting and Clinical Psychology*, 46: 806–34.

(1990). *Selected Philosophical and Methodological Papers*. University of Minnesota Press.

Mercer, N. (1996). 'Using English at Work'. In J. Maybin and N. Mercer (eds.), *Using English from Conversation to Canon*. Oxford: Routledge.

Milgram, S. (1974). *Obedience to Authority*. New York: Harper & Row.

Mohamedbhai, G. (2008). *The Effects of Massification on Higher Education in Africa*. Accra: Association of African Universities.

Moon, C. (2010). 'The *British Journal of Sociology* in the 1990s: Disintegration and Disarray?' *British Journal of Sociology*, 61: 261–9.

Moscovici, S. (1961). *La Psychanalyse: son image et son public*. Paris: Presses Universitaires de France.

(1963). 'Attitudes and Opinions'. *Annual Review of Psychology*, 14: 231–60.

(2000). *Social Representations: Studies in Social Psychology*. Cambridge: Polity Press.

Moxley, J. M. (1992). *Publish, Don't Perish: The Scholar's Guide to Academic Writing and Publishing*. Westport, CT: Praeger.

Muntigl, P. (2002). 'Politicization and Depoliticization: Employment Policy in the European Union'. In P. Chilton and C. Schäffner (eds.), *Politics as Talk and Text*. Amsterdam/Philadelphia: John Benjamins.

Murray, J. (2008). *Now That's What I Call Jargon*. Dublin: New Island Books.

Myers, G. (2006). '"In My Opinion": The Place of Personal Views in Undergraduate Essays'. In M. Hewings (ed.), *Academic Writing in Context*. London: Continuum.

Nash, W. (1993). *Jargon*. Oxford: Blackwell.

Ngok, K. (2008). 'Massification, Bureaucratization and Questing for "World-Class" Status: Higher Education in China since the Mid-1990s'. *International Journal of Educational Management*, 22: 547–64.

Nichols, T. (2005). 'Industry'. In T. Bennett, L. Grossberg and M. Morris (eds.), *New Keywords*. Oxford: Blackwell.

Northey, M., Tepperman, L. and Russell, J. (2002). *Making Sense in the Social Sciences: A Student's Guide to Research and Writing*. Ontario: Oxford University Press.

O'Leary, Z. (2007). *The Social Science Jargon Buster: The Key Terms You Need to Know*. London: Sage.

Okulska, U. and Cap, P. (2010). 'Analysis and Political Discourse: Landmarks, Challenges and Prospects'. In U. Okulska and P. Cap (eds.), *Perspectives in Politics and Discourse*. Amsterdam/Philadelphia: John Benjamins.

Orwell, G. (1946/1975). 'Politics and the English Language'. In G. Orwell, *Inside the Whale and Other Essays*. Harmondsworth: Penguin.

    (1949/2008). *Nineteen Eighty-Four*. Harmondsworth: Penguin.

Osborne, T. and Rose, N. (1999). 'Do the Social Sciences Create Phenomena? The Example of Public Opinion Research'. *British Journal of Sociology*, 50: 367–96.

Pahta, P. and Taavitsainen, I. (eds.). (2004). *Medical and Scientific Writing in Late Mediaeval English*. Cambridge University Press.

Parakh, P., Hindy, P. and Fruthcher, G. (2011). 'Are We Speaking the Same Language? Acronyms in Gastroenterology'. *American Journal of Gastroenterology*, 106: 8–9.

Pepitone, A. (1999). 'Historical Sketches and Critical Commentary About Social Psychology in the Golden Age'. In A. Rodrigues and R. Levine (eds.), *Reflections on 100 Years of Experimental Social Psychology*. New York: Basic Books.

Poole, G. (2009). 'Academic Disciplines: Homes or Barricades?' In C. Kreber (ed.), *The University and its Disciplines*. New York: Routledge.

Potter, J. (2012). 'Rereading "Discourse and Social Psychology": Transforming Social Psychology'. *British Journal of Social Psychology*, 51: 436–59.

Prior, P. A. (1998). *Writing/Disciplinarity: A Sociohistoric Account of Literate Activity in the Academy*. Mahwah, NJ: Lawrence Erlbaum.

    (2005). 'Re-situating and Re-mediating the Canons – Reflections on Writing Research and Rhetoric'. Plenary talk at Conference on Writing Research in the Making. Santa Barbara, California, 6 February.

Prosser, M. and Webb, C. (1994). 'Relating the Process of Undergraduate Essay Writing to the Finished Product'. *Studies in Higher Education*, 19: 125–38.

Rapport, N. and Overing, J. (2006). *Social and Cultural Anthropology: The Key Concepts*. London: Routledge.

Reicher, S. (2011). 'Promoting a Culture of Innovation: BJSP and the Emergence of New Paradigms in Social Psychology'. *British Journal of Social Psychology*, 50: 391–8.

Reider, B. (2008). 'Acronyms and Anachronisms'. *American Journal of Sports Medicine*, 36, 2081–2.

Reynolds, J. (2010). 'Writing in the Discipline of Anthropology – Theoretic, Thematic and Geographic Spaces'. *Studies in Higher Education*, 35: 11–24.

Richardson, R. D. (2007). *William James: In the Maelstrom of American Modernism*. Boston, MA: Mariner.

Rocco, T. S. (2011). 'Reasons to Write, Writing Opportunities and Other Considerations'. In T. S. Rocco and T. Hatcher (eds.), *The Handbook of Scholarly Writing and Publishing*. San Francisco, CA: Jossey-Bass.

Rose, N. (1996). *Inventing Our Selves*. Cambridge University Press.

Rose, N. and Miller, P. (2010). 'Political Power Beyond the State: Problematics of Government'. *British Journal of Sociology*, 61: 271–303.

Rose, N., O'Malley, P. and Valverde, M. (2006). 'Governmentality'. *Annual Review of Law and Social Science*, 2: 83–104.

Rowley-Jolivet, E. and Carter-Thomas, S. (2005). 'The Rhetoric of Conference Presentation Introductions'. *International Journal of Applied Linguistics*, 15: 45–71.

Rumbley, L., Pacheco, I. and Altbach, P. G. (2008). *International Comparison of Academic Salaries: An Exploratory Study*. Chestnut Hill, MA: Boston College Center for International Higher Education.

Russell, D. R. (2002). *Writing in the Academic Disciplines*. Carbondale, IL: Southern Illinois University Press.

Sacks, H. (1984). 'On Doing "Being Ordinary"'. In J. M. Atkinson and J. Heritage (eds.), *Structures of Social Action*. Cambridge University Press.

(1995). *Lectures on Conversation*. Oxford: Blackwell.

Sacks, H., Schegloff, E. A. and Jefferson, G. (1974). 'A Simplest Systematics for the Organization of Turn-Taking for Conversation'. *Language*, 50: 696–735.

Sánchez, D. and Isern, D. (2011). 'Automatic Extraction of Acronym Definition from the Web'. *Applied Intelligence*, 34: 311–27.

Schafer, R. (1976). *A New Language for Psychoanalysis*. New Haven, CT: Yale University Press.

Schaffer, R. (2006). *Key Concepts in Developmental Psychology*. London: Sage.

Scheff, T. J. (1990). *Microsociology*. University of Chicago Press.

(1997). *Emotions, the Social Bond and Human Reality*. Cambridge University Press.

(2006). *Goffman Unbound! A New Paradigm for Social Science*. Boulder, CO: Paradigm.

Scheff, T. J. and Fearon, D. S., Jr. (2004). 'Cognition and Emotion? The Dead End in Self-esteem Research'. *Journal for the Theory of Social Behaviour*, 34: 73–90.

Schegloff, E. (2000). 'Overlapping Talk and the Organization of Turn-taking for Conversation'. *Language and Society*, 29: 1–63.

Schroder, K. C. (2002). 'Discourses of Fact'. In K. B. Jensen (ed.), *Handbook of Media and Communication Research*. London: Routledge.

Schulz, W. (2004). 'Reconstructing Mediatization as an Analytical Concept'. *European Journal of Communication*, 19: 87–101.

Schuster, J. H. and Finkelstein. M. J. (2008). *The American Faculty*. Baltimore, MD: Johns Hopkins University Press.

Scott, J. (2005). 'Sociology and its Others: Reflections on Disciplinary Specialisation and Fragmentation'. *Sociological Research Online*, 10: 1. Retrieved 28 May 2012, www.socresonline.org.uk/10/1scott.html.

(2006). *Sociology: The Key Concepts*. Oxford: Routledge.

Scott-Lichter, D. (2011). 'Got Content, Get Attention'. *Learned Publishing*, 24: 245–6.

Sennett, R. and Cobb, J. (1993). *The Hidden Injuries of Class*. New York: W. W. Norton.

Shalit, I. and Bargh, J. A. (2011). 'Use of Priming-based Interventions to Facilitate Psychological Health: Commentary of Kazdin and Blasé'. *Perspectives on Psychological Sciences*, 6: 488–92.

Shaw, P. and Vassileva, I. (2009). 'Co-Evolving Academic Rhetoric Across Culture: Britain, Bulgaria, Denmark, Germany in the 20th Century'. *Journal of Pragmatics*, 41: 290–305.

Shore, C. and Wright, S. (2000). 'Coercive Accountability: The Rise of the Audit Culture in Higher Education'. In M. Stathern (ed.), *Audit Cultures*. London: Routledge.

Slaughter, S. and Rhoades, G. (2004). *Academic Capitalism and the New Economy*. Baltimore, MD: Johns Hopkins University Press.

  (2009). 'The Academic Capitalist Knowledge/Learning Regime'. In A. S. Chan and D. Fisher (eds.), *The Exchange University: Corporatization of Academic Culture*. Vancouver, BC: University of British Columbia Press.

Smart, L. E. and Moore, A. E. (2005). *Solid State Chemistry: An Introduction*, 3rd edn. London: Taylor and Francis.

Smeby, J.-C. (2003). 'The Impact of Massification on University Research'. *Tertiary Education and Management*, 9: 131–44.

Smith, E. R. and Mackie, D. M. (2000). *Social Psychology*, 2nd edn. Philadelphia, PA: Psychology Press.

Smyth, M. M. (2001). 'Fact Making in Psychology: The Voice of the Introductory Textbook'. *Theory & Psychology*, 11: 609–36.

Sokal, A. D. (2010). *Beyond the Hoax: Science, Philosophy and Culture*. Oxford University Press.

Sokal, A. D. and Bricmont, J. (1999). *Fashionable Nonsense*. New York: St Martin's Press.

Souder, L. (2011). 'The Ethics of Scholarly Peer Review: A Review of the Literature'. *Learned Publishing*, 24: 55–74.

Spears, R. (1995). 'Social Categorization'. In A. S. R. Manstead and M. Hewstone (eds.), *The Blackwell Encyclopedia of Social Psychology*. Oxford: Blackwell.

Stanley, L. (2005). 'A Child of its Time: Hybridic Perspectives on Othering in Sociology'. *Sociological Research Online*, 10, 3. Retrieved 28 May 2012, www.socresonline.or.uk/10/3/stanley.html.

Starfield, S. (2004). 'Word Power: Negotiating Success in a First-year Sociology Essay'. In L. J. Ravelli and R. A. Ellis (eds.), *Analysing Academic Writing*. London: Continuum.

Steele, C. (2006). 'Book to the Future: Twenty-first-century Models for the Scholarly Monograph'. In B. R. Bernhardt, T. Daniels, K. Steinle and K. Strauch (eds.), *Charleston Conference Proceedings 2005*. Westport, CT: Libraries Unlimited.

Stroebe, W., Hewstone, M. and Jonas, K. (2008). 'Introducing Social Psychology'. In M. Hewstone, W. Stroebe and K. Jonas (eds.), *Introduction to Social Psychology*. Oxford: BPS Blackwell.

Swales, J. M. (1990). *Genre Analysis*. Cambridge University Press.

  (2006). *Research Genres: Explorations and Applications*. Cambridge University Press.

Tajfel, H. (1969). 'Cognitive Aspects of Prejudice'. *Journal of Biosocial Science*, Supplement 1: 173–91.

(1981). *Human Groups and Social Categories*. Cambridge University Press.

Tajfel, H., Billig, M., Bundy, R. P. and Flament, C. (1971). 'Social Categorization and Intergroup Behaviour'. *European Journal of Social Psychology*, 1: 149–78.

Tang, R. and Suganthi, J. (1999). 'The "I" in Identity: Exploring Writer Identity in Student Academic Essays Through the First Person Pronoun. *English for Specific Purposes*, 18, Supplement 1, S23–S39.

Tarrant, M., Dazely, S. and Cottom, T. (2009). 'Social Categorization and Empathy for Outgroup Members'. *British Journal of Social Psychology*, 48: 427–46.

ten Have, P. (2009). 'Conversation Analysis: Analysing Everyday Conversations'. In M. H. Jacobsen (ed.), *Encountering the Everyday*. Basingstoke: Palgrave Macmillan.

Tenopir, C., Allard, S., Bates, B. J., Levine, K. J., Kings, D. W., Birch, B., Mays, R. and Caldwell, C. (2011). 'Perceived Value of Scholarly Articles'. *Learned Publishing*, 24: 123–32.

Thomas, L. (2005). *Widening Participation in Post-Compulsory Education*. London: Continuum.

Thompson, J. B. (1995). *The Media and Modernity*. Cambridge: Polity Press.

(2005). *Books in the Digital Age*. Cambridge: Polity Press.

Thorne, T. (2006). *Shoot the Puppy: A Survival Guide to the Curious Jargon of Modern Life*. Harmondsworth: Penguin.

Todd, R. W. (2003). 'EAP or TEAP?' *Journal of English for Academic Purposes*, 2: 147–56.

Tracy, K. (1997). *Colloquium: Dilemmas of Academic Discourse*. Norwood, NJ: Ablex.

Trow, M. A. (2000). *From Mass Higher Education to Universal Access: The American Advantage*. Berkeley, CA: Center for Studies in Higher Education.

(2005). 'Reflections on the Transition From Elite to Mass to Universal Access: Forms and Phases of Higher Education in Modern Societies since WWII'. University of California at Berkeley: Institute of Government Studies. Retrieved 28 May 2012, http://escholarship.org/uc/item/96p3s213.

Tucker, A. (1768). *The Light of Nature Pursued*, Vol. 1, Part I. London: T. Payne.

Turner, J. C. (1987). *Rediscovering the Social Group*. Oxford: Blackwell.

University Standards Report (2009). *Students and Universities*. Westminster, London: Innovation, Universities, Science and Skills Committee, House of Commons.

Urry, J. (2000). *Sociology Beyond Societies*. London: Sage.

(2010). 'Mobile Sociology'. *British Journal of Sociology*, 61: 347–66.

Vaihinger, H. (1924/2009). *The Philosophy of 'As If'*. London: Routledge and Kegan Paul.

Valsiner, J. and van der Veer, R. (2000). *The Social Mind*. Cambridge University Press.

van Dijk, T. A. (2003). 'Critical Discourse Analysis'. In D. Schiffrin, D. Tannen and H. E. Hamilton (eds.), *The Handbook of Discourse Analysis*. Oxford: Blackwell.

(2008). 'Critical Discourse Analysis and Nominalization: Problem or Pseudo-problem?'. *Discourse & Society*, 19: 821–8.

(2010). 'Critical Discourse Studies: A Sociocognitive Approach'. In R. Wodak and M. Meyer (eds.), *Methods of Critical Discourse Analysis*. London: Sage.

van Leeuwen, T. (2010). 'Discourse as the Recontextualization of Social Practice: A Guide'. In R. Wodak and M. Meyer (eds.), *Methods of Critical Discourse Analysis*. London: Sage.

van Leeuwen, T. and Kress, G. (2011). 'Discourse Semantics'. In T. A. van Dijk (ed.), *Discourse Studies*, 2nd edn. London: Sage.

Waldo, M. L. (2004). *Demythologizing Language Difference in the Academy*. Mahwah, NJ: Lawrence Erlbaum.

Wells, B. and Macfarlane, S. (1998). 'Prosody as an Interactional Resource: Turn-projection and Overlap'. *Language and Speech*, 41: 265–94.

Wheen, F. (2004). *How Mumbo-Jumbo Conquered the World*. London: Harper Perennial.

Wodak, R. (2006). 'Critical Linguistics and Critical Discourse Analysis'. In J.-O. Östman and J. Verschueren (eds.), *Handbook of Pragmatics*. Amsterdam/ Philadelphia: John Benjamins.

Wodak, R. and Meyer, M. (2010). 'Critical Discourse Analysis: History, Agenda, Theory and Methodology'. In R. Wodak and M. Meyer (eds.), *Methods of Critical Discourse Analysis*. London: Sage.

Wooffitt, R. (2001). 'Researching Psychic Practitioners: Conversation Analysis'. In M. Wetherell, S. Taylor and S. J. Yates (eds.), *Discourse as Data*. London: Sage.

Yule, G. (2010). *The Study of Language*. Cambridge University Press.

Zijderveld, A. C. (1979). *On Clichés*. London: Routledge and Kegan Paul.

Ziliak, S. T. and McCloskey, D. N. (2008). *The Cult of Statistical Significance*. University of Michigan Press.

Zimbardo, P. G. (1969). 'The Human Choice: Individuation, Reason and Order Versus Deindividuation, Impulse and Chaos'. *Nebraska Symposium on Motivation*, 17: 237–307.

Index